U.S. IMMIGRATION STEP BY STEP

Third Edition

Edwin T. Gania
Attorney at Law

SPHINX® PUBLISHING
AN IMPRINT OF SOURCEBOOKS, INC.®
NAPERVILLE, ILLINOIS
WWW.SPHINXLEGAL.COM

Published by: **Sphinx® Publishing, An Imprint of Sourcebooks, Inc.®**

<u>Naperville Office</u>
P.O. Box 4410
Naperville, Illinois 60567-4410
630-961-3900
Fax: 630-961-2168
www.sourcebooks.com
www.SphinxLegal.com

This publication is designed to provide accurate and authoritative information in regard to the subject matter covered. It is sold with the understanding that the publisher is not engaged in rendering legal, accounting, or other professional service. If legal advice or other expert assistance is required, the services of a competent professional person should be sought.
From a Declaration of Principles Jointly Adopted by a Committee of the
American Bar Association and a Committee of Publishers and Associations

This product is not a substitute for legal advice.

Disclaimer required by Texas statutes.

Library of Congress Cataloging-in-Publication Data
Gania, Edwin T.
  U.S. immigration : step by step / by Edwin T. Gania. -- 3rd ed.
      p. cm.
  Includes index.
  ISBN-13: 978-1-57248-555-6 (pbk. : alk. paper)
  ISBN-10: 1-57248-555-8 (pbk. : alk. paper)
  1. Emigration and immigration law—United States—Popular works. I.
Title. II. Title: US immigration.

KF4819.6.G36 2006
342.7308'2--dc22
                                                                2006018545

Printed and bound in the United States of America.
SB — 10 9 8 7 6 5 4 3 2

CONTENTS

USING SELF-HELP LAW BOOKS

Before using a self-help law book, you should realize the advantages and disadvantages of doing your own legal work and understand the challenges and diligence that this requires.

The Growing Trend

Rest assured that you will not be the first or only person handling your own legal matter. For example, in some states, more than 75% of the people in divorces and other cases represent themselves. Because of the high cost of legal services, this is a major trend, and many courts are struggling to make it easier for people to represent themselves. However, some courts are not happy with people who do not use attorneys and refuse to help them in any way. For some, the attitude is, "Go to the law library and figure it out for yourself."

We write and publish self-help law books to give people an alternative to the often complicated and confusing legal books found in most law libraries. We have made the explanations of the law as simple and easy to understand as possible. Of course, unlike an attorney advising an individual client, we cannot cover every conceivable possibility.

Cost/Value Analysis

Whenever you shop for a product or service, you are faced with various levels of quality and price. In deciding what product or service to buy, you make a cost/value analysis on the basis of your willingness to pay and the quality you desire.

When buying a car, you decide whether you want transportation, comfort, status, or sex appeal. Accordingly, you decide among choices such as a Neon, a Lincoln, a Rolls Royce, or a Porsche. Before making a decision, you usually weigh the merits of each option against the cost.

When you get a headache, you can take a pain reliever (such as aspirin) or visit a medical specialist for a neurological examination. Given this choice, most people, of course, take a pain reliever, since it costs only pennies; whereas a medical examination costs hundreds of dollars and takes a lot of time. This is usually a logical choice because it is rare to need anything more than a pain reliever for a headache. But in some cases, a headache may indicate a brain tumor, and failing to see a specialist right away can result in complications. Should everyone with a headache go to a specialist? Of course not, but people treating their own illnesses must realize that they are betting, on the basis of their cost/value analysis of the situation, that they are taking the most logical option.

The same cost/value analysis must be made when deciding to do one's own legal work. Many legal situations are very straightforward, requiring a simple form and no complicated analysis. Anyone with a little intelligence and a book of instructions can handle the matter without outside help.

But there is always the chance that complications are involved that only an attorney would notice. To simplify the law into a book like this, several legal cases often must be condensed into a single sentence or paragraph. Otherwise, the book would be several hundred pages long and too complicated for most people. However, this simplification necessarily leaves out many details and nuances that would apply to special or unusual situations. Also, there are many ways to interpret most legal questions. Your case may come before a judge who disagrees with the analysis of our authors.

Therefore, in deciding to use a self-help law book and to do your own legal work, you must realize that you are making a cost/value analysis. You have decided that the money you will save in doing it yourself outweighs the chance that your case will not turn out to your satisfaction. Most people handling their own simple legal matters never have a problem, but occasionally people find that it ended up costing them more to have an attorney straighten out the situation than it would have if they had hired an attorney in the beginning. Keep this in mind while handling your case, and be sure to consult an attorney if you feel you might need further guidance.

Immigration law is federal, which means that the same law and forms will apply to all *United States Citizenship and Immigration Services* (USCIS) offices across the country. However, there may be important differences in filing procedures depending on the particular local USCIS office. For example, offices have different procedures to inquire about a delayed or problematic case. If you are unsure, it may be wise to confirm a procedure by visiting the website for that office or dropping by the USCIS building and asking an employee.

You should not necessarily expect to be able to get all of the information and resources you need solely from within the pages of this book. This book will serve as your guide, giving you specific information whenever possible and helping you to find out what else you will need to know. This is just like if you decided to build your own backyard deck. You might purchase a book on how to build decks. However, such a book would not include the building codes and permit requirements of every city, town, county, and township in the nation; nor would it include the lumber, nails, saws, hammers, and other materials and tools you would need to actually build the deck. You would use the book as your guide, and then do some work and research involving such matters as whether you need a permit of some kind, what type and grade of wood is available in your area, whether to use hand tools or power tools, and how to use those tools.

Before using the forms in a book like this, you should check with your court clerk to see if there are any local rules of which you should be aware or local forms you will need to use. Often, such forms will require the same information as the forms in the book, but are merely laid out differently or use slightly different language. They will sometimes require additional information.

Changes in the Law

Besides being subject to local rules and practices, the law is subject to change at any time. The courts and the legislatures of all fifty states are constantly revising the laws. It is possible that while you are reading this book, some aspect of the law is being changed.

In most cases, the change will be of minimal significance. A form will be redesigned, additional information will be required, or a waiting period will be extended. As a result, you might need to revise a form, file an extra form, or wait out a longer time period. These types of changes will not usually affect the outcome of your case. On the other hand, sometimes a major part of the law is changed, the entire law in a particular area is rewritten, or a case that was the basis of a central legal point is overruled. In such instances, your entire ability to pursue your case may be impaired.

INTRODUCTION

Immigration is one area of life prone to false rumors. Too often, the truth of a rumor bears no relation to the speed with which it disseminates. I have seen too many instances where people have wound up in immigration court because they applied for permanent residence based upon a nonexistent amnesty, for example.

The popular media sometimes unwittingly fuels the fire. The details of a new immigration statute may not make interesting reading or may be difficult to understand, so they are left out of the article. By making the story simpler, details are left out that may affect a significant number of people.

Hopefully, this book can assist in separating fact from fiction. More than just a description of the eligibility requirements for a particular category (much of which can be obtained elsewhere), this book provides a feel for the reality of the process itself and where it might go awry.

The process of applying for a green card is a notoriously challenging undertaking. For the potential immigrant, it is no small accomplishment to understand this country's evolving eligibility requirements. Indeed, one veteran immigration prosecutor told me that immigration regulations are more confusing to her now than when she first started prosecuting cases. It is equally difficult to file the correct forms and supporting documents and then guide the application through the *United States Citizenship and Immigration Services* (USCIS).

Many immigration cases can simply be filed, go through the system, and be granted. But there is an incredibly fine line between an easy case and an impossible one. If an alien files a case for which he or she is not eligible, then that person has just turned him- or herself in to a federal law enforcement agency along with all relevant information needed to deport him or her. Imagine a thief filing with the local police station a signed confession, copies of ID documents and other personal information, tax returns, photos and fingerprints, and hundreds of dollars in filing fees—and then saying hurry up and schedule me for an interview. It sounds funny, but many thousands of hopeful aliens do the equivalent each year.

However, immigration cases vary widely in complexity. At one end of the scale are naturalization cases, which are typically straightforward, especially when the applicant has good command of the English language and no criminal background. (see Chapter 21.) Further, the stakes are lower for the naturalization applicant who already has a green card and can, in any event, normally reapply for naturalization if something goes unexpectedly wrong. If there is no criminal record, a naturalization applicant should not be deportable.

At the other end of the scale are those who are in immigration court. (see Chapter 19.) Such persons really should not proceed without expert advice. At the very least, anyone who is in immigration court must consult with an immigration attorney or competent organization so that his or her right to relief is confirmed. Mistakes made in immigration court may not be reversible. (See Chapter 22 for information on attorneys.)

In the broad middle area of the immigration scale are those seeking to apply for the green card through one of the eligibility categories discussed in Chapters 4 through 12. Some cases are easier than others. The easiest of these cases are usually the family-based applications, if there are no complicating factors. A key aspect of this book is to identify where the applicant can proceed without outside assistance, and Chapters 13 through 20 give you this information.

Using this Book

The U.S. immigration system is essentially a *closed system*, meaning you have to qualify in a specific category in order to obtain a green card. A person cannot normally self-petition. An instructive contrast is with the Canadian immigration system, which can be considered an *open system*. If a person can accumulate seventy points according to the Canadian point scheme, he or she can self-petition for permanent residence.

Therefore, to become a U.S. permanent resident, you must first find a category for which you are eligible. This book is organized to assist that search. Section 1 will help you understand terms, immigration cases, and the first steps before applying for anything. Section 2 contains the various green card eligibility categories. They have been arranged starting with the most available visas or those for which it is easiest to apply. In other words, if you are not certain which visa you might qualify for, you can look at the chapters in order until you see one that might apply to you.

While the various categories might seem confusing, there are basically four ways through which the vast majority of applicants will qualify for a green card: through their families, through their jobs, as asylees or refugees, or through the diversity visa lottery. The other categories are fairly restrictive and will only apply to a limited number of qualified people, but it never hurts to consider each of them.

The majority of filings are in the family-based categories. These applications may be attempted without outside assistance. The only exception is for adopted children. However, there are certain eligibility categories for which you should not attempt to apply on your own. The employment-based categories, for example, require familiarity with technical requirements well beyond the scope of this book.

Section 3 of this book contains background information regarding the green card process. It may either be read through or used as a reference for the information contained in any eligibility chapter.

NOTE: *Throughout the book, there are references to various supporting documents. Many of these are explained in detail in Chapter 13 as opposed to explaining them each time they are mentioned.*

The glossary is designed to be a unique resource. Not only does it contain complete definitions for all immigration terms, but it also attempts to provide perspective of the term in the overall immigration scheme. While such generalizations will not always prove accurate, they are still useful as a starting point.

Appendix A contains USCIS Field Office listings. Appendix B contains USCIS Service Centers. Appendix C contains websites and contact information. Appendix D contains a fee chart. Appendix E contains reproduced USCIS forms for your use.

NOTE: *Any reference to a section of law refers to the Immigration and Nationality Act (INA).*

Anyone who wishes to comment on any aspect of this book can contact the author at:

Edwin Gania
Mark Thomas and Associates
11 South LaSalle Street
Suite 2800
Chicago, IL 60603
312-236-3163
312-236-3894 (fax)
edgania@cs.com

SECTION 1:
BASIC IMMIGRATION
CONCEPTS

I — YOUR IMMIGRATION STATUS

A good place to begin is to understand the different types of immigration status, including your own. Every person in the U.S. has an immigration status. It is one of the following, in rough order of preference.

1. *U.S. citizen (USC).* A person who was born in the U.S., naturalized, or born abroad to a U.S. citizen parent. These are the only people in this list who are not subject to deportation proceedings.

2. *lawful permanent resident (LPR).* A green card holder who is eligible to reside permanently in the U.S. and apply for naturalization.

3. *asylee/refugee.* A person who was either granted asylum in the U.S. or who entered the U.S. officially as a refugee and has not yet been granted permanent residence.

4. *nonimmigrant.* A person who has come to the U.S. temporarily on a valid nonimmigrant visa for a specific purpose, such as to visit, study, work, or invest.

5. *temporary protected status (TPS).* A person who has obtained status as a citizen of a country that Congress has designated to receive protected

status on account of armed conflict, natural disaster, or other extraordinary circumstance. Such a person is in a position to possibly benefit from legislation allowing permanent residence.

6. *out of status.* A person who initially lawfully entered on a nonimmigrant visa, but the visa has expired or its terms have been violated.

7. *undocumented alien.* A person who has entered the U.S. without inspection (EWI), such as across the Mexican or Canadian border, or on a false passport.

This book is intended to assist those in categories 3 through 7 gain permanent residence status in the U.S. The primary focus of this book is applying for *adjustment of status* in the U.S. as opposed to applying for permanent residence (an immigrant visa) at a U.S. embassy or consulate in a foreign country. While the eligibility requirements are the same and some parts of the process are identical, the information in this book is not sufficiently detailed to be a guide to the entire process of applying abroad.

NOTE: *All of the above terms are explained in more detail where relevant in the text, or in the glossary at the back of the book. Also, many of the documents you need to support your petitions are described in Chapter 13.*

UNDERSTANDING IMMIGRATION TERMS AND WHERE TO FILE

Immigration law is already complex without the use of numerous difficult terms. While you will never need to know most terms, there are several terms that are widely used in the immigration field. It is helpful to learn these right from the beginning and to understand where the *United States Citizenship and Immigration Services* (USCIS) will be deciding on your application.

Important Terms to Know

It is important to fully understand some of the terms that are used most frequently in any immigration process.

Perhaps the most commonly used term is *visa*. Most often, a visa is a travel permit stamped into a passport by a consulate abroad that allows the alien to whom it is issued to travel to the U.S. (e.g., to board a plane, train, or ship) to apply for admission at a U.S. port of entry. Except for aliens traveling on the Visa Waiver Program, Mexicans with Border Crossing Cards, Canadian citizens, or those seeking asylum at the border, all aliens are expected to present valid visas to enter the U.S.

NOTE: *At an embassy, one is said to be applying for an immigrant visa, as opposed to in the U.S., where one applies for adjustment of status.*

There are approximately thirty types of nonimmigrant classifications. The letter name of the visa comes from the section of the statute that authorizes it. The nonimmigrant classification usually requires that the person maintain a permanent residence abroad in addition to qualifying for the particular category. A nonimmigrant status may or may not permit employment. The most common nonimmigrant visas are the tourist or student visa. See Chapter 5 for nonimmigrant classifications. With few exceptions, nonimmigrant visas do not lead directly to a green card. On the other hand, there is only one type of immigrant visa; that is, the visa which allows entry into the U.S. to assume permanent residence status.

Change of status refers to the process by which an alien present in the U.S. seeks to change from one valid nonimmigrant status to another. One is *in status* if the time period reflected on the I-94 card stapled into the passport upon entry into the U.S. has not yet expired.

Adjustment of status is the process whereby an alien in the U.S. applies to become a permanent resident. As a contrast, an alien in a foreign country seeking to reside in the U.S. as a permanent resident is said to *make an application* for an immigrant visa.

Petitioner and Beneficiary

A *petitioner* is one who applies for the benefit of a second person, the *beneficiary*. The petitioner is either a U.S. citizen, a green card holder, or a U.S. corporation. It is the beneficiary who will at some point acquire the immigrant or nonimmigrant status.

NOTE: *Refer to the detailed glossary at the back of the book if you come across any term that you do not understand.*

Supporting Documents

Throughout the book, you will notice that each petition or filing requires certain documents to help prove your case. Many of these forms are self-explanatory, such as a passport or birth certificate. For those that are not self-explanatory, you may find Chapter 13 helpful. It explains many of the major supporting documents. Refer there whenever a document is mentioned in the text that you do not understand.

Filing a Case: Local USCIS Office, Service Center, or Embassy

Before discussing the specific eligibility categories in Section 2 of this book, it will be helpful to provide some orientation as to where an application is filed.

There are four departments of the federal government that handle immigration: the Departments of Homeland Security, Justice, State, and Labor. The State Department runs the U.S. embassies and consulates in foreign countries, where it issues immigrant and nonimmigrant visas that a person requires to enter the U.S. The Labor Department has a limited but important role in the initial phase of an *employment-based application*. (An historical note is that it was initially the Labor Department that issued green cards in the early 1900s. They made them green to reflect the fact that the card allowed one to work in the U.S. and therefore were the equivalent of money.)

USCIS Offices   Once an alien is in the U.S., he or she is under the jurisdiction of the Department of Homeland Security, which most likely means the United States Citizenship and Immigration Services (USCIS). For the most part, the former *INS* is now referred to as USCIS. Those under deportation proceedings are under the jurisdiction of the *Executive Office for Immigration Review* (EOIR), which runs the immigration court and the appeals court (Board of Immigration Appeals) and which remains part of the Department of Justice.

There are two places where USCIS decides adjustment applications. These are either at a local USCIS office found in many cities or at one of the four USCIS service centers. Service centers are responsible for a particular state, or sometimes, other certain types of applications. The Department of State, at a U.S. embassy in a foreign country, also adjudicates applications for permanent residence.

Those already in the U.S. will want to file their application and complete processing in the U.S. Those abroad will most likely file at their embassy. However, with the recent changes in the law, it will be increasingly likely that a person will have no option except to leave the U.S. and attempt adjustment at his or her embassy. (As you might expect, there are several problems associated with this option.)

Service Centers

For those already in the U.S., adjustment applications are increasingly filed and adjudicated at one of the four regional USCIS service centers. If a case at the service center is determined to require an interview, the file is then transferred to the local USCIS office. In fact, the general rule is that most applications are now filed at the service centers. The only applications that are principally handled at a local office are those that are family- and diversity-based. Even these are now filed nationally.

In case you have not heard of the service centers, they are relatively new processing and adjudication centers. These centers are increasingly handling much of the paperwork and decision making, particularly for cases that are not commonly interviewed or do not require contact with the applicant. They are located in remote areas and for the most part do not have any public access, except for very busy telephone numbers. Nonetheless, the system appears to be a success. By their very removal from the public, they appear to be fair, uniform, and uninfluenced by outside factors. The cases that require interviews, such as marriage cases, citizenship, or processing for work permits, are handled by the local USCIS office.

One advantage of having your case at a service center is that it much easier to keep track of it. You can call customer service at 800-375-5283 and by continually pressing "1" on the telephone keypad, eventually get to the automated case system. You will then punch in your case number located at the top left corner of the receipt notice or any form you receive from USCIS. The automated system gives out important update information, such as that the petition is still pending or that an approval or a *Request for Evidence* (RFE) has been mailed. The same information is now available online at **www.uscis.gov**. (The exact link can be found in Appendix C.)

Based on this information, you can call back during business hours to talk to an information officer if necessary. The information officers may be helpful in clearing up a bureaucratic problem with the application. They are not, however, responsible for making a decision on the case.

Cases at the local office can be difficult to track. If your application is lost or drags on, information is hard to come by. At most local offices there is a mail-in inquiry system.

NOTE: *The status information available on the USCIS website, at present, only relates to cases filed at a service center and not to cases filed at a local office.*

U.S. Embassy or Consulate

You also have the option of obtaining permanent residence at the embassy or consulate in your native country. An application at an embassy is decided by a *consular officer* as opposed to an immigration officer in the U.S. However, under the new laws passed in 1996, there are severe restrictions on leaving the U.S. to process your case at the embassy.

If a person is *out of status* more than 180 days starting from April 1, 1997, he or she is barred from the U.S. for three years after leaving the U.S. If you are out of status more than one year starting from April 1, 1997, then you are barred for ten years from obtaining any *immigration benefit* (either an immigrant or nonimmigrant visa).

There is a *waiver* possible to avoid the harsh effects of the three- or ten-year bar. However, this waiver is difficult to obtain in normal circumstances. Moreover, this waiver is only available to those who have a U.S. citizen or lawful permanent resident parent or spouse. Also, it must be demonstrated that there would be an *extreme hardship* to that qualifying relative if the alien is not allowed to enter the U.S. (See Chapter 11 for more information.) Such waivers are often denied unless they are carefully documented.

Any case being processed by an embassy can become problematic for various reasons. Many cases are in effect a partnership between the USCIS service center and the embassy. For example, an alien relative or fiance petition is first approved by the service center and then the file is shifted to the embassy to complete immigrant visa processing. Tension may be created when the embassy thinks the service center's approval of a petition was in error. However, unless a consular officer finds substantial evidence of ineligibility that was unknown and unavailable to USCIS at the time it approved the petition, they must accept the approved petition and process the visa accordingly.

Additionally, there are difficulties in communicating with anyone in authority, particularly the consular officer in charge of the case, and there is a lack of oversight, such as an appeal process, over actions taken by an embassy. Therefore, if there is a choice of venue, it is always preferred that the case be processed in the U.S.

3 CHANGING IMMIGRATION LAWS

Immigration laws are in constant flux. While it is popular to blame the USCIS for its harsh treatment of aliens, it must be kept in mind that they are only carrying out the laws enacted by Congress and signed by the president. In fact, it would be an illegal act if a particular immigration officer did not carry out federal law and instead thought, *well, this person should get a green card anyway because he or she really deserves it.*

The U.S. is certainly in a period of restrictive immigration laws. Immigration laws underwent a drastic revision in 1996 in response to the tragic bombing of the federal building in Oklahoma City on April 22, 1995. In the days that followed, many believed that the bombing was the work of a Middle Eastern terrorist, even though the bombing turned out to be the work of an American. Nonetheless, Congress vowed to pass restrictive legislation affecting criminal aliens, if not all aliens.

The statute passed on April 22, 1996, exactly one year after the bombing, *severely affected* criminal aliens. Then, in July 1996, Congress enacted another highly restrictive statute affecting aliens more generally. These laws targeted and eliminated critical avenues for immigration benefits.

Section 245(i) and the LIFE Act

The change with possibly the biggest impact may have been the demise of Section 245(i) of the *Immigration and Nationality Act* (INA). Under it, a person who overstayed his or her nonimmigrant visa or entered the U.S. without inspection by an immigration officer (that is, snuck into the country) paid a $1,000 fine and was able to adjust status in the U.S.

As a compromise, Congress had passed the *LIFE Act*, which allowed those out of status to apply for a green card if they had filed an alien petition prior to April 30, 2001, and were physically present in the U.S. on December 20, 2000.

Many people ask if immigration laws changed drastically after the September 11, 2001, tragedy. Perhaps surprisingly, the answer is no, with only a few exceptions. However, existing laws are being enforced much more harshly and, in the case of deportations, more quickly. Prior to September 11, 2001, it appeared as though there was support to ease immigration law and reinstate Section 245(i). President Bush had even referred to a type of amnesty, at least for Mexicans. However, the fact that the tragic events of September 11th were caused by foreigners set back immigration reform for years to come.

NOTE: *The previous law had been that if someone was the beneficiary of an I-130 petition or a labor certification application filed prior to January 18, 1998, then the beneficiary was Section 245(i) eligible.*

Homeland Security Act

As of March 1, 2003, the *Immigration and Naturalization Service* (INS) ceased to exist. With the passage of the *Homeland Security Act of 2002,* the largest restructuring of the federal government in the past fifty years occurred. It created a new *Department of Homeland Security* (DHS) that consolidated twenty-two existing agencies and 170,000 employees, including the former INS.

The INS was absorbed into the DHS and separated into several separate bureaus including: the *United States Citizenship and Immigration Services* (USCIS) and the *Bureau of Immigration and Customs Enforcement* (ICE), among several other smaller ones. One goal was to formally separate the services side of immigration from enforcement. It remains to be seen whether this separation will produce any meaningful change.

So far, there has been no meaningful change. Since USCIS and ICE still share not just the same file system, but also the same actual alien files and still coordinate every operational detail, the separation into two agencies is mere window dressing.

REAL ID Act

The REAL ID Act will create very significant problems for aliens without valid status. Beginning May 2008, all people living in the U.S. will need a federally approved ID card to travel on an airplane, open a bank account, collect Social Security payments, or take advantage of nearly any government service. Drivers' licenses will be reissued to meet federal standards. A person must demonstrate valid nonimmigrant or immigrant status in order to be issued a driver's license. Some states already enforce these provisions.

State motor vehicle departments will have to verify that these identity documents are legitimate, digitize them, and store them permanently. In addition, Social Security numbers must be verified with the Social Security Administration.

In short, aliens without valid status will have difficulty functioning in society. It is hoped that the hardship suffered by millions of aliens will give rise to ameliorative legislation.

Proposed Amnesty

We are at a milestone in U.S. immigration history. It has been front-page news that Congress is attempting to resolve the issue of illegal aliens. At stake is who gets to acquire status and remain in the U.S. and who must continue in undocumented status facing possible eventual deportation. The decisions Congress makes will impact the lives of millions of aliens and millions more family members.

A very important first step has taken place towards a broad-based *amnesty*. On May 25, 2006, the U.S. Senate passed a compromise bill (S. 2611) creating a legalization program for certain individuals depending on how long they have been present in the U.S. Those present in the U.S. more than five years would eventually acquire permanent residence while those present more than two years would also acquire benefits. (See Chapter 10 for a more detailed discussion.)

In order for the Senate bill to become law, however, the House of Representatives must also enact the same provisions. While the compromise bill that passed the Senate has the full support of the Bush administration, early indications are that the House is not inclined to enact similar broad-based benefits. In fact, on December 16, 2005, the House passed a very harsh immigration bill (H.R. 4437) that dealt only with enforcement of the U.S.-Mexican border and further restricted the rights of illegal aliens inside the U.S. It is reasonable to expect that the House will significantly curtail the Senate bill. As of the summer of 2006, the best that can be said is that there is a 50/50 chance that the House will agree to some of the Senate provisions. Now is the time to contact your congressional representative to have your opinion heard.

SECTION 2:
CATEGORIES ELIGIBLE FOR PERMANENT RESIDENCE

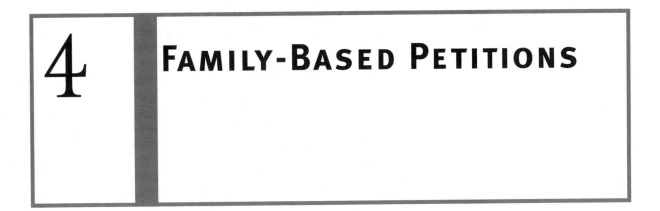

4 FAMILY-BASED PETITIONS

Family-based petitions are probably the largest group of permanent residence petitions. They encompass family members, widows, fiancés, and various others into *immediate* and *preference categories*. These categories are discussed later in this chapter. Furthermore, there are even some family-based petitions that allow an immigrant to have *temporary nonimmigrant status* prior to obtaining permanent residence. These, too, will be discussed later in this chapter.

Because this category of family-based petitions is so large, this chapter will naturally include a lot of information. Do not let this overwhelm you. If you fall into one of the family-based categories, you need only concern yourself with the information pertaining to that particular section.

Minor Children and Parents of U.S. Citizens— Immediate Relatives

An *immediate relative* is actually an appropriately named category. Immediate relatives are relatives who may immediately file for and obtain permanent residence status. U.S. citizens may apply for the following family members:

✪ parents;

✪ minor children; or,

✪ spouse (see "Spouses of U.S. Citizens—Immediate Relatives" on page 19).

The parent, spouse, or minor child of a U.S. citizen is an immediate relative. This means several things. Most importantly, it means there is no wait for a visa number, since Congress has placed no limitation on the number of immediate relatives who may enter the U.S. each year. For other relatives, those in *preference categories*, there is a set number that can come to the U.S. each year. (This has resulted in a waiting list and is discussed later in this chapter.)

Qualifying as a Minor Child The following are important points regarding a U.S. citizen parent who is applying for minor children.

✪ The children being applied for must be under the age of 21. (If they are 21 or over, they fall into a preference category as described later in this chapter.)

✪ A separate I-130 petition must be filed for each child.

✪ The minor children must be unmarried. (If they are married, they also fall into a preference category.)

✪ Any children of minor, unmarried children may be included.

✪ A stepparent may apply for a stepchild if the parent's marriage took place before the stepchild turned 18.

✪ A parent may apply for adopted children if the adoption took place before the adopted child turned 16 and the parent and child have lived together for at least two years.

(All forms, documents, and filing procedures are discussed in detail in Chapter 13.)

Qualifying as a Parent The following are important points when a U.S. citizen applies for his or her parents.

✪ The U.S. citizen child must be 21 years of age or over.

✪ A separate I-130 petition must be filed for each parent.

✪ A petition for the parents does not include the minor children of the parents—that is, the brothers or sisters of the petitioner. (The siblings fall into the fourth preference category—see page 25.)

✪ The U.S. citizen may apply for a stepparent (that is, someone who is married to his or her natural parent) if the marriage took place before the child's 18th birthday.

Spouses of U.S. Citizens— Immediate Relatives

The prevailing wisdom at the USCIS is that a high percentage of marriage cases are fraudulent. Even those that have a legitimate case often have to fight for respect from the USCIS because of the false cases. Estimates as to the amount of fraud vary, but the expectation is that half of the 80,000 or so marriage cases filed annually might be false.

Nonetheless, a minority of cases are actually denied. In the past, USCIS would sit on the case or send it to their investigations branch. Now, if there is not sufficient evidence, it is more likely to make a quick decision denying the application often claiming fraud as the basis.

NOTE: *If you are still married to a spouse overseas or cannot get a copy of a foreign divorce decree, it is very easy to simply get divorced in the U.S. In most states, it is a very short and inexpensive process to get divorced if the spouse resides outside the state. While this type of divorce serves only to dissolve the marriage and the court has no authority to order alimony, division of property, or child support, it is sufficient as a divorce for any immigration or other purpose.*

Note that an I-130 petition filed for the spouse does not include that spouse's children. Separate petitions must be filed for each stepchild.

See page 18 under the minor children and parents section for a list of supporting documents the U.S. citizen must have to establish his or her citizenship.

A marriage certificate is required to establish that the petitioner is in fact legally married to the beneficiary spouse. This certificate must establish that both the husband and wife were present at the ceremony.

In some cases, other documents must be provided. If either the husband or wife was previously married, then a divorce decree must also be submitted. If any name has been changed from one of the supporting documents, then documentation as to this change must be provided.

Again, provide only photocopies of all documents. The originals will be brought to the interview, as discussed in Chapter 17. All official certificates must have been issued by (or registered with) the proper civil authority in the foreign country. If a document is not in English, it must be submitted along with a certified English translation. (see page 142.) If any document is unavailable, see page 143 for more information.

The most important supporting documents are to establish that the marriage is *bona fide*—that is, it was entered into for love and affection rather than for a green card. The following list contains examples of useful supporting documents for proving a bona fide marriage. The more of these documents that are obtained, the quicker and easier the case will be granted.

Proving a Bona Fide Marriage

The critical aspect of a marriage case is to prove that the marriage was entered into for love and affection rather than a green card. In order to do so, the following should be demonstrated:

✪   joint obligations for housing and living expenses;

✪   joint management of finances;

✪   joint ownership of property; and,

✪   evidence that the couple hold themselves out as married.

The following documents are useful to prove that a marriage is bona fide:

✪ birth certificates of children born of the marriage;

✪ tax returns showing the couple filed as "married filing jointly";

✪ joint bank accounts or loans;

✪ wedding ceremony, reception, and honeymoon photos;

✪ a selection of photos that show the couple together with family or friends over as long a period of time as possible;

✪ evidence of vacations taken together such as airline tickets, photos, bills;

✪ joint apartment lease, or letter from parent or landlord that says you have been living together;

✪ joint property deed or mortgage;

✪ if the spouse has taken the married name, any document showing that married name such as Social Security card, driver's license, state I.D. card, credit cards, club cards, etc;

✪ joint car title or registration;

✪ joint car insurance;

✪ letter from current or former employer of one spouse showing a change in records to reflect new marital status;

✪ letter from current or former employer of one spouse showing other spouse was designated as person to be notified in event of accident, sickness, or emergency;

✪ health insurance plans naming spouse as member or beneficiary;

✪ life insurance policy naming spouse as member or beneficiary;

✪ any proof of correspondence between couple;

✪ utilities (phone, gas, electric, cable, etc.) in joint names;

✪   joint credit cards or department store cards;

✪   receipts, invoices, or installment contracts for major purchases made together such as car, furniture, television, VCR or DVD player, stereo, refrigerator, washer, and dryer, showing date, address, and name of one or both spouses;

✪   religious marriage certificate if there was a religious ceremony wedding;

✪   joint membership in clubs or other organizations;

✪   statements (on letterhead) from churches, civic groups, or other organizations in which the couple has joint investment;

✪   receipt for wedding reception;

✪   receipt for purchase of wedding rings;

✪   mail received at house (or old address now being forwarded);

✪   correspondence, invitations, or greeting cards (and envelopes if possible) sent to the couple;

✪   day care or school records showing spouse as parent or guardian;

✪   medical or dental records that name other spouse as contact person; or,

✪   affidavits from family or friends.

This is a fairly comprehensive list meant only to offer suggestions. By no means would (or should) any couple come to an USCIS interview with all or even most of the above items. For example, if you have a wedding album showing a large reception attended by family and friends, then that already goes a long way to proving the marriage. However, if a couple has a wide age difference, or is of clearly different ethnic, religious, or language backgrounds, then more pieces of evidence are required.

Special challenges are faced when the spouse or intended spouse resides in a foreign country, as this makes it much more difficult to obtain documentation. In such a case, the following might help:

✪ telephone records showing long-distance calls between the couple (if it is necessary to use calling cards that do not facilitate recordkeeping, try **www.onesuite.com**);

✪ letters, cards, and emails between the couple before or during marriage (with their postmarked envelopes if possible);

✪ other correspondence received by either the petitioner or the beneficiary that refers to the parties as a couple;

✪ evidence of meetings between the couple;

✪ evidence of trips taken together—including the honeymoon trip—with passport stamps, bills or receipts reflecting hotel stays, car rentals, plane tickets, postcards sent to family members while on the trip, color photocopies of photos; and,

✪ evidence of financial support or gifts.

Breaking Up   At least half of all marriages end in divorce. It is likely that for recent immigrants the percentage might be higher. It is difficult enough to maintain a relationship, without adding on all of the problems of adjusting to a new culture, being without status, or even likely being in a lower income bracket. Plus, it is disheartening to see how a U.S. citizen spouse will use his or her leverage over the immigration status of the other.

The legal standard to be granted permanent residence is whether the marriage was bona fide *at the time it was entered into.* It is not the state of the marriage by the time of the interview, except to the extent that this indicates whether the marriage was initially bona fide. While the USCIS tends to ignore this distinction, an immigration judge should not.

So what if your marriage falls apart before the initial interview? Unfortunately, the only answer is to fix the relationship. If that requires marriage counseling, then do it. That constitutes good evidence of a bona fide relationship.

Conditional Resident   If at the time of the *adjustment of status* (becoming a permanent resident) the marriage was less than two years old, then the alien becomes a *conditional resident* (CR). The classification is CR1 (if processed at an embassy) or CR6 (if processed in the U.S.). This status expires within two years. If the marriage has been in existence for more than two years at the time of the interview, then a permanent green card is issued.

The purpose of the two-year conditional resident status is so that the USCIS has another opportunity to determine whether the marriage was in fact bona fide. (The conditional resident must file *Form I-751* to remove conditions within the ninety-day period prior to the expiration date on the conditional green card, which is discussed in Chapter 13.)

If you miss the two-year deadline, then you have to show exceptional circumstances for late filing. The exceptional circumstances should be supported with documentation. For example, if you were travelling outside the U.S. around the deadline, show proof of travel. If the deadline is missed, you will have to re-file the original adjustment packet, discussed in Chapter 13. However, this time permanent status will be granted (as IR6).

Adopted Children— Immediate Relatives

If a child is under the age of 16 and cannot qualify for permanent residence through his or her own family, adoption by a U.S. citizen or green card holder might be an excellent means for the child to obtain permanent residence—even if both parents of the child are still alive. For example, a U.S. citizen or permanent resident over the age of 21 can apply for his or her niece, nephew, or grandchild, or even a child not related to the resident.

NOTE: *This process would only provide status for the child and not for his or her natural parents. Even when the child turns 21 and is a U.S. citizen, he or she would not be able to apply for his or her natural parents.*

Because of the technicalities involved with qualifying through an adoption, this book cannot provide details about the specific process and required applications. The child has to be eligible to be adopted according to the laws of the particular state or foreign country. To proceed with such a case, the person will need to consult with an immigration attorney or organization familiar with adoptions. However, this discussion will help to identify children who would benefit from the adoption process.

The adopted child would become an immediate relative to the adopting U.S. citizen—meaning there is no wait for a visa. Adoption may also work for a lawful permanent resident parent, although there would be an approximate five-year wait for a visa.

The main hurdle to overcome in an adoption case is the requirement that the child has lived with the U.S. citizen adopted parent for two years before filing the I-130 alien relative petition. These two years may be either in the native country or in the U.S. If the U.S. citizen adoptive parent lives in the U.S. and the child is in the other native country, then the two-year residence requirement may be difficult to satisfy. In this event, it may be necessary for the child to enter the U.S. on a type of *nonimmigrant visa*, such as a student or tourist visa.

Illegal Entry A child that enters the U.S. illegally (across a border without documentation) may not qualify for permanent residence in the U.S. unless he or she is Section 245(i) eligible. (see Chapter 5.) However, after he or she accumulates two years of residence with the adopted parents, he or she may return to the native country and apply there for an immigrant visa. If he or she is under the age of 17, he or she does not accumulate unlawful presence in the U.S. and so there is no bar on returning.

NOTE: *Orphan petitions are treated under different rules. Cases involving orphans are too complex for any person unfamiliar with the process. Orphan petitions require an analysis of state laws and also the laws of the foreign country where the child is from. USCIS must perform a home study. Contact an immigration attorney or a nonprofit organization for assistance.*

Preference Categories

In addition to the immediate visa categories mentioned already, U.S. citizens may also apply for certain other relatives—together called the *preference categories*. There are four separate preference categories, and the second preference category has two parts (2A and 2B). There is, however, a waiting period for a visa number for each category. A U.S. citizen may apply for the following relatives:

- ✪ a single child 21 years of age or over—adult child (first preference);
- ✪ a married child of any age (third preference); and,
- ✪ a brother or sister of any age (fourth preference).

If a parent only has a green card and is not a U.S. citizen, then he or she may only apply for the following relatives:

✪ a spouse and single child under the age of 21 (preference 2A); and,

✪ a single child 21 years of age or over (preference 2B).

Unlike an immediate family visa category, the preference visa categories are *backlogged*. You must consult the *visa chart* published by the Department of State to determine when to file the adjustment application.

It is extremely important to understand the visa chart in order to know when to apply for adjustment of status. The chart tells those who have already filed the *Petition for Alien Relative* (I-130) when they may file for *Adjustment of Status* (I-485).

The Department of State publishes an updated visa chart each month. This chart reflects the waiting times for each of the preference visas. The priority date is the date reflected on the I-130 approval notice. It is the date on which you filed the Petition for Alien Relative (I-130). For the preference visas, you may only apply for adjustment once a petition becomes current (i.e., once a visa becomes available as reflected in the State Department chart). A petition is *current* when the date the particular preference category moves past the priority date on the I-130 petition.

In order to check the visa chart for the status of the petition, you must be familiar with the visa categories.

First Preference   The single adult children of the U.S. citizen petitioner must be unmarried. If they are married, they fall into the third preference category and must start the waiting period anew. Any minor children of the unmarried adult child may be included. Furthermore, the petitioner may apply for stepchildren if the parent's marriage took place before the stepchild turned 18. Prove citizenship and the parent, child relationship with the same documents listed for immediate relatives earlier in this chapter.

Second Preference– Spouses (2A)   *Permanent residents* may apply for a spouse under the same guidelines as a U.S. citizen spouse. (see page 19.) The difference is that there is a wait of approximately four or five years for a visa number. However, if the permanent resident spouse *naturalizes* (becomes a U.S. citizen), then the alien spouse may apply immediately for permanent residence. The permanent resident spouse will need a copy of the green card in place of proof of U.S. citizenship. Otherwise, the required documents are the same as for a U.S. citizen spouse. (see p.20.)

In contrast to the immediate relative spousal petition, the preference petition does include the beneficiary's children.

Second Preference–Unmarried Children (2B)

The following are important points regarding lawful permanent resident petitioners who are applying for an unmarried child (of any age).

✪ The children of permanent U.S. residents must be unmarried. If they are married, they can only be applied for by a U.S. citizen parent.

✪ Any children of the unmarried child may be included.

✪ The permanent resident parent may apply for stepchildren if the parent's marriage took place before the children turned 18.

✪ The permanent resident parent may apply for adopted children if the adoption took place before the child turned 16 and the parent and child have lived together for at least two years.

The same documents are required here as for immediate relatives listed on page 85. However, a copy of the parent's green card replaces proof of U.S. citizenship in this situation.

Third Preference

The U.S. citizen petitioner who is applying for a married adult child may include the spouse of the adult child in the petition. The single unmarried children of the adult children being applied for may be included as well. Such children must normally *adjust status* (become a permanent resident) prior to turning age 21 or they will be excluded from the petition. The *Child Status Protection Act* may assist in some cases. (see page 34.)

The U.S. citizen must establish his or her citizenship by one of the documents indicated on page 18. The birth certificate of the adult child must be filed to establish the qualifying relationship. This birth certificate must show the name of the parent who is filing the petition. If the father is petitioning, then his marriage certificate must also be provided. Finally, if any name on a supporting document has changed, a legal document to evidence the name change is required, such as a marriage certificate, adoption certificate, or court order.

Fourth Preference

Typically, the fourth preference category takes many years to become current. Some people do not file a petition on the theory that it will take too long, but time has a way of passing quickly. Plus, benefits may accrue by simply being the beneficiary of a petition filed before a certain date. It is an easy and inexpensive petition to file. It should be filed in all circumstances as soon as possible.

The following are important points regarding the U.S. citizen petitioner who is applying for a brother or sister:

✪ the U.S. citizen petitioner must be 21 years of age or over;

✪ the spouse of the adult sibling is included;

✪ half-brothers and -sisters may petition for one another; and,

✪ the single unmarried children of the adult sibling may be included. (Such children must adjust status prior to turning 21 years or be excluded from the petition.)

Visa Bulletin Chart

The Visa Bulletin Chart applies only to preference visas. Those in an immediate category may apply for adjustment at any time. The chart looks confusing, but it is not really that complicated. The following five steps will help you to easily use the chart, especially for the first time.

1. Get a current version of the monthly visa chart. You can either find it on the Internet at **www.travel.state.gov** or else call 202-663-1541. It is sometimes easier to call the recorded message. Immediately, the dates like those on the sample chart will be read off in the same order.

2. Know which preference visa category you fall into. This table contains only a short description of each category. The preference category is also contained on your approval notice. If you need further assistance, refer back to the explanations on pages 26–27.

3. Check your I-130 approval notice for your priority date. This will normally be the date that you filed the I-130 petition. The date is often found in one of the boxes in the upper left corner, or on the right side of an older approval notice.

4. Find the applicable cut-off date corresponding to your preference category and country. (Only one of the country columns on the right will apply to you.)

5. Compare your priority date to the reported cut-off date. If your *priority date* is earlier than the cut-off date, you will have to wait before filing the adjustment application. If your priority date has passed the cut-off date, you may go ahead and file for adjustment of status.

Sample Visa Bulletin Chart

Family Preference Categories	*All Other Countries*	*India*	*Mexico*	*Philippines*
1st single child 21 or over of a U.S. citizen	22 APR 01	22 APR 01	08 AUG 94	22 AUG 91
2A spouse or single child under 21 of a permanent resident	22 FEB 02	22 FEB 02	15 MAY 99	22 FEB 02
2B single child 21 or over of a permanent resident	08 JUL 96	08 JUL 96	01 JAN 95	08 FEB 91
3rd married child of a U.S. citizen	22 JUL 98	22 JUL 98	01 JAN 95	08 FEB 91
4th brother or sister of a U.S. citizen	01 OCT 94	22 MAR 94	22 MAY 93	01 OCT 83

Do not despair if there appears to be a long wait based on your priority date and the cut-off date. Cut-off dates can move backwards and forwards rapidly. However, over the past several years, the third and fourth preference categories have typically progressed less than one month for each calender month. (Unavailable categories sometimes become available again after October 1st of each year, which is the start of the government fiscal year and a fresh allocation of visa numbers.)

NOTE: *In contrast to the family-based categories, all employment categories are for the most part current.*

You must wait until the date passes. It cannot just be in the same month. The USCIS officer may check at the interview that the visa was actually current at the time the petition was filed. If it was not current, the application will be denied, although they may allow a new application to be filed and paid for on the same day.

Recently, there has been a problem with the visa numbers in preference categories. Some categories have progressed only one month in the past year. The cause of this backup is that the USCIS is processing an unusual number of cases to clear up the long backlog of adjustment applications pending at the local USCIS offices.

Death or Illness of Petitioner

If the petitioner is deceased prior to filing the adjustment, consult with an immigration attorney to determine whether you have any options. If the petitioner becomes ill while the adjustment application is pending, notify the local USCIS office and request that the interview be scheduled as soon as possible. Include a letter from the physician and other evidence of the medical condition.

Self-Petitions

There are two main family-based categories whereby a person can petition on his or her own to immigrate to the U.S. One way is as a widow or widower of a deceased U.S. citizen. A second way is as an abused spouse of a U.S. citizen.

Widows or Widowers

An individual may obtain permanent residence through a deceased U.S. citizen spouse if:

✪ the alien spouse was married for at least two years to a U.S. citizen;

✪ the U.S. citizen was a citizen for at least two years at the time of death;

✪ the petition is filed within two years of the death of the U.S. citizen spouse;

✪ the alien spouse was not legally separated from the U.S. citizen spouse at the time of death; and,

✪ the alien spouse has not remarried.

The widow or widower's unmarried children under 21 years of age may also obtain status.

Abused Spouse

An individual may obtain permanent residence through a U.S. citizen spouse if:

✪ the alien spouse is married to or was divorced from a U.S. citizen within the past two years;

✪ the alien spouse is a person of good moral character;

✪ the alien spouse has resided with the U.S. citizen spouse;

✪ the marriage was entered into in good faith; and,

✪ the alien spouse (or his or her minor child) was battered or was the subject of extreme cruelty.

The rules recently changed for *former* spouses of abusive U.S. citizens or lawful permanent residents. It used to be that one was *ineligible* to self-petition if the abused spouse was *not* legally married to the U.S. citizen or legal permanent resident spouse on the day the petition was filed. Now a petition may still be filed if the divorce took place during the two-year period immediately *preceding* the filing of the self-petition. It must also be shown that the divorce was connected to the battery or extreme mental cruelty, although this may already be proven by the other evidence. However, the divorce judgment need not specifically state that the divorce was caused by domestic violence.

5

NONIMMIGRANT VISAS AND MAINTAINING VALID STATUS

If you are in the U.S. on a *nonimmigrant visa*, it is critical that you remain in *valid status*. This will preserve your right to obtain permanent residence or change status to another nonimmigrant visa classification.

Those seeking to become a permanent resident in the future will normally need to be in a valid status to do so, unless they fall within one of two exceptions—if the person is Section 245(i) eligible, or if he or she is eligible to adjust through an immediate family visa.

Section 245(i)

People are 245(i) eligible if they have an I-130 filed on their behalf prior to April 30, 2001, during the *mini-amnesty* period, and if they were present in the U.S. on December 20, 2000. Or, if the I-130 was filed before January 18, 1998, then the person is 245(i) eligible whether or not he or she was present in the U.S. on December 20, 2000.

Immediate Family

The other exception to being in valid status is if the person is the beneficiary of an immediate family visa petition such as:

✪ marriage to a U.S. citizen;

✪ parent of a U.S. citizen; or,

✪ minor, unmarried child of a U.S. citizen.

These people must have made a lawful entry into the U.S. and not have worked without authorization in the U.S. (However, in most cases, USCIS currently does not appear to be enforcing this last provision.)

Child Status Protection Act

On August 6, 2002, President Bush signed into law the *Child Status Protection Act* (CSPA). This Act provides important benefits to those who are turning 21 and consequently will age out of their eligibility to adjust status. The CSPA applies to children seeking benefits only in the following types of cases:

✪ family based (except K visas);

✪ employment based;

✪ diversity visa; and,

✪ asylum and refugee.

It does not apply to nonimmigrant applications at all. However, the benefit that the CSPA may provide depends very much on the type of petition and the specific preference category. Certainly, anyone who may age out or has already aged out of any category should check this section to see if it preserves or restores eligibility.

The first step is to determine whether the CSPA applies to the case at all, since the CSPA is not retroactive. It will only apply to a petition:

✪ filed after August 6, 2002;

✪ filed before August 6, 2002, but was still pending on that date (i.e., not approved) or was denied but an appeal or motion to reopen was timely filed; or,

✪ approved before August 6, 2002, if the beneficiary either:

• aged out after August 6, 2002 or

• aged out before August 6, 2002, but prior to aging out, had applied for an immigrant visa and no final decision was made prior to that date.

If the *CSPA* does apply, what benefit does it provide to the child who may have otherwise aged out or is about to age out? It depends on the benefit.

✪ *Immediate relatives:* The age of the child is fixed on the date the I-130 petition was filed. Therefore, the child will never age out of the benefit.

✪ *Preference categories:* The age of the child is fixed on the date the immigrant visa number becomes available (i.e., I-130, I-140 or I-360 petition becomes current) and not when it is filed. However, the age of child is reduced by the period of time the petition was pending (i.e., before it was approved). In order to retain this benefit, the adjustment of status *must* be filed within on year of the visa number becoming available.

✪ *Diversity visas.* The age of the child is fixed on the first day of the diversity visa mail-in application period.

✪ *Asylum/refugee applications.* The age of the child is fixed on the day that the parent files the application.

There are numerous memos available on the USCIS website that go into detail about specific situations. Keep in mind that the policy is developing and there is considerable room for creative argument.

Travel Outside the U.S.

The other important aspect of maintaining nonimmigrant status is the right to travel outside the U.S. during the time you wait for the adjustment interview. If you were out of status more than six months at the time you filed an application for adjustment of status, then you would not qualify for *advance parole* on account of unlawful presence. Thus, you may not travel outside the U.S. until your status is adjusted. While the backlog for adjustment interviews have decreased substantially in recent months, your case can still drag on for various reasons after the interview.

Keep a copy of both sides of each *I-94* and turn it into the airline, whether the airline's employees ask for it or not. The airline personnel at the gate are supposed to have this information. If the airline is not collecting the I-94s, then it is possible to go to the U.S. embassy and hand it in. The other option is to keep a copy of the airline ticket and perhaps proof that you actually arrived in the foreign country. When applying for a new visa, you can show it to the consulate that you honored the terms of your last visa by leaving in time. Also, if applying for an immigrant visa at an embassy, it might be useful to show you returned to the U.S. and were not *unlawfully present*, which may bar approval of the visa.

Types of Nonimmigrant Visas

Most nonimmigrants enter as one of the following:

- ✪ tourists;

- ✪ students;

- ✪ business-related visitors; or,

- ✪ temporary employees.

Following is a fairly complete list of the nonimmigrant categories. The rest of this chapter, however, will only detail the family-based ones. (The rest are beyond the scope of this book.) The nonimmigrant categories are:

✪ *A-1, A-2, A-3:* foreign government employees (such as diplomats and officials) and their families, servants, and private employees;

✪ *B-1, B-2:* business visitors (to attend conferences, trade shows, etc.) who are not employed in the U.S., and tourists visiting for pleasure (obtaining medical treatment, conventions, incidental school attendance);

✪ *C-1, C-2, C-3:* aliens in transit through the U.S. or en route to the United Nations;

✪ *D-1, D-2:* foreign crew members of ships and aircrafts;

✪ *E-1, E-2:* aliens entering the U.S. to engage in trade or investment pursuant to a bilateral treaty between the U.S. and their country of nationality. (This classification authorizes employment in the U.S. to manage the trade or investment enterprise.);

✪ *F-1, F-2:* foreign students authorized to study in the U.S. Limited work authorization available during and after completion of the course of study;

✪ *G-1, G-5:* employees of international organizations and their families and servants;

✪ *H-1, H-2, H-3, H-4:* certain qualified temporary workers, trainees, and their families. (The *H-1B* category is accorded to individuals employed in a specialty occupation and is one of the most important nonimmigrant categories for employers wishing to hire a foreign national in a professional or highly technical position.);

✪ *I:* media representatives;

✪ *J-1, J-2:* exchange visitors and their families. This certification allows nonimmigrants to enter the U.S. for purposes of engaging in lecturing, research, study, observation, or training. (Most individuals in J status are subject to a requirement that they return to their home country for at least two years upon completion of the J program. Waivers of this requirement are available in some circumstances.);

✪ *K-1, K-2:* fiancés of U.S. citizens and their minor children;

✪ *K-3, K-4:* spouses of U.S. citizens with an I-130 petition pending, and their minor children;

✪ *L-1, L-2:* intracompany transferees who are managers, executives, and employees with specialized knowledge of international corporations to the U.S.;

✪ *M-1, M-2:* vocational students and their families;

✪ *N:* family members of G-4 special immigrants;

✪ *O-1, O-2, O-3:* aliens of extraordinary ability in the sciences, arts, education, business, or athletics, and accompanying family members. These nonimmigrants must be at the top of their field to qualify. (Although there are lower standards for artists and entertainers, they must have achieved prominence.);

✪ *P-1, P-2, P-3:* athletic teams and entertainment groups who are recognized internationally;

✪ *Q:* international cultural exchange aliens;

✪ *R-1, R-2:* ministers, religious workers, and their families;

✪ *S-5, S-6:* also called the *Snitch visa*. Promised frequently, but awarded sparingly in the U.S. to individuals who assist with a criminal investigation;

✪ *TN:* Canadian and Mexican citizens qualified as temporary workers under NAFTA; and,

✪ *V:* the spouse and minor children of an LPR whose I-130 petition was filed prior to December 20, 2000, and has been pending more than three years. (see Chapter 4.)

In addition to the above specific criteria, there are requirements that are common to many nonimmigrant visas, such as the applicant must not be an *intending immigrant* (that is, the person intends to return to his or her native country before expiration of the visa).

Procedure   The procedures for obtaining a nonimmigrant visa varies with the type of visa. If the person is in the U.S., he or she must be in status on a valid nonexpired visa to extend or change status. The I-94 will be marked with the date of expiration for the visa regardless of the date of expiration on the visa stamped in the passport.

Then an application is made on the I-539 form to either extend or change status.

A common scenario is to enter the U.S. as a tourist and then attempt to change status to that of a student. This application is not as easy as simply registering at a school to be a full-time student. First, under rules enacted in August 2003, the only people who can change status to that of a student are those who have their I-94 card annotated *prospective student* by an inspections officer at the place of entry. If you wish to enroll as a student, you may still travel back to your country and obtain a student visa at your embassy. The procedure to enter the U.S. as a nonimmigrant may be either a two- or three-step process, depending on the type of visa.

For some petitions, it may be necessary to file a petition first with the service center in the U.S. that has jurisdiction over the petitioner or sponsoring company. For example, the H, L, and E visas require an approved petition from a service center. The service center will transmit the file to the designated embassy upon its approval.

Then, the applicant will process through the consulate or embassy to obtain the visa. In some cases, the application is filed directly at the consulate. For example, tourist visas, student visas, and religious worker visas are directly filed with the consulate.

Finally, the visa is given a final lookover by the inspections officer at the place of entry. The inspections officer has the right to deny entry on the visa if he or she suspects the terms of the visa may be violated. This is much less likely to happen where a petition was approved first by a service center and then by an embassy. (It is the B visa that tends to come under closer scrutiny at the place of entry.)

K-1 Visa

A U.S. citizen may apply to bring his or her fiancé into the U.S. through an embassy or consulate. The fiancé enters on a K-1 visa. (The fiancé's minor unmarried children under the age of 21 enter in K-2 status.)

Several documents are required to support the *fiancé* petition. The U.S. citizen must establish his or her citizenship. Other documents may be required. For example, if a person was previously married, then a divorce decree must also be submitted. If any name has been changed from one of the supporting documents, then documentation as to this change must be provided.

The supporting documents establish that the engagement is *bona fide*; that is, that it was entered into for love and affection rather than for U.S. immigration status. The petitioner should draft a short statement as to the history of the relationship, and in particular when marriage was proposed. There is a strict requirement that the couple have met in person within the past two years. The list in Chapter 14 contains examples of useful supporting documents. The more of these documents that are obtained, the quicker and easier the case will be granted.

K-1 Benefits and Eligibility

A person in K-1 status is immediately eligible to work based on his or her status. As a practical matter, the K-1 alien may require a work permit in order to demonstrate to an employer his or her eligibility to work.

The K-1 beneficiary must marry the U.S. citizen petitioner within three months. This is a very strict deadline. There are no extensions of the K-1 visa, which is a single entry visa. Nor may the beneficiary change to other nonimmigrant status. However, there is no deadline to apply for adjustment of status—you may apply with an expired visa.

After marriage, a Form I-485 must be filed, as in marriage cases. (See Chapter 13.) A new medical exam is not required if the adjustment of status application is filed within one year of the medical exam presented at the embassy. However, it will be necessary to complete the vaccination supplement. The I-130 petition is not required for the spouse, but separate I-130 petitions are required for the children. The Affidavit of Support form, the *I-864*, is also required. If any type of waiver (Form *I-601*) was required to obtain the K-1 visa, the waiver will remain valid for adjustment of status purposes, unless there is a new ground of inadmissibility.

There are harsh consequences if the intended marriage does not take place. If the beneficiary does not marry the petitioner within ninety days, he or she may not pursue adjustment of status by any other avenue. Even Section 245(i) (which helps applicants who enter illegally) does not assist the K-1 fiancé who does not marry. The only possible exception is to apply for asylum within one year of entry. (see Chapter 9.)

K-3 Visa

The K-3 visa is a nonimmigrant classification to speed the entry of spouses and minor unmarried children of U.S. citizens into the U.S. These visas came into being with the *LIFE Act,* and they are issued to spouses and children of U.S. citizens for whom I-130 petitions have been filed and are pending. The K-3 petition is approved for a period of four months, which may be extended if visa processing is not completed. Unlike an immigrant visa application, K-3 and K-4 visa applicants do not take the full medical exam and there is no Affidavit of Support requirement. A person applies for the K-3 visa as a faster route to entry to the U.S., or where the U.S. citizen petitioner has not been resident in the U.S. and cannot presently meet residence requirement for the Affidavit of Support.

K-3 visas are issued for two years (multiple entry) with extension available for good cause. The subsequent application for adjustment of status must be based on marriage to the K-3 petitioner and can be filed prior to approval of the I-130. Each K-4 dependent needs a separate I-130.

NOTE: *A person can apply for a K-4 Visa for a minor child only if the parent is the beneficiary of a K-3 Visa. If the parent is already in the U.S., then the minor child must wait until the parent adjusts status.*

K-1 and K-3 visas are unusual in that they are both nonimmigrant and immigrant visas at the same time. Also, careful inspection of the approval notice will indicate that these visas have expiration dates. A K-1 visa, for example, expires after four months. It normally takes more than four months from the time of DHS approval for a beneficiary to be interviewed at the consulate. Thus, if more time is required, it is necessary to formally ask the embassy for an extension of the petition, otherwise, it may expire necessitating a brand new petition.

Which type of cases are most problematic? The following scenarios typically serve as a red flag to the service center or consular officer, prompting a delay or outright denial:

- ✪ a very brief courtship followed by a plunge into matrimony;

- ✪ a marriage ceremony arranged only a short time after petitioner arrives in the beneficiary's country and they meet for the first time;

- ✪ no common language;

- ✪ petitioner resides with family members of the beneficiary in the U.S.;

- ✪ petitioner is employed by or has a business relationship with a relative of the beneficiary;

- ✪ petitioner submits phone records that show he or she uses a residential phone number that is listed in the name of another person;

- ✪ U.S. divorce followed very quickly by an engagement to foreign beneficiary;

- ✪ little or no documentary evidence of the relationship prior to the actual engagement;

- ✪ long gaps of time between the petitioner and beneficiary being together in person;

- ✪ failure to disclose previous marriages; and,

- ✪ failure to disclose previous petitions filed on behalf of other beneficiaries.

Any case reflecting one or more of the above characteristics requires more thorough documentation and explanation.

6 EMPLOYMENT-BASED PETITIONS

The *employment-based* permanent residence process can be long and arduous, particularly where *labor certification* is required. Labor certification means that after a supervised recruitment period, a state employment agency certifies that there is no qualified U.S. worker who can assume the job offered to the alien. If a labor certification is required, then the case may require an additional six months to one year (or more) depending on locality. Normally, an attorney will be required to process an employment-based application.

With the demise of Section 245(i) (described in Chapter 3), an individual must be *in status* (i.e., on an unexpired nonimmigrant visa) at the time the application for adjustment of status is filed. However, there are a couple of exceptions. If an individual filed a *labor certification application* or was the beneficiary of an immediate relative petition before April 30, 2001, then he or she may apply for adjustment if he or she was physically present in the U.S. on December 20, 2000. Otherwise, if the labor certification or an I-130 petition was filed before January 18, 1998, then he or she may also adjust without regard to presence in the U.S. on December 20, 2000.

First Preference: Extraordinary Ability, Outstanding Researcher, Multinational Executive

The first preference category is comparable to the nonimmigrant O and P visas. These include aliens of extraordinary ability in the sciences, arts, education, business, or athletics, and accompanying family members. In the case of P Visa holders, athletic teams and entertainment groups that are recognized internationally are included.

Federal regulations define *extraordinary ability* as a level of expertise indicating that the individual is one of a small percentage who have risen to the very top of a particular field in the sciences, arts, education, business, and athletics. Such a person will have received national or international acclaim.

The extraordinary ability category is a very difficult standard to meet. For example, only the top players in the major, professional sports leagues would qualify. A wide variety of artists, such as those in the culinary and visual arts, may qualify with a slightly lower standard of having achieved *prominence*.

Further, this category does not necessarily require a job offer, but most applications will likely need one, or at least correspondence with prospective employers. There is no labor certification required. The petition may be filed by a prospective employer or by the alien him- or herself. As these petitions are difficult to document and are not easily approved by the service center, the assistance of an attorney will be necessary.

Outstanding Professor or Researcher

Generally, professors and researchers with a demonstrated record of excellence in the field and who have been offered a tenure-track position with a U.S. institution of higher education, a similar position at a research institution, or an established research division of a corporation meet the extraordinary ability requirements. This category does not require a labor certification.

Multinational Executives and Managers

The multinational executives and managers category is intended to facilitate the transfer of key managerial and executive personnel within a multinational corporation. This classification is generally available to an individual who has been employed abroad in a managerial or executive capacity by a branch, subsidiary, affiliate, or parent of a U.S. company for at least one year, and who is being transferred to the U.S. company. Such people may be in the U.S. on an L-1A visa. This category does not require labor certification.

Second Preference: Exceptional Ability, Advance Degree Professionals

The second preference classification is available to individuals demonstrating exceptional ability in the sciences, arts, or business. Federal regulations define *exceptional ability* as a degree of expertise significantly above that ordinarily encountered in the sciences, arts, or business. Labor certification and a job offer are required unless they are waived by approval of a national interest waiver.

Professionals with Advanced Degrees or Experience

Qualification in the professionals category requires demonstration that the beneficiary holds an advanced degree in the field and that the position offered requires an individual with an advanced degree. The equivalent of an advanced degree is where the position requires a bachelor's degree plus five years of progressive experience. Labor certification and a job offer are required unless they are waived by approval of a national interest waiver.

Third Preference: Skilled Workers

The third preference is the most common category in which employment-based applications are filed. This category requires a job offer and labor certification. It includes entry-level professionals with a bachelor's degree and skilled workers in occupations that require at least two years' experience, training, or education. Presently, there is a significant backlog for visa numbers.

Fourth Preference: Unskilled Workers

The fourth preference group includes unskilled workers in occupations that require less than two years of experience, training, and education. Almost any occupation should qualify here. Often, there is a significant backlog in this category, such as at present. This classification does require labor certification.

Shortage Occupations

At the present time, only two occupations—registered nurses and physical therapists—have been designated by the Department of Labor as *shortage occupations*. These are called *Schedule A* occupations, since that is how they are named in the Department of Labor regulations. The benefit of such a designation is that labor certification is not required.

The Labor Certification Process

Labor certification is required for most employment-based adjustment applications. It is an actual recruitment of U.S. workers, under the supervision of the *Department of Labor* and the *State Employment Security Agency* (SESA) in order to establish that there is no U.S. worker who is ready, willing, able, and qualified to take the position offered to an alien. A labor certification may be approved when there is no U.S. worker who can do a certain job. A wide variety of jobs can fit into this category, such as nanny, ethnic chef, or software engineer.

As of March 2005, a new system called PERM (Certification for the Permanent Employment of Aliens in the United States) went into effect, completely replacing the former arduous labor certification process. As the former process was prone to long delays, the goal of the redesigned process is for streamlined processing and fraud reduction. The PERM program is showing itself to be a success. In the first year of its operation, over 100,000 cases have been filed, the vast majority processed within forty-five to sixty days. Even in the substantial number of cases where an audit was requested, processing was still handled expeditiously.

Now the process is under the near complete control of the U.S. Department of Labor and requires much more participation by the employer. In order to file permanent labor certification applications online, the employer must open an online account. Once the employer information is verified by the Department of Labor, a password and PIN are sent to the employer. An employer must have a valid Federal Employer Identification Number (FEIN) in order to use the system. The application may be filed electronically or on paper.

Before filing the labor certification, recruitment must have been completed. Such recruitment must have taken place no more than six months before filing the application. There are specific types of requirements that must be met.

Employers have the option of submitting the new form, the **APPLICATION FOR PERMANENT EMPLOYMENT CERTIFICATION (ETA FORM 9089)** electronically, directly to a national processing center. Supporting documentation is not submitted with the application.

Recruitment   Recruitment provisions are divided into professional and nonprofessional occupations, and additional recruitment steps are required for professional occupations. Sunday edition newspaper advertisements are required. A language requirement may be included within the job description, but business necessity will likely have to be demonstrated.

The following recruitment efforts may be utilized:

- ✪ job order with the state workforce agency;

- ✪ internal company recruitment;

- ✪ company and commercial Internet web page ads;

- ✪ community, college, or other job fairs;

- ✪ private employment agency; or,

- ✪ newspaper or other print advertisements.

In addition to the results of the above, the Department of Labor may consider its own experience with such jobs and obtain general job market information as well.

Once the labor certification is approved, the petitioning company then files **IMMIGRANT PETITION FOR ALIEN WORKER (FORM I-140)** on behalf of the alien. The purpose of the I-140 petition is to prove that the alien meets the job and experience requirements and all other requirements of the position, that the job offer is legitimate, and that the employer has the ability to pay the required wage.

If the alien is present in the U.S. and eligible to apply for adjustment of status, then the entire adjustment package for the alien and his or her dependents may be filed concurrently with Form I-140. However, if there is any question as to the approval of the I-140 petition, then it may be most prudent to file the petition initially and await its adjudication before going to the considerable expense of applying for adjustment.

Religious Workers

The religious worker is actually part of the employment-based fourth preference category, but is separated here since the documentation required is unique. It is available to certain qualified ministers and religious workers coming to the U.S. to practice their vocation. Labor certification is not required.

The religious worker program has been extended by Congress through September 30, 2008. (Despite the substantial fraud in this category, Congress appears likely to keep extending the duration of this program.)

Eligibility   The nonimmigrant R-1 visa for religious workers has different eligibility requirements than those required for the immigrant visa. For this nonimmigrant visa, a person merely has to show that he or she was a member of the religious organization for two years and has an offer of employment from the organization. As for most nonimmigrant visas, the person must demonstrate that he or she will return to his or her native country at the end of the visa period.

The petitioning organization does not have to actually be a church, but it must be a section 501(c)(3) organization that meets certain requirements. Its nonprofit classification must be due to religious factors, it must be organized for religious purposes, and it must operate under the principles of a particular faith. For example, religious schools should qualify. Detailed guidance is set forth at 9 FAM 42.32(d)(1), 9 FAM 41.58 Notes, 9 CFR 214.2(r), and 8 CFR 204.5(m).

The type of person who may qualify for the immigrant visa is more limited than for the nonimmigrant visa. A petition may be filed for an alien who for the past two years has been a member of a religious denomination that has been a bona fide nonprofit, religious organization in the U.S.

This person must also have been carrying on the vocation, professional work, or other work described below, continuously for the past two years. The person must seek to enter the U.S. to work solely as one of the following:

✪   as a minister of that denomination;

✪   in a professional capacity in a religious vocation or occupation for that organization; or,

✪   in a religious vocation or occupation for the organization or its non-profit affiliate.

The religious worker must have a full-time job offer by the religious organization. There must also be a demonstration that the alien's services are needed by the organization in the U.S. Such a demonstration requires an analysis of the staff size, congregation size, specific duties, prior experience of the alien, and prior staffing of a particular position. The organization must also demonstrate it has sufficient funds to pay the salary. (See pages 132–134 for information on filing a religious worker petition.)

7 | INVESTORS

The investor category is actually a fifth preference employment-based petition. However, it deserves separate treatment for the purposes of this book because of its unique qualifications.

Qualifications

An alien investing a specified amount of capital *at risk* in a commercial enterprise may be eligible in the investor category. The enterprise must generate full-time employment for U.S. workers, and permanent residence is granted conditionally.

The following criteria must be met for a new commercial enterprise:

- ✪ the investor must be engaged in a managerial or policy-making capacity;

- ✪ the investor must invest or be actively in the process of investing at least $1 million in the enterprise, or $500,000 if the investment is in a rural area or high unemployment area;

✪ the enterprise must benefit the U.S. economy and create full-time employment for at least ten U.S. citizen workers not related to the investor;

✪ the capital must have been obtained through a lawful means; and,

✪ the investment must be made in a new commercial enterprise (such as a new business), the purchase and restructuring of an existing business, or the expansion of a business so as to result in a 40% increase in net worth or number of employees.

Multiple investors may pool their money into an investment as long as each investor meets the above requirements. Investment funds may come from any legal source, including gifts and divorce settlements.

> **Warning:** Investor petitions are highly technical and also involve substantial sums of money. Given these factors, you should definitely not proceed with such a petition without expert assistance.

The initial petition is filed on *Form I-526*. (See page 134 for information on how to complete this form.) It is important to realize that the entire investment need not be made at the outset. However, you must demonstrate the ability to do so by the end of the initial two-year conditional period. A detailed business plan will normally be necessary to make such a showing.

Permanent residence is granted only for a conditional two-year period. Within the three-month period prior to its expiration, you must file *Form I-829* in order to remove the conditions. (see pages 136–137.)

8 | GREEN CARD DIVERSITY LOTTERY

Once a year, normally in November, the Department of State holds a *green card diversity lottery* with 50,000 green cards up for grabs. This lottery has provided major relief to hundreds of thousands of immigrants. There is some discussion, however, of ending this category.

The idea behind this category is to create diversity by offering green cards to people in countries that do not normally immigrate to the U.S. in large numbers. Therefore, those from countries that send more than 50,000 immigrants to the U.S. in the previous year are prevented from applying. In 2006, the barred countries were Mexico, Canada, China, Colombia, the Dominican Republic, El Salvador, Haiti, India, Jamaica, Pakistan, the Philippines, Poland, Russia, South Korea, the United Kingdom, and Vietnam.

The problem with the lottery is that it has became hugely popular in recent years. Over ten million applications were received last year. Considering that almost three million applications were thrown out for not following instructions and that 100,000 acceptance letters are sent out, the odds of winning are approximately 1 in 100. If a person is married and both file a separate application, the odds are cut in half to 1 in 50. If one were to file applications over a five-year period, then the odds might drop to 1 in 20 over that time. These odds vary by region.

Since there is no fee to file the application and it is an easy application to complete, it is well worth doing each year. The most difficult part of the process might be to get the timing right. The application period changes slightly, but recently it has been starting in early November of each year. An application must be properly filed and received within the specified application period.

Qualifications

Other than not being from one of the excluded countries, you easily qualify for the diversity lottery by being a high school graduate. If you are not a high school graduate, but have more than two years' work experience within the past five years in an occupation or trade that requires at least two years of training or experience to perform, you also qualify. You also need to meet all of the normal requirements for a green card, such as having a valid affidavit of support. Both spouses may submit an application and include any unmarried children under the age of 21.

Beginning in 2003, the State Department replaced the old mail-in system with an online application system and lengthened the application period. Now you apply by accessing the new system at **www.dvlottery.state.gov**. The availability of an online system is welcome news for those who were applying outside the U.S. and previously had to rely on their own country's and the U.S. mail system for the application to be received within the thirty-day period.

Prior to making the application, it is necessary to obtain a digital photo of each member of the family. The photograph must be in the JPEG format. You may check online to see if a photograph meets the specifications.

In approximately May through July of the next year, winners begin to be notified through receipt of an acceptance letter. Although there are only approximately 50,000 visas (including dependents) available each year, the State Department mails out approximately 100,000 acceptance letters each year. The timing of visa processing for diversity visa winners coincides with the government fiscal year, which starts on October 1st and ends on September 30th of each year. The visa numbers become available on October 1st and then expire on September 30th of the next year. Any lottery applicant who has not received a letter by July of the next year was probably not be selected.

Any person who has not adjusted by September 30th will simply not become a permanent resident, including derivative family members who are overseas. The visa numbers cease to exist after September 30th, with no exceptions whatsoever.

Every year, there are people who do not complete their case by September 30th and are excluded. There is almost no recourse if you fail to adjust status before September 30th.

Since there are more diversity visa winners than visa numbers, a shortage of visa numbers may develop—especially towards the end of the government fiscal year. In August and September, the diversity visa numbers start to become scarce. While a single individual can probably always scrounge up a number, a family of five may not.

9 | Asylum

It is possible to qualify for permanent residence through a grant of *asylum*. One whose asylum application is granted, whether by the asylum office or by an *immigration judge* (IJ), is called an *asylee*. After one year in asylee status, that individual may apply for a green card. It will actually take a number of years thereafter to receive the green card, due to the multiyear backlog in visa numbers for asylees.

Refugees

You may have heard of the term *refugee*. The use of this term is somewhat confusing in regard to immigration law. In common usage, a refugee is a person who has had to escape his or her native country for whatever reason, usually war or natural disaster. In the immigration sense, a refugee is a person who is granted specific status allowing that person to enter the U.S. and apply for adjustment after one year's residence in the U.S.

The legal definition of refugee, according to the United Nations, is one who has a *well-founded fear of persecution* and therefore cannot return to his or her country of citizenship. The persecution must be on account of one of five grounds:

1. political opinion;

2. race;

3. religion;

4. gender; or,

5. social group.

An applicant for asylum must meet the same legal standard. The next section explains these concepts in more detail.

Refugee Status versus Asylum

If a potential immigrant is outside the U.S., he or she applies for refugee status at one of the several refugee processing centers. Asylum, on the other hand, is for a person who is able to enter the U.S. either on a type of visa (such as a tourist or work visa), illegally through Canada or Mexico, or with a false passport.

There are numerous advantages to applying for asylum in the U.S. rather than refugee status abroad. The first advantage is there is no limit on the number of asylum cases that may be granted in the U.S. The limitation does come in when the asylee applies for a green card, but he or she is allowed to live and work in the U.S. during this time as well as travel abroad, so the hardship is reduced. The problem for those applying for refugee status is there are relatively few visa numbers allowed per year—approximately 50,000. Even these numbers are fewer than it seems, since there are restrictions by region. This means that there may be a longer wait for a number, even if the case is granted.

The other principal advantage is that it is easier to get the case approved in the U.S. consular officers at an embassy, though they are not the easiest people to convince as to the genuineness of any case. (Neither are the asylum officers in the U.S.) However, the advantage is that a case that is not granted by the asylum office, but rather is referred to the *immigration court*, allows a second (and a better) opportunity to the asylum applicant to prove his or her case. The hearing process is about as fair a process that can be provided to an alien, at least before most immigration judges.

Those applying for asylum are often concerned about the effect their manner of entry will have on their application. While a person does not earn points for making any type of unlawful entry, it is generally understood that a person fleeing persecution will enter the U.S. in any possible way if his or her life or well-being is at stake.

If you are intending to seek asylum upon entry or attempted entry at an airport or border, it makes a difference where you choose to enter. If you do not have valid entry documents, you will be subject to expedited removal, unless you can demonstrate a *credible fear* of harm in your home country. According to a 2005 United States Commission on International Religious Freedom report, the worst place to attempt entry was at New York's Kennedy Airport, where the ratio of applicants immediately sent back to their home country compared to the number allowed in for interview with the asylum office was 5:1. Contrast this with Miami Airport, where the ratio was 1:2. Atlanta and Newark were also particularly unlikely to find that the credible standard had been met.

Ironically, those who enter the U.S. on a work visa, such as an H-1B, are sometimes viewed more suspiciously, since they waited to obtain a job in the U.S. before escaping from persecution. It is more important to be able to explain the type of entry you made and why it was necessary than to enter in any particular way.

NOTE: *The post-September 11 climate appears to have chilled the Asylum Office. The Chicago Asylum Office reports that their approval rate prior to September 11, 2001 was 33%. Six months after, the approval rate dropped to 18%. It has since recovered to its normal levels. There are also fewer applications being filed on account of the one-year filing deadline.*

Qualifications

A claim of well-founded fear of persecution must be *subjectively genuine* and *objectively reasonable*. The *Board of Immigration Appeals* (BIA) has said that if there is a 10% chance of actual persecution happening in the native country, then asylum should be granted.

The conditions in certain countries render their citizens most likely to be granted asylum. The former Soviet bloc countries certainly dominated the asylum top ten charts before the breakup of the Soviet Union. Today, countries such as China, Iraq, Iran, and Ethiopia are probably the easiest countries from which to be granted asylum. There are, however, many countries where repressive regimes and persecution are a way of life.

Of course, the present approval rate of the asylum offices, which is roughly 33%, does not give one much hope. However, one's chances before the immigration court, in most cities, are substantially greater. Chicago, in particular, has very principled and fair immigration judges who seek to find reasons why a case should be granted. This is in contrast to the asylum office, where the officers are really looking to find reasons why the case should be denied.

If you have a real case where you did have problems with the authorities in your country or with groups the government is unwilling or unable to control on account of one of the five protected grounds, then you have a good chance. The more documentation you have, the better your chance.

Useful documentation is anything that proves any part of your claim, including:

❂   photos documenting any part of your claim;

❂   medical records;

❂   police records;

❂   newspaper articles that mention you, your family, or relatives;

❂   an expert witness to testify on your behalf;

❂   personal information, including photos, school records, participation in a relevant political or religious group, etc.;

❂   proof of membership in a specific political or religious party or organization, such as membership cards, a membership certificate, or a letter confirming the date you joined the organization and the activities you undertook after becoming a member;

❂   affidavits from members of the party or organization of which you claim membership;

✪ affidavits from witnesses to specific instances of arrests, or encounters under adverse circumstances with the police or other authorities in your native country; and,

✪ if you have a scar or marks on your body that are part of your claim, you should obtain a letter from the treating physician detailing the injuries and the date, type, and duration of treatment.

The more the asylum officer or IJ knows about you, the more he or she becomes involved and sympathetic to your case. The likelihood of an asylum grant increases substantially.

You should go to the State Department's human rights section of its website at **www.state.gov/gldrl/hr**, print out the *Country Report* for your country, and be familiar with the report.

The *Profile of Asylum Claims and Country Conditions* could also be referenced. It is hard to find a copy, as it was last printed in 1997, but it is authoritative with the immigration court. If it is not helpful, do not include it in evidence. But if you are lucky enough to have it support your claim, it could be entered and the pertinent sections highlighted.

Check out the websites in Appendix C under "human rights organizations." Find reports and articles that help your claim. Search for other supporting documents on the Internet. Your public library might help you do a search on Nexis, which is a database containing all articles of the leading newspapers, journals, and newswires around the world. You can search using words that might appear in an article. The information is out there—you just have to find it. With the advent of easy access to information through the Internet, it is expected that a valid asylum application will be documented. An applicant who expects to simply show up and be granted asylum is taking a big risk. (See page 122 for more information on filing an asylum application.)

Asylum Office Interview

Your application will first be reviewed by an asylum officer. Unfortunately, with any system involving humans, the end result may depend on who the officer is. This really holds true in a close case, which many applications are.

NOTE: *If you want to get a background on the asylum interview process, there is an excellent documentary called* Well-Founded Fear, *which analyzes the asylum process, including the interview.*

These days the asylum office gives an answer on an application fairly quickly. It used to be that many asylum cases would drag on for months or years. After ten days for those who are out of status, you will go to the asylum office to pick up the result. It may be either a grant of asylum or a referral to the immigration court.

The reason a case is referred will not be detailed. In a few sentences, it will simply say that the applicant did not meet the standard for asylum. That is, he or she did not demonstrate a well-founded fear of persecution.

It almost does not matter what is written on the referral notice except if it says that there is a finding of a lack of credibility. Essentially, this means the applicant was thought to be dishonest with regards to his or her testimony before the asylum officer. This may catch the eye of the immigration judge or the trial attorney during the court.

If the applicant is in status, the procedure is substantially different. He or she will not be asked to pick up a decision, but rather will be mailed either an *approval letter* or a *Notice of Intent to Deny.*

The latter consists of a detailed summary of your testimony and the precise reasons why the case is intended to be denied. The applicant will then have sixteen days to respond to this notice and provide detailed reasons and documentation to overcome the denial. This opportunity is provided for those in status, because they will not have a chance to contest the decision in immigration court. (Since they are in status, they cannot be placed into deportation proceedings.)

In the end, if the case is referred, bear in mind that the best opportunity still lies ahead. As previously discussed, the chances of winning an asylum case are much better in immigration court.

Benefits of Applying for Asylum

Applying for asylum grants some important benefits to the applicant, including obtaining work authorization, delaying deportation, and stopping the accrual of unlawful presence.

Obtaining Work Authorization

A major benefit of an asylum case is that the applicant becomes eligible for a work permit five months after the application is filed. While an application for asylum is pending, the applicant may apply for *work authorization*. There is no filing fee for the first application.

To discourage asylum filings to only obtain work authorization, the first application for work authorization may only be filed 150 days after the asylum application itself is filed. However, if the asylum applicant requests a continuance from either the asylum office or the immigration court during the 150 day period, the 150-day clock stops and only starts again after the next interview or hearing is held.

Congress has mandated that an asylum applicant have both his or her asylum interview and hearing before the immigration judge within six months after filing. This is a tough haul just to get work authorization. It has proven effective in decreasing the number of frivolous applications and reducing the burden on the system. (See Chapter 13 to apply for work authorization five months after filing the asylum application.)

Delaying Deportation

If you are placed into proceedings, even a weak asylum case may be helpful simply as a means to delay deportation. It will take perhaps one year for the individual hearing date, two or more years for an appeal to the BIA, and then another year for the appeal to one of the federal circuit courts.

During this four-year period, the alien can hope that a family-based or employment-based petition becomes approved. If the asylum case is still pending with the BIA, then a *motion to remand* may be filed. That will bring the case back to the immigration judge for a decision on the adjustment application. Finally, there is always the hope that in the meantime an *amnesty* or other immigration benefit will be enacted by Congress.

Stopping Accrual of Unlawful Presence

An alien begins to accrue *unlawful presence* once the nonimmigrant visa expires, or once he or she enters the U.S. without inspection. Accrual of six months of unlawful presence will prevent that person from reentering the U.S. for three years. One year of unlawful presence serves as a ten-year bar. These bars go into effect only if the person departs the U.S. and then seeks to reenter.

One of the several exceptions to accruing unlawful presence is if the alien has a pending *bona fide* asylum application. It does not matter whether the application is eventually denied. The fact that it is *pending* stops the accrual of unlawful presence.

Applying for Family Members

A person who was granted asylum or was admitted to the U.S. as a refugee within the past two years may apply for a family member. Only the principal individual who was granted asylum or refugee status may apply for family members. Such a person may apply for his or her spouse or unmarried child under 21 years of age. He or she must follow these rules.

- ✪ An asylee may apply for family members, whether they are in the U.S. or not.

- ✪ The relationship must have existed on the date of asylum approval or the date the applicant was admitted to the U.S. as a refugee and continues to exist as such at the time of filing.

- ✪ Both husband and wife must have been physically present at the marriage ceremony, or if not, they must have met since.

- ✪ A child may be conceived only on the date of asylum approval or admission to U.S. as refugee.

- ✪ An applicant may apply for stepchildren.

- ✪ An applicant may apply for an adopted child. (Submit the adoption decree and proof of two years' residence with the child.)

- ✪ Persons granted *derivative status* may not apply for their family members.

(See page 122 for more information.)

Applying for Permanent Residence

One year after the grant of asylum, an asylee may apply for adjustment of status. All asylee-based adjustment applications are filed at the Nebraska Service Center in Lincoln, Nebraska.

The Real ID Act, passed in May 2005, drastically changed the time frame in which asylees may obtain permanent residence. This statute abolished the 10,000 person annual limit on the number of asylees who could obtain permanent residence, thereby eliminating the five-year waiting list.

NOTE: *The official date adjustment of status is backdated one year from the date of approval.*

Refugee Filing

The filing for a refugee application is very similar to filing for an asylee application. Refugees may apply for adjustment one year after their entry. There is no filing fee for the refugee adjustment application or for fingerprints. The affidavit of support form is also not required.

NOTE: *The official date of adjustment of status is backdated to the date of original entry into the U.S.*

10 AMNESTIES

Amnesties are not a frequent occurrence in the U.S., as they are fraught with numerous problems. For one thing, they cause a tremendous burden on the system in terms of a huge number of applications in a very short period of time. The system is already running at capacity and subject to long backlogs.

Another problem is fraud. An amnesty usually means people qualify by proving residency in the U.S. prior to a certain distant date. With the availability of computers and laser printers, it is too easy to falsify documents.

Amnesties also reward those who have violated immigration laws and not those who are waiting patiently in their home country for a visa number.

It used to be thought that granting amnesty might solve the problem of illegal immigrants. However, it is now realized that it only exacerbates illegal immigration by encouraging future illegal aliens.

Recent Amnesty

The *LIFE Act* passed on December 20, 2000, is referred to by some as a *mini-amnesty*. It allowed a person who was the beneficiary of an I-130 petition, or who filed a labor certification by April 30, 2001, to be eligible to adjust status in the future on that petition or any other petition for which he or she might be eligible. It does not matter if the petition is later approved or not, so long as it was approvable when filed. The applicant needs to preserve proof that he or she was present in the U.S. on the day that the statute was passed—December 20, 2000.

Congress appears about to pass an extension of Section 245(i) that may not prove helpful to many people. It requires that the family relationship take place prior to August 15, 2001. For a marriage case, this means the marriage had to have taken place by that time. This will be disheartening to many couples who would have married had they known there might be a deadline. Some states recognize a common-law marriage. In these states, it may be possible to claim an earlier official marriage date by qualifying through the *common-law marriage* criteria.

NOTE: *You must talk to a domestic relations attorney to determine if you can qualify through this common-law marriage criteria.*

Late Amnesty Class Members

Approximately 400,000 *late amnesty* class members had a deadline of June 4, 2003, to file an application for adjustment of status. These are individuals who claim to have resided in the U.S. before 1982, but were improperly denied an opportunity by the INS to file for the 1986 amnesty announced by President Reagan by the amnesty's 1988 deadline because they had traveled abroad. These individuals later registered because of one of the three class action lawsuits filed against the Department of Justice. Many class members have been living in *immigration limbo* with work authorization since 1990. The LIFE Act gave class members one last chance to file for a green card if they could prove they entered the U.S. prior to 1982 and resided continuously in the U.S. through May 1988.

Be warned, however, that merely being a class member does not entitle an applicant to a grant of permanent residence It still has to be proven that you resided illegally in the U.S. between 1982 to 1988. The USCIS is insisting on substantial evidence beyond just letters or affidavits from friends or other private sources.

On May 25, 2006, the U.S. Senate passed a compromise bill (S. 2611) creating a legalization program for the following four groups of individuals:

✪ Group 1: Earned Adjustment

- individuals in the U.S. before April 5, 2001

- must have been employed for at least three years

- were not in lawful status on April 5, 2006

- can apply for a work permit for the first six years, then apply for permanent residence

✪ Group 2: Deferred Mandatory Departure

- individuals who entered the U.S. after April 5, 2001, but before January 7, 2004

- have been *continuously* employed

- not in lawful status on January 7, 2004

- can apply for a work permit of three years' duration; renewals may have to be applied for outside the U.S. (possibly at border)

- may be able to apply for permanent residence after Group 1 backlog clears

✪ Group 3: Agricultural Workers

- individuals who worked in agriculture over a two-year period

- first apply for *blue card*, then after three or five years (depending on hours worked) apply for green card

✪ Group 4: DREAM Act (Development, Relief, and Education for Alien Minors Act)

- minors who entered the U.S. before the age of 16

- have resided in U.S. for at least five years

- at least graduated high school

- individual becomes conditional permanent resident for six years, then may apply to remove conditions

The above are only the key provisions of the Senate bill. There are exceptions to many of these and additional relatively minor requirements that are too numerous to discuss at this time. For example, those who have outstanding orders of deportation or removal would be ineligible to apply for the above benefits. However, it may be possible to reopen the removal proceedings in order to erase the outstanding order and then be qualified to apply.

Other than the above key requirements listed above, it is simply too early in the political process to begin looking at the details that are sure to change, if any are enacted at all.

While the Senate bill is widely regarded as favorable to aliens, it also deals harshly with those aliens who do not qualify for benefits. For example, it includes a six month prison sentence for one failure to notify DHS of an address change, and deportation for two failures. It overturns the U.S. Supreme Court and authorizes indefinite detention. It not only makes illegal entry into the U.S. a misdemeanor crime, it renders it a continuing offense in order to encourage local law enforcement. In general, the Senate bill greatly increases the effect of minor crimes and immigration offenses, makes many DHS discretionary decisions unchallengeable, actively encourages local law enforcement to prosecute federal immigration laws, and allocates significant resources for detention facilities.

Needless to say, the stakes could not be higher for the millions of illegal aliens in the U.S. to see where the dividing line for benefits is to be drawn and whether they fall on the right side of it. There will not be any middle ground in the minefield that immigration law has become.

II CANCELLATION OF REMOVAL: 10 YEARS IN THE U.S.

A person may qualify for permanent residence if he or she has lived in the U.S. for the past ten years and meets other criteria. This type of relief is only available to those who are in *removal proceedings* before the immigration court. This can be frustrating to someone who feels he or she has a strong case and wants to be placed in proceedings. Ironically, those who wish to be placed in proceedings may not receive the cooperation of the USCIS.

As described earlier, removal proceedings are initiated when the Department of Homeland Security serves a document called a *Notice to Appear*. This document lists certain factual allegations and the *grounds of removability*. These are the sections of the *Immigration and Nationality Act* (INA) that make you removable. Often, the ground is simply overstaying your nonimmigrant visa or entering the U.S. without inspection.

Qualifications

To qualify for cancellation of removal, a person must demonstrate the following to an immigration judge:

- ☻ ten years' presence in the U.S. prior to the service of the Notice to Appear;

- ☻ a person of good moral character throughout this period;

- ☻ not been convicted of a criminal offense in sections 212(a)(2), 237(a)(2) or 237(a)(3) of the INA. These are a long list of crimes, including multiple misdemeanor offenses such as retail theft, drug possession, and the majority of felony offenses; and,

- ☻ removal would result in exceptional and extremely unusual hardship to a U.S. citizen or lawful permanent resident spouse, parent, or child.

These cases are very difficult to win. One immigration judge says that he has only granted three out of fifty cancellation cases. (Plus, in each of those cases, there was a U.S. citizen child who had a birth defect requiring treatment or therapy only available in the U.S.) More recently, the standards have eased significantly.

Living Continuously in the U.S. The first part of the case is to prove you entered the U.S. at least ten years ago and lived continuously in the U.S. You may have left the U.S., but for no more than three months at a time or six months in total. It can be difficult to prove continuous presence in the U.S. if one does not have a Social Security number and did not have accounts in his or her name. Also, many people do not keep records going back ten years, especially when they might be moving frequently or living with others.

The fourth ground in particular—*exceptional and extremely unusual hardship*—is what the case will be fought over. As you can imagine, it is very difficult to establish hardship to this extent.

Several recent opinions from the Board of Immigration Appeals provide a comparison from which you can evaluate your own case. These cases are the most important guidelines for determining whether cancellation of removal should be granted. They can be obtained from the *EOIR Virtual Law Library.* Go to **www.usdoj.gov/eoir**, then click on "Virtual Law Library." The cases are:

- ☻ *Matter of Andazola,* 23 I&N Dec. 319 (BIA 2002) (not granted);

- ☻ *Matter of Monreal,* 23 I&N Dec. 805 (BIA 2001) (not granted); and,

- ☻ *Matter of Recinas,* 23 I&N Dec. 467 (BIA 2002) (granted).

These are the factors that courts consider to prove hardship:

- ✪ age of the qualifying family member;

- ✪ family ties in the U.S. and abroad;

- ✪ length of residency in the U.S.;

- ✪ conditions of health requiring treatment in the U.S.;

- ✪ economic hardship;

- ✪ acculturation; and,

- ✪ balance of the equities.

Essentially, those who create a life for themselves in the U.S. by marrying, having children, or starting a business are the ones who are more likely to win this case. Those who were cautious and waited to have status will not have as much ammunition in trying to prove a cancellation case.

To demonstrate continuous physical presence, provide:

- ✪ leases or property deeds;

- ✪ mortgage company loan records;

- ✪ utility bills or a letter from a utility company;

- ✪ driver's and other types of licenses;

- ✪ purchase receipts or letters from companies;

- ✪ correspondence;

- ✪ documentation issued by governmental or other authorities;

- ✪ birth records of children, if born in the U.S.;

- ✪ hospital or medical records;

✪ church records;

✪ school records for yourself or your children;

✪ employment records;

✪ letter from employer;

✪ W-2 forms;

✪ tax returns;

✪ bank records;

✪ personal checks with cancellation stamps;

✪ credit card statements;

✪ USCIS documents such as work permits; or,

✪ insurance policies.

To demonstrate good moral character, provide:

✪ police records from each jurisdiction where you resided in the past ten years;

✪ affidavits of two U.S. citizens attesting to good character;

✪ an affidavit or letter from your current employer; or,

✪ evidence of tax payments.

To prove hardship, provide:

✪ an affidavit of an expert witness;

✪ medical records, where relevant;

✪ school records of children;

- ✪ records of participation in community organizations or a church (or letter from minister or officer of organization);

- ✪ records of volunteer work; or,

- ✪ if self-employed, records showing the number of people employed.

To prove date of entry into the U.S., provide:

- ✪ a passport with entry stamp;

- ✪ *form I-94* (arrival-departure record);

- ✪ nonimmigrant visa issued;

- ✪ *form I-20* (certificate of eligibility for student status); or,

- ✪ *form IAP-66* (certificate of eligibility for exchange visitor status).

Other useful documents are court conviction records and proof of child support payments.

Family Members

Bear in mind that, as difficult as these cases are, only the applicant will obtain permanent residence. The applicant's spouse and foreign-born children, unless they are in proceedings themselves, will not also obtain status from the judge. They will have to be applied for by the legal permanent resident, which may take about five years, and that is if the beneficiaries are eligible to adjust under Section 245(i).

***Battered Spouse
or Child***

There is a special rule that applies to a battered spouse or child. The immigration judge may grant cancellation of removal if a person has been battered or subjected to extreme cruelty in the U.S. by a spouse or parent who is a U.S. citizen or lawful permanent resident, the person has been present in the U.S. for at least three years, and the person is of good moral character.

12 | MISCELLANEOUS CATEGORIES

The categories in this chapter stand on their own and usually have unique circumstances. It is beyond the scope of this book to give any detail on how to file for them. An attorney should be consulted for assistance.

U.S. Citizen Grandparent: Transmitted Citizenship

If someone has a grandparent who is a U.S. citizen, then that person may be able to obtain citizenship through the parent, who may unknowingly be a U.S. citizen. These laws, contained in Section 301 of the INA, are complex and vary with the date of birth of the parent.

NOTE: *Consult an immigration attorney to confirm a particular situation.*

Private Bills

A *private bill* is an option of final and last resort. It involves having a member of Congress sponsor an individual to become a permanent resident. Or, more realistically, a private bill removes a bar to permanent residence, such as a criminal record. A private bill is one that affects only one individual or a small group of people. (A *public bill* affects the public generally.)

In a recent session of Congress, fourteen private bills were introduced and two passed. It is not a realistic option in most cases. However, with a combination of the right contacts, facts, and marketing ability, it is worth a try.

A private bill must be approved by the House Judiciary Committee's Subcommittee on Immigration and Claims and by the Senate Judiciary Committee's Immigration Subcommittee before going to each respective chamber for a *floor vote*. Clearly, the passage of a private bill is a long and difficult road at best.

The House Subcommittee on Immigration and Claims has recently put together a very helpful guide to the private bill process at **www.house.gov/ judiciary.**

This guide describes the criteria used by the subcommittee in considering a bill. The Senate also published a set of rules in 1993, which are not available on the Internet but can be ordered at **www.senate.gov**.

Cubans

Any native or citizen of Cuba who was admitted or paroled into the U.S. after 1958 may apply for adjustment of status. He or she must have been physically present in the U.S. for one year.

S "Snitch" Visa

The *S Visa* category allows for those who assist a Department of Homeland Security (DHS) investigation to be given nonimmigrant status. They can then later apply for adjustment of status. While this visa is often promised by agents of the DHS, it is rarely delivered. The *S Visa* is also known as the *snitch* visa.

NOTE: *Any promise to be petitioned for by a DHS officer should be put in writing.*

T and U Visas

The new T and U nonimmigrant visa categories are for victims of smuggling or people-trafficking, who can show they would suffer extreme hardship if removed from the U.S. After three years in this status, such a person may apply for adjustment of status.

Registry

On account of the rather ancient cutoff date, the registry is rarely used anymore as a basis for adjustment of status. To qualify, an individual must have entered the U.S. prior to 1972 and have resided in the U.S. continuously since. For the most part, anyone who qualifies under this law would likely qualify under other categories, such as the 1986 amnesty. It is conceivable that someone who was barred from the 1986 amnesty on account of criminal convictions could meet the less restrictive registry requirement of being a person of good moral character at the time of application.

There is talk in Congress of amending the cutoff date for the registry to something more realistic, such as 1986.

Minors Dependent on a Juvenile Court

A minor can qualify for a green card as a special immigrant if he or she has been declared dependent on a juvenile court located in the U.S., it has been determined by that court to be eligible for long-term foster care, and it is in the best interests of the child to not be returned to his or her native country. A child who acquires permanent residence status on this basis may not ever petition for his or her natural or adoptive parents.

Military Translators

As of 2006, a native of Afghanistan or Iraq who has been employed for at least twelve months as a translator by the U.S. military may apply for permanent residence. Such individuals who are already present in the U.S. may file Form I-360 with the Nebraska Service Center, while those in Afghanistan or Iraq file with the Islamabad, Pakistan, or Rome, Italy, embassies, respectively.

SECTION 3:
THE PERMANENT RESIDENCE
APPLICATION PROCESS

13 REQUIRED FORMS AND INSTRUCTIONS

Each eligibility category has its own specific required forms and documents. Keep in mind that the actual forms are just the starting point. The supporting documents are most critical to getting a case timely processed and granted. Carefully read the section in this chapter that applies to you in order to get started with the proper requirements.

The following forms are covered in detail in this chapter:

✪ **RELIGIOUS WORKERS** **132**
I-360 Petition filing
I-485 Adjustment of Status filing
(see also, Labor Certification filing, p.110)

✪ **INVESTORS**. **134**
I-526 Petition filing
I-829 Petition to Remove Conditions filing

✪ **CANCELLATION OF REMOVAL**. **137**
Form EOIR-42B Application filing

Immediate Relative Petitions

If the alien relative is already in the U.S. and eligible for adjustment of status, then the petition is normally filed as a *one-stop package*—that is, along with the adjustment of status application. However, when the beneficiary resides outside the U.S. or will be adjusting status outside the U.S., it is often the case that an I-130 petition is filed on its own with the appropriate service center.

Applying for a Minor Child

The required documents for a U.S. citizen applying for a minor child are as follows:

✪ **FORM I-130 ALIEN RELATIVE PETITION**;

✪ filing fee of $130;

✪ proof of the petitioner's U.S. citizenship (birth certificate if born in the U.S.; naturalization certificate, certificate of citizenship, or U.S. passport identification page if not born in the U.S.);

✪ birth certificate showing the names of the petitioner and the child (and if the father is petitioning, his marriage certificate);

✪ legal termination of any previous marriage of father or stepfather, if he is the petitioner;

✪ evidence of legal name change, if necessary (marriage certificate, adoption decree, or court order); and,

    ✪   if the child is adopted, certified copy of adoption decree showing adoption before age 16, any legal custody decree, and a statement listing the dates and places the parent has lived with the adopted child (must be more than two years).

The listing on page 85 is the entire **I-130** packet that will be filed.

The **I-130** must be carefully completed (see page 87) and signed. It must then be supported by several documents. First, the U.S. citizen must establish his or her citizenship by one of the documents previously indicated. The birth certificate of the minor child must be filed to establish the qualifying relationship. This birth certificate must show the name of the parent who is filing the petition. If the father is petitioning, then the marriage certificate must also be provided. Finally, if any name on a supporting document has changed, a legal document to evidence the name change is required.

The following points apply to any required document. Provide only photocopies of all documents. All birth and marriage certificates must have been issued by or registered with the proper civil authority in the foreign country. If a document is not in English, it must be submitted along with a certified English translation (see page 142). If any document is unavailable, see page 143 for more information.

After the **I-130** petition is completed and the above documents assembled, refer to page 87 for a description of how and where to file the I-130 petition packet.

Applying for a Parent   The required documents for a U.S. citizen applying for a parent are as follows:

    ✪   **Form I-130 Alien Relative Petition**;

    ✪   filing fee of $130;

    ✪   proof of the petitioner's U.S. citizenship (birth certificate if born in the U.S.; naturalization certificate, certificate of citizenship, or, U.S. passport identification page if not born in the U.S.);

    ✪   birth certificate showing the names of the petitioner and the parent (and if the father or a stepparent is the beneficiary, his or her marriage certificate);

- ✪ legal termination of any previous marriage of father or stepfather, if he is the petitioner; and,

- ✪ evidence of legal name change, if necessary (marriage certificate, adoption decree, or court order).

The listing on the previous page is the entire **I-130** packet that will be filed. The I-130 must be carefully completed (see the next section) and signed.

It must then be supported by several documents. First, the U.S. citizen must establish his or her citizenship by one of the documents previously indicated. The birth certificate of the petitioner must be filed to establish the qualifying relationship. This birth certificate must show the name of the petitioner and the parent who is being filed for. If the father is being filed for, then the marriage certificate must also be provided. Finally, if any name on a supporting document has changed, a legal document to evidence the name change is required.

The following points apply to any required document. Provide only photocopies of all documents. All birth and marriage certificates must have been issued by or registered with the proper civil authority in the foreign country. If a document is not in English, it must be submitted along with a certified English translation. (see page 142.) If any document is unavailable, see page 143 for more information.

After the **I-130** petition is completed and the above documents assembled, refer to the next section for a description of how and where to file the I-130 petition packet.

Spouses

A U.S. citizen may apply for an alien spouse for whom there is no wait for a visa number. The first stage is the **I-130** petition, which depending on certain circumstances may or may not be filed with the adjustment of status packet. This first section deals with preparing the I-130 petition.

I-130 Petition   An **I-130** petition filing requires the items listed on page 94. The items listed consist of the entire I-130 packet that will be filed. The I-130 form itself must be carefully completed. Page 94 contains detailed instructions on how to do so.

An **I-130** petition filing requires the following:

✪ **Form I-130**;

✪ filing fee of $130;

✪ **Form G-325A** for husband;

✪ **Form G-325A** for wife;

✪ one passport-style photo for both husband and wife;

✪ proof of the petitioner's U.S. citizenship (birth certificate, if born in U.S.; naturalization certificate, certificate of citizenship, or, U.S. passport identification page if not born in the U.S.);

✪ marriage certificate;

✪ documentation of legal termination of any previous marriages; and,

✪ documentation as to a name change on a supporting document (marriage certificate, adoption decree, or court order).

G-325A   The other required form is the **G-325A** biographic information form. This form must be completed by both the husband and wife.

The documents listed in Chapter 4 for proving a *bona fide marriage* do not need to be filed with the I-130 petition if the I-130 is filed locally. They may be gathered while the application is pending and brought to the interview. However, if the I-130 is to be filed with a service center, there probably will not be an interview. In that instance only should you gather sufficient evidence and file it with the I-130 petition.

If both spouses are not at the interview, the application will be denied. It is better to ask that the interview be rescheduled to allow time to work out the problem. This should be done well before the interview, in writing. Any rescheduling letter must be sent by certified mail with a return receipt. Then if the case is closed out by the USCIS, you will have proof of mailing.

If the U.S. citizen spouse dies before the interview, then it may be possible to self-petition. There is a requirement that the marriage have lasted longer than two years prior to the death of the spouse. (The *I-360* should be filed first with the service center, but this is beyond the scope of this book.) See Chapters 17 and 21 for more information about the interview.

Where to file. File the I-130 petition and the G-325A form with a service center or a local USCIS office.

I-751 Removing Conditions

The conditional resident must file *Form I-751* to remove conditions within the 90-day period prior to the expiration date on the conditional green card.

The following constitutes a complete I-751 filing:

✪ Form I-751;

✪ filing fee of $145;

✪ two passport-style photos;

✪ a copy of the conditional green card;

✪ joint tax returns;

✪ an apartment lease or joint deed;

✪ substantial evidence as to a bona fide marriage (see page 21); and,

✪ any court dispositions if arrested after conditional adjustment.

The filing fee of $145, in the form of a money order, should be attached to the completed I-751 form, along with two passport-style photos. On the back of the photos, the person's name and number should be written in pencil or with a felt pen. A photocopy of the green card must be submitted. The most important part of the filing is the evidence that the marriage was bona fide. As many of the documents listed on page 21 as possible should be attached, to establish beyond any doubt that the marriage is real.

If sufficient documents to prove a bona fide marriage are submitted, then the petition will be approved by the service center. Otherwise, the petition will be forwarded to the local USCIS office for an interview.

Where to file. The I-751 packet is filed with the service center responsible for your jurisdiction. You will receive a receipt notice within several weeks, which will serve to extend your permanent residence status and provide evidence of employment authorization.

Even though the conditional green card stamp in your passport may have expired, you do not need to get a renewal stamp placed in your passport. You may simply travel on your now expired conditional green card, your passport, and the original receipt notice.

NOTE: *If you get divorced after being granted adjustment, but before filing the I-751, there is no deadline for filing the I-751. However, your file will certainly be transferred to the local USCIS office for interview.*

Grounds for filing. There are two grounds for filing the I-751. The first is that the marriage was entered into in good faith and the second is extreme hardship. However, it is apparently very rare to proceed on the second standard only. The USCIS officer may not even know how to proceed. Be prepared to show that this second standard exists if you wish to rely upon it.

In this instance, it is important to carefully prepare for the interview. You will need fairly extensive documentation of the bona fide marriage. These cases are scrutinized carefully by the USCIS. It is not unusual for the officer to call the former spouse to get his or her side of the story. This is problematic because the former spouse may resent that the alien received status through him or her.

NOTE: *If your I-751 application is pending and it has been at least two years and nine months since you became a lawful permanent resident, you may still file a citizenship application. The USCIS will schedule your interview with an officer who is familiar with adjudicating both citizenship and the I-751 petitions. At the time of the interview on the N-400, bring your U.S. citizen spouse and all necessary documents in order to complete the I-751 interview.*

If it is denied, the I-751 application is reviewable in immigration court by an immigration judge. There may be a substantial delay before being placed in proceedings. Many USCIS offices have a large room full of files to be processed for immigration court. However, once in court, the judge will review the entire application and take testimony from the alien and any witnesses. In many ways, it may be a much fairer proceeding than the interview at the USCIS. As in any proceeding before the immigration court, it will require the services of an immigration attorney.

Immediate Relatives— One-Stop Filing

You may file the **I-130 ALIEN RELATIVE PETITION** with a local USCIS office *along with* the **I-485 ADJUSTMENT OF STATUS APPLICATION**, if the relative is already in the U.S. and eligible to adjust in the U.S. Filing these together is called a *one-stop application.*

The different purposes of the I-130 petition and I-485 form are important to understand. The I-130 petition establishes the petitioner's relationship to the alien relative. It is not an application for a green card by itself, but it is the first step. The I-485 form, on the other hand, is filed by the alien relative on his or her own behalf and relates only to his or her own eligibility for permanent residence.

Those alien relatives who fall into a preference category, such as married children, will first file only the I-130 petition with a service center. After they receive a visa number, they will file the I-485 adjustment application along with the I-130 approval notice with the local USCIS office. These procedures will be explained in detail later in this chapter.

A one-stop adjustment of status application packet consists of numerous forms and supporting documents. However, the required forms and documents vary slightly by case. The following outline is a useful checklist of all of the possible forms and documents. A more detailed explanation follows the outline.

One-Stop Adjustment

The following are required for filing the one-stop adjustment:

✪ **FORM I-130 ALIEN RELATIVE PETITION** and supporting documents (see page 94) or approval notice;

✪ filing fee for form I-130 of $130;

✪ **FORM I-485 ADJUSTMENT APPLICATION** (see page 96);

✪ filing fee for form I-485 depends on age (see chart in Appendix D);

✪ fingerprint fee of $50;

✪ **FORM G-325A** biographic information for applicant (see page 88 for more information on this form);

✪ two passport-style photos;

✪ **FORM I-485 SUPPLEMENT** OR proof of legal entry, such as copies of the visa page in the applicant's passport, I-94s and relevant approval notices, or a copy of Canadian citizenship;

✪ a copy of the applicant's birth certificate and translation;

✪ *Form I-693 Medical Form* and vaccination sheet in sealed envelope;

✪ *Form I-864 Affidavit of Support* (the petitioner's most recent tax returns and W-2s may be included or brought to the interview); and,

✪ a job letter.

The following may be required in some cases:

✪ proof of eligibility under Section 245(i);

✪ physical presence in the U.S. on December 20, 2000;

✪ *Form I-601 Waiver of Inadmissibility* and supporting documents;

✪ cable request for overseas dependents;

✪ marriage certificate;

✪ divorce decrees or documentation of termination of any previous marriages;

✪ birth certificates of the beneficiary's children; and,

✪ documents related to convictions or other special circumstances.

How to File   To properly file the one-stop application, follow these suggestions:

✪ make a copy of all documents and keep them in a safe place;

✪ write the name and *A number* (the eight-digit number assigned by the USCIS that appears on your work permit, fingerprint, and interview notices) or date of birth in pencil on the back of the photos;

✪ attach a money order or cashier's check made out to USCIS;

✪ make sure the name of the applicant is on the check;

✪ if the case requires special processing, such as expedited processing, place a colored sheet of paper on top of the application and state clearly the reason;

✪ mail the package to:

U.S. Citizenship and Immigration Services
PO Box 805887
Chicago, IL 60680

✪ or, for non-United States Postal Service (USPS) deliveries (e.g. private couriers):

U.S. Citizenship and Immigration Services
Attn: FBASI
10 West Jackson Boulevard
Chicago, IL 60604

✪ if a deadline needs to be met, file using express mail through the U.S. Post Office. They deliver to post office boxes, unlike FedEx. If no deadline is involved, file using regular mail; and,

✪ any address changes must be sent by certified mail, return receipt requested, since such requests may not be processed by the USCIS and will result in a closed case.

I-130 Petition   An **I-130** petition filing requires the following:

✪ **FORM I-130**;

✪ filing fee of $130;

✪ proof of petitioner's U.S. citizenship (birth certificate, if born in U.S.; naturalization certificate, certificate of citizenship, or U.S. passport identification page if not born in the U.S.);

✪ documentation of legal termination of any previous marriages; and,

✪ documentation as to a name change on a supporting document (marriage certificate, adoption decree, or court order).

The above listing consists of the entire **I-130** packet that will be filed with the local USCIS office. The **I-130** form itself must be carefully completed. Fill it in as follows.

◈ Part A. Relationship: Fill in the correct category of the alien relative for whom you are applying. If the wrong box is checked, the approval notice may reflect the wrong relationship.

◈ Part B. Information about you: This means the petitioner's personal information. Enter your name as it is currently being used. If a different name is on an official document such as the naturalization certificate or birth certificate, enter this name in response to Question 7. Also include in Question 7 all other names used, such as married or maiden names.

◈ Question 10 asks for the alien registration number. It may be found on the naturalization certificate just below the certificate number or on the green card if the petitioner is a permanent resident.

◈ Question 13 may be a little confusing. A petitioner who obtained U.S. citizenship through naturalization will check the "Naturalization" box and enter the certificate number, and date and place of issue. The "Parents" box is used for those who have a citizenship certificate rather than a naturalization certificate. Such persons were never permanent residents but were later determined to be U.S. citizens at birth.

◈ Part C. Information about your alien relative: This means the person being applied for and his or her personal information. If the alien relative is abroad, enter his or her mailing address as opposed to physical address.

◈ Question 13 asks whether the alien relative is presently in the U.S. If so, Question 14 seeks the status of the relative upon entry. Typically, this will be as B-2 visitor or F-1 student. If the relative entered illegally across the border, then the correct answer is EWI. The I-94 number is found on the white I-94 card issued at the point of entry. If this card is lost, so indicate.

◈ Question 15 asks for employment information. Be careful—working without USCIS authorization may prevent future adjustment of status.

◈ Question 16 asks whether the relative is in proceedings. If the answer is yes, the service center will ask for documents concerning the type and outcome of the proceedings.

◈ Question 17 also asks that the spouse or children of the alien relative be listed. It is particularly important that any children of the relative be listed, especially if they will also be seeking permanent residence status.

◈ Question 22 should be answered carefully. If a person has any intent of filing in the U.S., then mark the second box. If the first box is marked, the file will be transferred to an embassy or consulate, who will continue processing the case. The embassy or consulate will look to cancel the visa petition if the beneficiary does not continue with permanent residence processing within one year. Marking the second box will allow the beneficiary to wait as long as necessary in the U.S. before applying. For example, a person may have to wait for an extension of Section 245(i) before applying. (You can always apply later at the embassy by filing form *I-824* with the appropriate service center, although this may cause a delay of several months.)

◈ Part D. Other Information: Question 1 asks whether other I-130 petitions are being filed for other relatives at this time. For example, are both parents or more than one child being applied for? If so, write down their names and relationship.

◈ Question 2 asks whether the petitioner has previously filed for any other relative. If so, write in the information. For example, you might put down: *John Smith; son; filed on 3/15/1990 at Nebraska Service Center; petition was approved on 10/15/1990.*

◈ Finally, the petitioning relative signs where indicated on the bottom of the second page.

After the **I-130** petition is complete and the previously described documents assembled, refer to page 94 for a description of how and where to file the **I-130** petition.

I-485 Adjustment of Status

The other important form is the **I-485**. This is the actual adjustment of status application. It should be carefully completed as follows.

◈ Part 1. Information about you: This means the applicant and his or her personal information. Fill in all required information. Many applicants may not have a Social Security number or alien registration number, in which case they should respond to these questions "N/A."

The I-94 number is found on the white I-94 card issued at the point of entry. If this card is lost, so indicate. If the alien crossed the border illegally, mark "N/A."

◈ The last questions ask for the current status of the applicant. Typically, this will be as B-2 visitor or F-1 student. If the relative entered illegally across the border, then the correct response is EWI. If the person has overstayed a B-2 visa, write in "B-2 overstay."

◈ Part 2. Application Type: Check the box that applies to the type of case. For example, if the applicant is being applied for by an immediate relative, check box (a). If the applicant was selected in the diversity visa lottery, check box (h) and write in "Diversity Visa Selection 2004."

◈ Part 3. Processing Information: Enter the specific background information requested. If the applicant did not make a lawful entry, there is no I-94, border inspection, or visa. Therefore, enter "N/A" in response to these questions.

◈ Section B asks for the names of all relatives. The applicant should fill in the names of any spouse and all children, regardless of status.

◈ Section C asks for the names of organizations of which the applicant has been a member. Military service in the U.S. or in a foreign country is probably most important and should be listed. Asylum applicants should also maintain consistency with their asylum claim.

◈ Page 3 has a list of questions that must be answered "yes" or "no." If any box is marked "yes," it may be necessary to consult with an attorney.

The most important of these is Question 1, regarding the applicant's criminal record. If the applicant has ever been arrested, let alone charged or convicted, it must be disclosed here. Check the "yes" box and write in something like *Arrested 2/20/02 in Chicago, Illinois, for retail theft; charge dismissed by Circuit Court of Cook County on 4/15/02.*

◈ Part 4. Signature: The applicant signs where indicated.

The filing fee is $255 if the applicant is 14 years of age and over and $160 if under. Likewise, those age 14 or over require fingerprints and must pay the $50 fingerprint fee. A completed **G-325A** form is required for all applicants 14 years of age or older.

Include two passport-style photos, no matter what the applicant's age.

I-485 Supplement A

If an immediate relative beneficiary entered the U.S. without a visa, then he or she must file the **I-485 SUPPLEMENT A** and pay the $1,000 filing fee. Care must be taken to ensure that the applicant is eligible to file this form. Those who are eligible to file the supplement are those whose I-130 was filed prior to April 30, 2001 or who were the beneficiary of another I-130 or labor certification filed prior to that date. (See p. 94 for further discussion.)

Fill in **SUPPLEMENT A** as follows.

◈ Part A. Information about applicant: This means the applicant and his or her personal information. Fill in all required information as on the **I-485** application.

◈ Part B. Eligibility: Question 1 really asks when the earliest I-130 or labor certification was filed or your behalf. Question 2 refers to the manner of entry. Many people will check only box (c).

◈ Part C asks whether the applicant belongs to a list of special adjustment categories. Those seeking adjustment based on a relative will not check any box.

◈ Part D. Signature: The applicant signs where indicated.

This list describes the minimum documents required for filing the adjustment packet. The remaining items may be brought to the adjustment interview or filed with the initial packet.

Where to file   Now that the **I-130** is completed and the correct supporting documents obtained (see Chapter 14), it can be filed. The question now is where to file it. If the parent or child seeking to immigrate is eligible to adjust in the U.S. as mentioned earlier, then file the **I-130** along with the **I-485** at the local USCIS office.

The following persons will file the **I-130** with a service center, rather than the local USCIS office:

- ✪   preference category relatives;

- ✪   immediate relatives residing outside the U.S.;

- ✪   immediate relatives in the U.S. who are ineligible to apply for adjustment; or,

- ✪   immediate relatives who are in deportation proceedings.

Be sure to make a copy of the petition and supporting documents and keep them in a safe place. Also attach the correct filing fee of $130 as a money order or cashier's check made out to "USCIS." Make sure the name of the petitioner is on the check, and confirm the correct address of the service center.

NOTE: *There is typically a specific post office box for an I-130 Petition. If you are close to a deadline, use express mail to the street address of the service center and place the P.O. Box on the label.*

Once the petition is approved, it will be sent to the National Visa Center, which will hold the file until a visa number is available. It will then forward the file to the appropriate embassy or consulate.

NOTE: *Most often, the I-130 and I-485 are filed simultaneously in a one-stop application.*

Family-Based Preference Categories

If the relative being applied for is in a *preference visa category*, then the I-130 is filed with the appropriate service center, the necessary time period is waited, and then the I-485 is filed at the local USCIS office. A copy of the I-130 approval notice will be included with the I-485 filing.

First Preference   The required documents for a *first preference* petition are similar to those for immediate relatives:

✪ **FORM I-130 ALIEN RELATIVE PETITION**;

✪ filing fee of $130;

✪ proof of the petitioner's U.S. citizenship (birth certificate if born in the U.S.; naturalization certificate, certificate of citizenship, or U.S. passport identification page if not born in the U.S.);

✪ birth certificate of the adult child, showing the name of the petitioner and child (and if the father is the petitioner, his marriage certificate);

✪ legal termination of any previous marriage of father, if he is the petitioner; and,

✪ evidence of legal name change, if necessary (marriage certificate, adoption decree, or court order).

The above listing consists of the entire I-130 packet that will be filed. The I-130 petition must be completed. (see page 94.) It then must be supported by several documents. First, the U.S. citizen must establish his or her citizenship by one of the documents previously indicated. The birth certificate of the adult child must be filed to establish the qualifying relationship. This birth certificate must show the name of the parent who is filing the petition. If the father is petitioning, then the father's marriage certificate must also be provided. Finally, if any name on a supporting document has changed, a legal document to evidence the name change is required.

Pages 94–95 contain detailed instructions on completing the **I-130** petition. This form should be carefully filled out and signed. After the I-130 petition is completed and the documents assembled, refer to page 94 for a description of how and where to file the I-130 petition packet.

Second Preference

For the three types of beneficiaries within the second preference category, prepare **FORM I-130** as follows.

✪ If filing for a spouse, then the I-130 petition is prepared in a similar fashion as described previously for a U.S. citizen spouse.

✪ If filing for a minor or adult child, then the I-130 petition is prepared in a similar fashion as just described for a first preference petition.

For these second preference petitions, of course, evidence of the petitioner's lawful permanent residence status (i.e., copy of green card) is provided instead of proof of U.S. citizenship.

The I-130 petition is filed with a service center, as are preference petitions. See pages 94-95 for detailed instructions on completing the I-130 petition. This form should be carefully filled out and signed.

After the **I-130** petition is completed and the documents assembled, refer to page 94 for a description of how and where to file the I-130 petition packet. Be sure you have all documents listed in Chapter 4 included in the packet.

Third Preference

A third preference petition is prepared in a similar fashion as just described for a first preference petition. (see page 99.)

Detailed instructions on completing the **I-130** petition are also found on that page. This form should be carefully filled out and signed. Be sure to include the names of the beneficiary's spouse and children where requested at the top of page 2 of the form.

After the I-130 petition is completed and the documents assembled, refer to page 94 for a description of how and where to file the I-130 petition packet.

Fourth Preference A similar I-130 packet that is filed for the other three preferences must be filed for the fourth preference:

✪ **FORM I-130 ALIEN RELATIVE PETITION**;

✪ filing fee of $130;

✪ proof of petitioner's U.S. citizenship (birth certificate, if born in U.S.; naturalization certificate, certificate of citizenship, or U.S. passport identification page if not born in the U.S.);

✪ birth certificate of petitioner and of brother or sister showing names of both parents;

✪ birth certificate of brother or sister showing names of both parents (if they have different mothers, then supply a marriage certificate of the father to both mothers and also legal termination of any of the father's previous marriages); and,

✪ evidence of legal name change, if necessary (marriage certificate, adoption decree, or court order).

The **I-130** petition must be completed. (see page 94.) Be sure to include the names of the beneficiary's spouse and children where requested at the top of page 2 of the form. It then must be supported by several documents described in the above outline. First, the U.S. citizen sibling must establish his or her citizenship by one of the documents indicated. The birth certificate of the U.S. citizen petitioner and that of the brother or sister must be filed to establish the qualifying relationship to an identical parent. These birth certificates must show that the siblings have the mother or father in common. If only the father is in common, then the marriage certificates of the father to both mothers is also required. Finally, if any name on a supporting document has changed, a legal document to evidence the name change is required. See pages 94-95 for detailed instructions on filling in the I-130 petition.

How to file. Persons filing for the preference categories file the **I-130** with the service center. Ensure that you have the I-130 petition complete. Attach the filing fee of $130 in a money order. Do not forget to include the supporting documents as described earlier, depending on which preference category the petitioner and beneficiary are in.

Remember to provide only photocopies of all documents. The originals will be brought to the interview (as discussed in Chapter 17). All birth and marriage certificates must have been issued by or registered with the proper civil authority in the foreign country. If a document is not in English, it must be submitted along with a certified English translation. (see page 142.) (If any document is unavailable, see page 143 for more information.)

Other points to follow in filing the **I-130** petition:

✪   make a copy of the petition and supporting documents and keep them in safe place;

✪   attach a money order or cashier's check in the amount of $130 made out to "USCIS";

✪   make sure the name of the petitioner is on the check; and,

✪   confirm the correct address of the service center. There is typically a specific post office box for an I-130 petition. (If a deadline needs to be met, file using express mail to the street address of the service center and place the P.O. Box on the label.)

Check Appendix B for your appropriate service center address.

These petitions may take an extended period of time to be decided on, since there are long waits for visa numbers in most preference categories. The service center will send a request for evidence if further information is required to approve the case. Once the petition is approved, it will be sent to the National Visa Center (NVC), which will hold the file until a visa number is available.

Once a visa number becomes available, the NVC will begin to process the immigrant visa. The NVC first sends *Form DS-3032*, Choice of Address and Agent, to the applicant. After this form is returned, the NVC sends an invoice for immigrant visa processing to the named agent. Upon receiving the fee, it sends an instruction package to the applicant or agent.

The NVC also sends an invoice for Affidavit of Support (Form I-864) processing to the petitioner. After the petitioner pays the fee, it sends Form I-864 to petitioner for completion.

All returned information is reviewed for technical correctness. Finally, the NVC sends the file to the appropriate embassy where the applicant will apply for an immigrant visa.

Family-Based Preference

Complete the adjustment package as described on page 96. Any spouse of the beneficiary will also need to include the marriage certificate and proof that the marriage is bona fide. A copy of the *I-864 Affidavit of Support* and its supporting documents should be included for the beneficiary's spouse and any children.

It is critical that preference petition adjustment applicants maintain valid work authorization while the application is pending, or else their applications may be denied.

Widows and Widowers

A filing for a widow or widower consists of the following:

- ✪ **FORM I-360**;

- ✪ filing fee of $130;

- ✪ U.S. citizenship of spouse;

- ✪ marriage certificate;

- ✪ death certificate of U.S. citizen spouse;

- ✪ divorce judgements or marriage terminations as applicable for either spouse;

- ✪ birth certificates of children of alien; and,

- ✪ evidence as to validity of relationship (may be required).

These petitions are filed with the appropriate service center. See the documents list contained in Chapter 4 and begin to gather evidence that the relationship was bona fide. This evidence may be required if the case is interviewed. The I-360 petition can be obtained from the USCIS website at **www.uscis.gov/ graphics/formsfee/forms**. Instructions for this form are also at this site.

Once the I-360 petition is approved, an adjustment application may be filed with the local USCIS office.

Abused Spouses

Abused spouse self-petitions are filed with the Vermont Service Center and include:

❂ **FORM I-360**;

❂ filing fee of $130;

❂ U.S. citizenship or lawful permanent resident (LPR) status of spouse;

❂ marriage certificate;

❂ evidence that the alien resided with spouse;

❂ evidence that the marriage was entered into in good faith;

❂ evidence of the abuse of the alien spouse:

• medical reports;

• police reports;

• affidavits;

• order of protection;

• photos;

✪ evidence of good moral character of the abused spouse;

✪ affidavits and police certificates;

✪ divorce judgments or marriage terminations as applicable for either spouse; and,

✪ birth certificates of the children of the alien.

Once the **I-360** petition is approved by the Vermont Service Center, the individual then files for adjustment of status with the local office. (see Chapter 4.) An affidavit of support form is not required for an abused spouse or child adjustment application.

NOTE: *You must read the section on page 96 entitled "Adjustment of Status" for the rest of the procedure to immigrate to the U.S.*

Family-Based Nonimmigrant Visas

See Chapter 5 for a detailed explanation of which visa you may qualify for.

K-1 Visa Packet— Fiancés

The first step in the K-1 visa packet is approval of the fiancé visa petition with the service center in the petitioner's jurisdiction. The following documents need to be filed:

✪ *Form I-129F;*

✪ one passport-style photo of the petitioner and one of the beneficiary;

✪ filing fee of $110;

✪ **FORM G-325A** for the petitioner;

✪ **FORM G-325A** for the beneficiary;

✪ the petitioner's naturalization certificate or birth certificate;

✪ the petitioner's statement as to the history of the relationship;

✪ evidence of the relationship;

✪ phone bill showing calls to the beneficiary;

✪ photos of vacation together;

✪ copy of airline tickets showing recent meetings;

✪ copies of letters, cards, or emails sent between the couple;

✪ evidence of gifts;

✪ any other document that verifies validity of relationship; and,

✪ photo of the petitioner and the beneficiary.

The previous listing consists of the entire packet that will be filed. Any derivative children of the alien are included on the same petition. Not every supporting document is necessarily required. The I-129F form itself must be carefully completed. This form is similar to the I-130 form. Consult the I-130 instructions on pages 94–95.

The other required form is the **G-325A BIOGRAPHIC INFORMATION FORM**. This form is completed by both the the U.S. citizen and the fiancé.

Then, the I-129F petition must be supported by documents demonstrating that the relationship is bona fide.

Embassy requirements. After approval of the I-129F, the service center will transmit the file to the designated embassy or consulate. It may take a month or more for the file to be transmitted. The consulate will issue a notice for an interview.

The documents required for the embassy to complete processing are:

✪ *DS-156* application form;

✪ a passport valid six months beyond the date of intended entry into the U.S. (K-4 may be included in K-3's passport);

✪ documents to prove the relationship is bona fide;

✪ birth certificates;

✪ local police certificates;

✪ court records;

✪ divorce decrees or death certificates for any previous marriage;

✪ IV medical exam minus vaccinations on form *DS-2053*; and,

✪ three passport-style photographs.

NOTE: *No affidavit of support is required, but you may be questioned to ensure you will not become a public burden. In such cases, Form I-134 may be required.*

K-3 and K-4 Visas—Spouse and Minor Children of U.S. Citizens

The first step to a K-3 visa is ensuring that an I-130 packet, discussed on page 94, was filed previously with the service center that has jurisdiction over the U.S. citizen petitioner. However, the I-130 only has to be *pending*. Any minor children of the U.S. citizen spouse may be included on the spouse's I-130. (See page 94 for information on filing an immediate relative I-130 petition.)

Then the U.S. citizen petitioner must also file a second petition, the I-129F, with the Missouri Service Center. This petition must be approved by the USCIS before the alien can continue processing for the K visa at an embassy. The I-129F again will include the petitioner's stepchildren.

The I-129F Packet. The following constitutes the I-129F filing:

✪ *Form I-129F*;

✪ filing fee of $110;

✪ **G-325A** for the beneficiary;

✪ two passport-style photos;

✪ I-130 receipt notice or approval notice or other proof of a pending or approved petition;

✪   petitioner's naturalization certificate or birth certificate; and,

✪   a copy of a marriage certificate (if the I-130 is pending).

This listing consists of the entire packet that will be filed. The I-129F form itself must be carefully completed. Clearly mark "K-3/LIFE" in the top margin. This form is similar to the I-130 form. Consult the I-130 instructions on pages 94–95.

The other required form is the **G-325A** biographic information form. This form is completed by the beneficiary. Also include two passport-style photos.

An I-130 receipt or approval notice must be attached to the I-129F form. If the I-130 petition is pending, a marriage certificate is required.

All I-129 documents are mailed to:

United States Citizenship and Immigration Services
P.O. Box 7218
Chicago, IL 60680

These petitions will be forwarded to the Missouri Service Center for processing. Once the petition is approved, the Missouri Service Center will forward the paper case file to the National Visa Center. The National Visa Center will scan the I-129F petition and perform a criminal records check. The National Visa Center will then email the case to the embassy in the country of marriage, or to the spouse's country of residence if married in the U.S.

The embassy will then send the beneficiary a letter describing the documents required for K-3 and K-4 issuance:

✪   *DS-156* nonimmigrant visa application (two copies);

✪   DS-156 nonimmigrant fiancé visa application;

✪   a passport valid six months beyond the date of intended entry (K-4 may be included in K-3's passport);

✪   documents to prove the relationship is bona fide;

- birth certificate;

- marriage certificate;

- police certificates from all places lived since age of 16;

- proof of financial support (form I-134 affidavit of support may be requested);

- divorce decrees or death certificates for any previous marriage;

- IV medical exam minus vaccinations on form DS-2053; and,

- two passport-style photographs.

NOTE: *No affidavit of support is required, but you may be questioned to ensure you will not become a public burden.*

Once in the U.S., the K-3 or K-4 status person may apply for a work permit with the Missouri Service Center by submitting the following:

- **FORM I-765**;

- filing fee of $120;

- a copy of K visa in passport or copy of I-94;

- a signature card; and,

- two passport-style photos.

The K-3 or K-4 recipient may then file an adjustment packet with his or her local USCIS office. If the I-130 petition is not approved, approval may be waited for or a duplicate petition may be filed. Attach the I-130 receipt notice as proof of payment.

Labor Certification Filing

Before filing the application for labor certification, appropriate recruitment must take place. The specific type of recruitment depends on whether the position is classified as professional or nonprofessional. At a minimum, two ads must be placed in a Sunday edition of a paper of wide circulation and a job order must be placed with the state employment agency. Professional positions require additional recruitment. The employer must categorize the lawful job-related reasons for rejection of U.S. applicants and provide the number of U.S. applicants rejected in each category.

Once recruitment is completed and a report is made, the application may be completed. On the application, the employer describes in detail the job duties, educational requirements, training, experience, and other special capabilities the employee must possess to do the work, and a statement of the prospective immigrant's qualifications.

The employer has the option of filing an application electronically or by mail. However, the Department of Labor recommends that employers file electronically. Not only is electronic filing easier, but it also ensures the employer has provided all required information, as an electronic application can not be submitted if the required fields are not completed. The employer goes to **www.plc.doleta.gov** and after registering and establishing an account, electronically fills out and submit an **APPLICATION FOR PERMANENT EMPLOYMENT CERTIFICATION, ETA FORM 9089**. If filing by mail, the same application is mailed to either the Chicago or Atlanta National Processing Center, depending on which has jurisdiction for the state where the job opportunity is located.

Prior to filing **ETA FORM 9089**, the employer must request a prevailing wage determination from the State Workforce Agency (SWA) having jurisdiction over the proposed area of intended employment.

If the appropriate National Processing Center approves the application, the ETA Form 9089 is *certified* (stamped) by the Certifying Officer and returned to the employer/agent who submitted the application.

The purpose of the **I-140** petition is to prove eligibility for the particular preference category that the alien satisfies all requirements, and that the employer has the ability to pay the required wage. Upon approval of the labor certification, the **I-140** form may be filed with the appropriate service center along with:

✪ filing fee of $135;

✪ approved labor certification (or *ETA Form 9089, Parts A* and *B* with proof qualifies as a Schedule A shortage occupation or approved national interest waiver);

✪ employer's letter;

✪ proof of employer's ability to pay the wage:

• annual reports;

• federal tax returns;

• audited financial statements; or,

• other evidence (e.g., bank accounts, profit and loss statements, payroll and personnel records);

✪ documentation to prove eligibility for a preference category; and,

✪ documentation to prove that the alien satisfies educational, training, and experience requirements of the *ETA Form 9089*.

Along with the **I-140** form, several documents need to be attached. These are the original approved labor certification obtained from the Department of Labor. An employer's letter on the company letterhead should be prepared, renewing the employee's job offer at the required salary. Documentation as to the alien's education and credentials are required to prove he or she meets with the educational, training, and experience requirements of the particular position. (For example, school transcripts or training certificates should be included.) Finally, the issue of ability to pay the wage is critical. The net income level on the corporate tax returns is the most important factor. This packet can then be filed with the appropriate service center. (See Appendix B for the correct address.)

I-140 petitions are now typically decided on by the service center within a couple of months. The service center will send a request for evidence if further information is required to approve the case. Once the I-140 is approved, the beneficiary may apply for adjustment of status.

Concurrent Filing

The USCIS now permits Form I-140 and the adjustment of status package to be filed at the same time, if desired. In situations where it is certain that the I-140 will be approved or work authorization is sought as soon as possible, then a simultaneous filing is advisable. Otherwise, the I-140 may be filed first, and then after approval the adjustment of status may be filed.

Filing for Adjustment of Status I-145

After the I-140 petition is approved, the applicant may apply for adjustment of status. Unlike an adjustment filing with a local USCIS office, where only certain forms and documents are initially required, a complete adjustment packet for an employment-based case should be filed with the service center. In this way, the chances of the case being referred back to a local USCIS office for interview are reduced.

NOTE: *Transfer of the file to a local USCIS office will cause a substantial delay.*

The adjustment filing consists of numerous forms and supporting documents. The following outline is a useful checklist of all of the possible forms and documents. A more detailed explanation follows the outline.

The following packet should be filed with the service center:

- ✪ **FORM I-485 ADJUSTMENT OF STATUS** form;

- ✪ filing fee of $255;

- ✪ fingerprint fee of $50;

- ✪ **FORM I-140 APPROVAL NOTICE**;

- ✪ two passport-style photos;

- ✪ **FORM G-325A BIOGRAPHIC INFORMATION** sheet;

- ✪ **FORM I-485 SUPPLEMENT** or proof of legal entry into the U.S. and maintenance of status:

- copies of the visa page in your passport;

- I-94s and relevant approval notices; or,

- a copy of Canadian citizenship (if any);

✪ Form I-693 medical examination form and vaccination supplement completed by physician in a sealed envelope;

✪ recent job letter confirming job offer;

✪ applicant's birth certificate;

✪ marriage certificate;

✪ cable request for overseas dependents;

✪ documents related to convictions;

✪ Form I-864 affidavit of support (only if a relative owns more than 5% of petitioning company);

✪ Form I-601 waiver of inadmissibility (if required) with supporting documents; and,

✪ *Form I-824* for overseas family members.

If you are filing under the LIFE Act, you need to additionally provide proof of physical presence on December 20, 2000. (This is not necessary for dependents.) Also, if this labor certification was filed after April 30, 2001, proof of prior I-130 or labor certification filing must be shown.

Work Authorization

If you want to work as soon as possible, you must file the following for work authorization:

✪ **FORM I-765 WORK PERMIT**;

✪ filing fee of $120;

✪ two passport-style photos; and,

✪ a copy of state-issued I.D.

Travel Permission

To travel in the meantime, file:

✪ **FORM I-131** travel permission (if eligible);

✪ filing fee of $110;

✪ two passport-style photos; and,

✪ a clear copy of an identity document.

The principal form is the **I-485** adjustment of status form. It should be carefully completed. See page 112 for detailed filing instructions. The filing fee is $255 if the applicant is 14 years of age over, and $160 if under 14 years of age. Likewise, those 14 or over require fingerprints and must pay the $50 fingerprint fee. A completed **G-325A** form is required for all applicants 14 years of age or over as well. Every applicant requires two passport-style photos to be included.

Eligibility. The next aspect that is critical to the permanent residence process is *eligibility.* If the applicant is in valid nonimmigrant status at the time of the filing of the application, then he or she is eligible to file for adjustment. If the applicant is out of status, then he or she must qualify under Section 245(i) (see Chapter 3 for a detailed discussion). Basically, if the labor certification was filed before April 30, 2001, then the applicant is eligible to file for adjustment. However, the applicant will then have to file the **I-485 SUPPLEMENT** and pay the $1,000 fee.

The medical examination form (Chapter 14) must be filed. Employment-based adjustment applicants do not typically require the affidavit of support (Chapter 14) since a job offer is pending. Only if a relative owns more than 5% of the petitioning company is the affidavit of support required to be filed by that relative. However, a current job letter stating that the position is offered to the alien at the required salary must be submitted.

If there is any *condition of inadmissibility* (see Chapter 15), such as for criminal record or entry on a false passport, the I-601 waiver must be filed and the fee must be paid. For any criminal record, original certified records of disposition must be obtained from the clerk of the court and included with the filing.

Since you will not be at an interview to fill in the missing holes and provide documents, these filings should be as complete as possible. If you wish to make the examiner's job easier, prepare a supplemental letter addressing the following.

✪ If the I-485 supplement is not being filed, document your entire nonimmigrant history: submit a road map for the entire time you have been in the U.S., and not just since the most recent entry. Include all available documentation such as copies of I-94s, passport visas, *I-797* approval notices, *I-20*s, *IAP-66*s, etc.

✪ Clarify that you have not worked without authorization (at all times—including during any nonimmigrant stays) and support this statement with copies of work permits, I-797 approval notices, passport visas, and the like.

✪ Provide complete documentation for dependent applications to establish a relationship to the principal alien (a birth certificate, and if the principal applicant is the father, a copy of the marriage certificate. If applicable, provide evidence of termination of any prior marriages). If the marriage occurred less than two years prior to filing, provide evidence as to the bona fides of the marriage.

✪ Submit a copy of the local USCIS office's current list of civil surgeons and highlight the name of the doctor who conducted the exam. You should remind your doctor that the form will be reviewed for eligibility. Therefore, the doctor should print his or her name clearly and be sure it is complete, including TB tests and vaccinations.

✪ Submit any history of appearing in immigration court, including documents such as a final order.

✪ If there are many documents, you can place tabs (for service centers, use the tabs along the bottom of the page, not along the sides).

Receipt notice. Several weeks after filing, a *receipt notice* will be received. This receipt contains your case number and should be safely kept. Depending on the backlog, the application will be decided in due course. If any information is missing or any documentation is incomplete, then a Request for Evidence (RFE) may be issued. You will then have an 84-day period to provide the required information.

NOTE: *This is a very strict deadline. Any response should be returned to the USCIS by overnight mail so that proof of mailing is available should the USCIS claim it was never received.*

You have generally one chance to comply with the RFE, so be sure you have enclosed all of the information. If some information is not available, provide a detailed explanation as to why.

The adjustment process varies by service center. You will need to go to the service center website to confirm the processing time before taking additional action.

If the processing time is past the time indicated on the receipt notice, wait an additional week or two. If nothing happens, you should call the number at the bottom of the receipt notice. It is possible to call the service center late at night when the phone lines are free. Eventually, you will be asked to punch in your case number, including the three-letter service center designation as a number. For example, "LIN" for the Lincoln service center is "546" on the keypad. You might get useful recorded information about your case. For example, the recording might say that an approval notice or request for evidence was sent.

Now there is an online case status information system for cases pending at a service center. Go to the USCIS website at **www.uscis.gov** and click "Case Status & Processing Dates" on the right side of the home page.

Processing problems and denial. To clear up processing problems, it is possible to call the service center and speak with an information officer. This is not an officer who will be adjudicating the application. The information officer will not have access to the file and may only have the same information that is in the automated system.

The question often arises as to whether the applicant must work for the petitioning company while the adjustment of status application is pending and the applicant has work authorization. Regulations do not require that the applicant actually work for the employer, merely that it is the intent of the employer to make the permanent position available for the foreign worker upon receipt of permanent residence status. However, the fact that the applicant is not working for the employer may evidence that it is not a legitimate job offer.

If the adjustment of status application is pending more than 180 days, an employee may *switch* or *port* to a new employer as long as the job description is substantially similar.

A case will not be denied without an opportunity to remedy the problem being allowed. You may reapply if the grounds for denial can be overcome. You will, however, need to be in status to do so, unless the petition is *grandfathered* under Section 245(i).

If the case is granted, an *approval notice* will be mailed to the applicant. The applicant will be required to appear at his or her local USCIS office for Alien Documentation, Identification, and Telecommunication System (ADIT) processing.

Interview The majority of applications filed with a service center will not be interviewed. An applicant may be interviewed if:

✪ the applicant's identity, legal status, admissibility, and/or qualifications are questionable;

✪ recent marriage to a dependent suggests the marriage may be a sham (particularly where no evidence of a bona fide marriage was included with application);

✪ the applicant fails to admit arrests or convictions and the service center learns about them through a fingerprint check;

✪ the applicant admits a conviction for one or more *crimes involving moral turpitude* (CIMT) and an I-601 waiver is required;

✪ the applicant entered the U.S. without inspection;

✪ the applicant is not presently employed by the petitioner; or,

✪ the application was selected as part of a random sample for purposes of quality assurance.

If the case requires an interview, the applicant will receive a transfer notice indicating that the file has been transferred to the local USCIS office. An interview should be scheduled in accordance with its filing date with the service center and not the date of the transfer to the local office. All further inquiries should be directed to the local office.

It would now be an excellent time to seek the advice of an immigration attorney to review the file, if one has not been previously consulted. It will be critical to identify the problem area and provide documentation to remedy it. See Chapter 17 for more information on the interview process.

If an interview is scheduled, you will need to bring an employment letter and a copy of your most recent tax return in order to verify employment with the petitioning company.

Diversity Visa Lottery

A diversity winner may apply in the U.S. or abroad at an embassy. It does not matter if the selection letter is received at an address in the U.S. or abroad—you may apply for a green card wherever you are eligible or it is more convenient.

If you are applying through the embassy, then carefully follow the directions contained in the acceptance packet. Recently, the process and the forms have changed for processing a diversity visa application. The packet must be carefully reviewed and directions must be followed. One of the forms is to be completed and returned immediately to the new processing center in Kentucky. From there, the State Department will send the immigrant visa processing packet to the address indicated. The procedure will vary with the particular embassy.

If the diversity winner is in the U.S., he or she will need to be in a valid nonimmigrant status (with certain exceptions). If a person is out of status and wishes to apply in the U.S., he or she must be eligible under immigration law (Section 245(i)). The criteria for eligibility in the U.S. is the same as for anyone applying for adjustment in any other category.

The following is an outline of the necessary adjustment packet to be filed with the local USCIS office:

✪ **FORM I-485 ADJUSTMENT APPLICATION** (see page 112);

✪ filing fee, which depends on age (see chart in Appendix D);

✪ fingerprint fee of $50;

✪ a copy of the diversity visa acceptance letter from the State Department;

✪ **FORM G-325A BIOGRAPHIC INFORMATION** for the applicant;

✪ two passport-style photos;

✪ **FORM I-485 SUPPLEMENT** OR proof of legal entry into the U.S., such as copies of the visa page in your passport, I-94s and relevant approval notices, or a copy of Canadian citizenship;

✪ a copy of the applicant's birth certificate and translation;

✪ proof of high school graduation or two years' work experience in a trade requiring two years' experience;

✪ Form I-693 Medical Form and vaccination sheet in a sealed envelope;

✪ *Form I-134 Affidavit of Support* with documentation; and,

✪ a job letter.

The following is required in some cases:

✪ proof of eligibility under section 245(i);

✪ physical presence in the U.S. on December 20, 2000;

✪ Form I-601 Waiver of Inadmissibility and supporting documents;

✪ cable request for overseas dependents;

✪ marriage certificate;

✪ divorce decrees or proof of termination of previous marriages;

✪ birth certificates of the beneficiary's children; and,

✪ documents related to criminal convictions or other special circumstances.

The principal form is the **I-485**. This is the actual adjustment of status application. It should be carefully completed. See page 112 for detailed filing instructions. The filing fee is $255 if the applicant is 14 years of age over and $160 if the applicant is under age 14. Likewise, those 14 or over require fingerprints and will pay the $50 fingerprint fee.

A completed **G-325A** form is required for all applicants 14 years of age or older. Every applicant requires two passport-style photos to be included as well.

The above outline describes the minimum documents required for filing the adjustment packet. The remaining items may be brought to the adjustment interview or filed initially.

The medical examination form (Chapter 14) and affidavit of support (Chapter 14) must be filed. This is the short I-134 form that requires only one year of tax returns or a job offer. If there is any condition of inadmissibility (see Chapter 15), such as for criminal record or entry on a false passport, the I-601 waiver must be filed and the fee must be paid. For any criminal record, original certified records of disposition must be obtained from the clerk of the court and included with the filing.

To properly file the adjustment application, follow these suggestions:

◈   make a copy of all documents and keep them in a safe place;

◈   write the name and A number or date of birth in pencil on back of photos;

◈   attach a money order or cashier's check made out to "USCIS" in the amount of the correct filing fee;

◈   make sure the name of the applicant is on the check;

◈   confirm the correct address. It is not the same address as the USCIS office. There is typically a specific post office box for an adjustment application. While an application sent to the local address might be forwarded, this is a risky proposition; and,

◈   send any address changes by certified mail return receipt requested, since such requests may not be processed by the USCIS, resulting in a closed case.

The timing of the filing is very important in a diversity visa case. If an applicant is seeking to adjust status in the U.S., then it is critical to wait until after October 1ˢᵗ to file the adjustment application. It may be hard to wait six months from when the acceptance letter is received to apply for adjustment, particularly where there is a race against time to complete the processing and obtain a first-come-first-served visa number. But an adjustment application filed before October 1ˢᵗ must actually be denied since there is no visa number in existence. If the USCIS is not considerate enough to mail the application back, they could deny the application and then process the file for immigration court.

It is also critically important to mark the outside of the mailing envelope: "Urgent—diversity visa filing." The same should be marked on a colored piece of paper on top of the application packet. Since the backlog at many USCIS offices is about a year, there is not time for the application to go through the normal application track. It must be treated as an expedited application so that it is interviewed on time.

What to Expect   As with any adjustment filing, a receipt notice should be received in the mail within several weeks. Then, a fingerprint notice will be received. The fingerprints should be taken as soon as possible.

Next is the wait for an interview notice. In some jurisdictions, the interview may be delayed until there is actually a visa number. It may be somewhat confusing that there should be a wait for a diversity visa number when the applicant has already won the lottery and is racing to complete processing by the end of the government fiscal year.

While 50,000 diversity visas are made available each year, there may still be a wait, depending on one's selection number. If one has a selection number in the low thousands, it is likely current right off the bat. A number over 5,000 for Europe or Africa may not become current for several months. Those with a selection number over 10,000 may be waiting until the summer for a visa number. Check the Visa Bulletin on the Department of State's website for the cutoff number. It used to be risky to even file an adjustment application for which there was no current number. Now the policy is to accept the filing and hold it until a visa number becomes available.

Interview   In many jurisdictions, the adjustment interview is scheduled for January, whether or not there is a visa number. It is critical that all remaining documents and applications be brought to the interview. If the case is not completed, then it may be extremely difficult to follow up with the officer later. At the end of the interview, ask the officer how to follow up on the case. The best scenario is that the officer holds on to your file and maintains responsibility for it. Be sure to ask the officer for his or her name and phone number so that you may contact him or her. Ask the officer when it will be appropriate to follow up.

1-551 Stamp   The U.S.-based adjustment applicant will want the *I-551* stamp in his or her passport as proof that the case is approved. It is somewhat risky to rely upon the officer or supervisor simply saying the case is approved.

NOTE: *If you have dependents waiting to process overseas, then bear in mind that they must not only complete processing at the embassy, but they must also actually enter the U.S. prior to September 30th.*

Asylum

There is now a one-year deadline to file for asylum from your last arrival in the U.S. If you were in the U.S. longer than one year, and then left and reentered, time starts from the date of reentry. Also, if you are in status, say, on a student visa, then you may apply for asylum as long as you are in valid status, even if that is more than one year. There are exceptions to this rule, such as for minor children or if there are changed conditions in your country.

There are two steps to an asylum application. It is first filed with the appropriate service center on **FORM I-589** with all necessary documentation:

✪   **FORM I-589** accurately completed;

✪   two passport-style photos for each family member;

✪   supplemental detailed statement as to problems;

✪   copies of all identification documents, marriage certificate, and birth certificates of all applicants;

✪   any documentation, such as news articles or reports, as to the problem; and,

✪   affidavits from witnesses.

NOTE: *There is no filing fee.*

The service center then sends the file to one of the nine asylum offices for interview. With the decreasing numbers of asylum applications, the interview will occur approximately six weeks after filing.

ASYLUM OFFICE QUESTION SHEET

This guideline, provided to asylum officers, demonstrates the types of questions that will be addressed in an asylum interview.

ASYLUM DECISION-MAKING FORMAT

I. Who is the Applicant?

✪   Name? Date of birth? Place of birth? Last habitual residence?

✪   What was the date and manner of Applicant's entry into U.S.?

✪   Time spent and countries transited en route to the U.S.?

✪   Family Members: In the U.S.? Still in the country of origin?

II. Why did the Applicant leave his or her country of origin? [Claim]

✪   Does the Applicant fear returning home? If so, why?

✪   What—specifically (summarize in assessment)—does he or she fear?

✪   Who does the Applicant fear will do these things?

✪   Why was the past harm done or future harm feared?

✪   Has anything—specifically (summarize in assessment)—yet been done to the Applicant [e.g., threats, harm, beating, arrest, detention]?

✪   If so, what? When? Where? How? Why? Who?

✪   Has anything—specifically (summarize in assessment)—yet been done to someone the Applicant knows/knows of [e.g. threats, harm, beating, arrest, detention]? If so, what? When? Where? How?

✪ Is there a reasonable "nexus" between the harm experienced by that someone else and the Applicant?

III. Is the Applicant's testimony credible?

✪ Is the evidence (direct or circumstantial) and/or testimony detailed and specific?

✪ Is the evidence and/or testimony consistent?

✪ Is the evidence/testimony plausible in light of country conditions?

✪ Does any specific country conditions info specifically refute claim?

IV. Is the Applicant a refugee? [Analysis]

✪ Is the harm experienced/feared "persecution" or does it "rise to the level of persecution" over time (cumulatively; in the totality of the circumstances)?

✪ Is the Applicant singled out, or similarly situated?

✪ Is the claim based on past persecution or future?

✪ If past, does the preponderance of evidence establish what country conditions have changed such that a fear of future harm is not a reasonable possibility?

✪ If so, has the Applicant presented compelling reasons why he or she should not return on account of the atrocious and severe character of his/her past persecution? (*Chen* Analysis.)

✪ If future, is the fear well-founded [use Mogharrabi/Acosta]?

✪ Is the fear reasonable, country-wide, or localized?

✪ Is the [feared] persecutor the government, or someone the government is unable or unwilling to control?

✪ Is the harm linked to "on account of" one of the five protected grounds of the statute? If so, which one?

✪ Is the Applicant willing to return to his or her country?

V. Are there any bars?

✪ Mandatory: Persecution of others? Firm resettlement?

✪ Multiple nationality? Conviction for particularly serious crime in U.S.? National security danger?

✪ Discretionary: Commission of crime outside the U.S.? Avoidance of overseas refugee processing? Fraudulent entry into U.S. [in connection with flight from harm/fear of harm]? Filed within one year of entry?

VI. Decision. [Conclusion on eligibility]

Immigration Court and Appeals

The procedure before the immigration judge is really a deportation proceeding. At the first brief master hearing, once the alien concedes that he or she is deportable, then the immigration judge will ask what relief he or she is seeking from the court. The alien should state that he or she is seeking to renew the asylum application. At the master hearing, the asylum applicant must decline to designate a country of deportation.

The immigration judge will then set an individual hearing date, at which time the applicant may again attempt to prove his or her asylum case. It is a brand-new hearing with an opportunity to submit evidence, testimony, and witnesses before the court.

Expert witness. It is highly recommended for all but the most compelling cases to have an expert witness brought in to assist with proving the case. Given the stakes involved for an asylum case before the immigration judge, it is necessary to pull out all the stops. It is the last realistic opportunity to win the case.

An asylum case is decided by the ability to convince the immigration judge as to the country's conditions as they relate to that particular applicant. An expert witness puts the government prosecutor on the defensive in trying to disprove his or her testimony, which is very difficult to do. This is a dangerous path for the trial attorney if he or she tries to confront the expert. It may end up merely giving the expert another opportunity to put across his or her point of view and discuss the basis for that opinion. In any event, it never hurts to have an expert. In a close case, it will certainly tip the balance in the alien's favor.

Further, one simply never knows what point an immigration judge will get stuck on with regard to your case. An expert can assist the court with any unique question arising from the case and provide critical background information. The expert is also useful in providing reports and articles that corroborate the case. (See Chapter 19 for more information on appearing in immigration court.)

Approval Rates

The success of an asylum application in the immigration court depends on many factors, the most important being the country of origin and the type of claim within that country. Therefore, an overall number for approvals may not be meaningful. Nonetheless, it is interesting to note that the overall approval rate for an affirmatively filed asylum application (one filed prior to being placed in removal proceedings) is 37%. For a defensive application, the approval rate is 26%.

Another major factor is the actual immigration court. The granting rate of immigration judges unfortunately varies widely. During the nine month period ending in June 2004, asylum approval rates ranged from 66% in Honolulu to 4% in Atlanta. Other large cities were as follows: New York (43%), San Francisco (26%), and Chicago (10%).

The Grant of Asylum

If the asylum application is approved by the asylum office, then the initial grant letter will indicate that it is a temporary grant pending a background check. This is almost always just a formality. There should be a final approval approximately a month later if there is no hitch in the fingerprint and bureaucratic process. A grant of asylum by the immigration judge constitutes a final grant.

Asylee status is an indefinite status since it has no set expiration. However, it can be determined by the Asylum Office that asylees from a certain country no longer require asylum if conditions in that country improve dramatically. It is a good idea to apply for adjustment at the first available opportunity, which is one year from the grant.

An asylee must apply for work authorization through the Nebraska Service Center each year. It is a good idea to apply about two months in advance.

Travel   In order to reenter the U.S., the applicant must obtain travel permission from the USCIS. Such travel permission can take two forms. First, travel authorization may be obtained through the Nebraska Service Center in the form of a *refugee travel permit*. This permit is a small white book that can substitute for a passport. It also allows reentry to the U.S. within one year. It typically takes about two to three months to obtain this travel permit from the USCIS.

If you need to travel on short notice, you can apply for *advance parole* on **FORM I-131** with your local office. Different offices have different procedures to obtain such parole. This filing is also made on **FORM I-131**. Gather the following to file:

✪   **FORM I-131**;

✪   filing fee of $110;

✪   two green card style-photos;

✪   a letter stating the reason for travel;

✪   proof of identity, such as a driver's license or passport asylum approval; and,

✪   a copy of the I-94.

You can expect to spend a number of hours at the USCIS in order to obtain the advance parole. Unlike the travel document, you will require a passport to travel. The grant of advance parole appears to be limited to sixty days when obtained at the local USCIS office. Thus, if you have time, it is much easier to apply through the Nebraska Service Center.

An asylee may not travel back to his or her home country under any circumstances. (Green card holders usually cannot travel back to their home countries either.)

Asylees and refugees are entitled to receive certain benefits through the Office of Refugee Resettlement, which administers various federal and state programs. These programs include cash and medical assistance, employment preparation, job placement, and English language training. Call 800-354-0365 or go to the website at **www.acf.hhs.gov/programs/orr**.

For assistance with a job search and training, call 877-US2-JOBS or go to **www.servicelocator.org**.

Family   A person granted asylum may apply for immediate family members within two years of being granted. The application is as follows:

✪   *Form I-730;*

✪   evidence of asylee or refugee status;

✪   evidence of family relationship, such as a birth certificate;

✪   a clear photo of the family member; and,

✪   a copy of I-94 if the beneficiary is in the U.S. in another status.

NOTE: *There is no filing fee.*

If petitioning for a spouse, also include:

✪   a marriage certificate and

✪   legal termination of any previous marriages.

If the mother is petitioning for a child, also include a birth certificate of the child showing the names of both child and mother. If a father is petitioning for a child, also include a birth certificate of the child showing the names of both child and father.

If the father is married to the child's mother, he should also include the marriage certificate and legal termination of previous marriages of the father and mother. If the father is not married to the child's mother, also include evidence the child was legitimated by civil authorities.

If not legitimated, also include evidence that a bona fide parent/child relationship exists; for example, the parent has emotional and financial ties to the child and has shown genuine concern and interest in the child's support, education, and general welfare. Such evidence may be:

- ✪ money order receipts or canceled checks showing financial support of child;

- ✪ IRS returns showing the child claimed as dependent;

- ✪ medical or other records showing the child as a dependent;

- ✪ school records for the child;

- ✪ correspondence with the child;

- ✪ affidavits of those knowledgeable about the relationship; or,

- ✪ evidence of a legal name change of the beneficiary, if necessary.

The above application is filed with the Nebraska Service Center. If the person is in the U.S., once approved he or she may file for a work permit. One year after approval, he or she can file for permanent residence. Those abroad must go to an embassy or consulate and receive a visa to enter the U.S.

The following comprises an application for an asylee-based adjustment of status application:

- ✪ **FORM I-485** adjustment application filing (see page 112);

- ✪ a filing fee of $255;

- ✪ fingerprint fee of $50;

- ✪ **FORM G-325A** biographic information sheet;

- ✪ proof of asylee status (asylum grant letter or immigration court order);

- ✪ copies of all pages of the passport and I-94s;

- ✪ birth certificate;

- ✪ two passport-style photos;

✪ minimal evidence of residence in the U.S. for the past year—lease, tax forms, etc.;

✪ dates and proof of any travel outside U.S., such as copies of stamps in the asylee's travel documents;

✪ if necessary, proof of any name change;

✪ documents related to criminal convictions, if applicable; and,

✪ *Form I-602* waiver of inadmissibility with supporting documents (if required for criminal convictions or if last entry was EWI or with false passport).

Form I-602 waiver of inadmissibility with supporting documents (if required for criminal convictions or if last entry was EWI or with false passport).

For derivative spouse: Same as above, but also include the marriage certificate.

NOTE: *The G-28 is the attorney appearance form and is only included if the applicant has an attorney. It would be included with all applications.*

Optional benefits can be applied for, such as a work permit or travel permission. (see Chapter 9.)

FORM I-765 work permit:

✪ **FORM I-765** (use category (a)(5));

✪ filing fee of $120;

✪ two passport-style photos;

✪ copy of state-issued I.D. or passport;

✪ asylum grant letter or immigration court decision;

✪ copy of last work permit; and,

✪ copy of I-94 front and back, if available.

FORM I-131 refugee travel document/advance parole (if eligible):

✪ **FORM I-131**;

✪ filing fee of $110;

✪ two passport-style photos;

✪ copy of state issued I.D. or passport;

✪ asylum grant letter or immigration court decision;

✪ copy of previous travel document or advance parole; and,

✪ copy of I-94 front and back, if available.

Form I-485   The principal form is the **I-485**. This is the actual adjustment of status application. It should be carefully completed. (See page 112 for detailed instructions.) The filing fee is either $255 if the applicant is 14 years of age or over or $160 if the applicant is under age 14. Likewise, those age 14 or over require fingerprints and must pay the $50 fingerprint fee.

Form G-325A   A completed **G-325A** form is required for all applicants 14 years of age or older. Every applicant requires two passport-style photos to be included. The medical examination form and vaccination supplement must be obtained. (see Chapter 14.)

Form I-864   There is no requirement for the I-864 Affidavit of Support, which normally accompanies an adjustment application. Further, the USCIS has stated that refugees and asylees can use any public benefits, including cash welfare, health care, food programs, and other non-cash programs without hurting their chances of obtaining permanent residence.

Form I-602   If there is any condition of inadmissibility for a criminal record only, the I-602 waiver must be filed and fee paid. (see Chapter 15.) For any criminal record including arrests, original certified records of disposition must be obtained from the clerk of the court and included with the adjustment packet.

Adjustment Application   To properly file the adjustment application, follow these suggestions.

✪ Make a copy of all documents and keep them in safe place.

- ✪ Write your name and *A number* (the eight-digit number assigned by the USCIS that appears on your work permit, fingerprint, and interview notices) or date of birth in pencil on the back of photos.

- ✪ Attach the correct filing fee—a money order or cashier's check made out to "USCIS" can be used for all of the fees.

- ✪ Make sure the name of the applicant is on the check.

- ✪ Confirm the correct address for the service center.

- ✪ Send any address changes by certified mail, return receipt requested, since such requests may not be processed by the USCIS, resulting in a closed case.

The applicant will receive a receipt notice a few weeks after filing. While the receipt notice may state the adjudication period as a reasonably short period of time, the current wait for adjudication does go back several years. Since there are no visa numbers for several years, there is no rush for the Nebraska Service Center to adjudicate the application.

The applicant will need to be fingerprinted prior to completion of the case. As fingerprints expire after fifteen months, the applicant is then in a race against time to get the case closed out before the prints expire.

NOTE: *The official date of adjustment of status will be backdated to one year before adjustment was granted.*

Religious Workers

The following is an outline of the complete packet to be filed with the appropriate service center for religious workers:

- ✪ **FORM I-360**;

- ✪ filing fee of $130;

- ✪ a detailed letter from an authorized official of the religious organization establishing that the proposed services and the alien qualify for the benefit;

✪ a detailed letter from the authorized official of the religious organization attesting to the alien's membership in the religious denomination and explaining, in detail, the person's religious work, all employment during the past two years, and the proposed employment;

✪ a copy of the applicant's religious training or ordination certificate;

✪ evidence establishing that the religious organization, and any affiliate that will employ the person, is a bona fide, nonprofit, religious organization in the U.S. and is exempt from taxation under Section 501(c)(3) of the Internal Revenue Code;

✪ financial statement from the religious organization;

✪ corporation papers of the religious organization;

✪ proof of employment as a religious worker for the past two years from an organization official;

✪ photos of previous employment as a religious worker; and,

✪ background information about the religious organization.

I-360 Petition

The purpose of the **I-360** petition is to prove eligibility as a religious worker. Along with the I-360 petition, the several documents just listed need to be attached in support of it. Specifically, an authorized official of the church must explain in detail the need for the alien's services and the qualifying credentials of the alien. A copy of the alien's religious training must be provided. Finally, a Section 501(c)(3) letter must be attached to prove the religious organization is tax-exempt and nonprofit. (This packet can then be filed with the appropriate service center. See Appendix B for the correct address.)

Adjustment

Once the **I-360** petition is approved, an adjustment application (I-485) may be filed with the local USCIS office. This application may be filed in the same manner as for a family-based one, except that an approved I-360 petition is substituted for the I-130 petition. Also, no affidavit of support is required with this adjustment packet.

While the adjustment filing does not require an affidavit of support, there may be a *public charge* problem on account of the low salaries paid to religious workers.

The religious worker will be required to demonstrate that he or she is employed with the religious organization in a full-time capacity and will not need financial support.

A religious worker with an adjustment application pending is eligible to apply for work authorization. However, it may be considered a red flag to the USCIS officer if the applicant is employed in a nonreligious field.

Investors

All investor petitions are filed with either the Texas or California service centers. Those in the jurisdiction of the Nebraska Service Center will file their petition with the California Service Center while those who would normally file with the Vermont Service Center will file with the Texas Service Center.

An investor visa application is normally too complex to handle without the assistance of an immigration attorney, but it is useful to know what type of documentation is required. A filing for an investor visa might look as follows:

✪ *Form I-526 Immigrant Petition by Alien Entrepreneur;*

✪ filing fee of $400;

✪ letter summarizing eligibility; and,

✪ supporting documentation:

- establishment of business (i.e., articles of incorporation);

- partnership agreement, joint venture agreement, lease, or proof of ownership of property;

- establishment in a rural or high unemployment area;

- proof of investment (i.e., bank statements, certified financial reports, assets or property transfers, loans or mortgages, or other borrowing secured by assets of the investor);

- capital obtained through lawful means (i.e., tax returns, evidence of source of capital);

- employment creation (i.e., tax records, Form I-9);

- investor involvement in management (i.e., statement of position title, description of duties);

- certificate evidencing authority to do business in a state or municipality; and,

- business plan evidencing job creation.

The above outline describes the initial filing for an investor visa. The principal form is the I-526 petition. This form requests standard biographic and immigration status information about the investor and basic information about the corporation. The major part of the application is to prepare a detailed cover letter describing the business venture and to specifically address each of the particular criteria previously set forth above. Documentation as to each of the criteria must be included.

To reduce the risk of denial of the visa on a sizeable financial investment, an *escrow account* may be used, so that the funds are committed to the enterprise only if the visa is approved and are returned to the investor if it is denied. The escrow agreement must state that the required initial capital contribution is actually committed to the new commercial enterprise immediately and irrevocably upon approval of the petition. The escrow agreement must unequivocally release the funds into the operations of the enterprise upon approval of the petition. These documents must be prepared carefully to meet the technical requirements of the USCIS.

If the service center requires additional information, it will send a request for evidence. It may also send the file to the local district office for interview.

Once the I-526 petition is approved, then the individual and his or her spouse and children may apply for conditional permanent residence. (see Chapter 4.) The process for adjustment is the same as for a family-based petition, except that an approved I-526 rather than an I-130 petition is submitted. This adjustment application is filed with the local USCIS office.

Conditional Grant   The visa is initially granted on a conditional basis, similar to the conditional residence granted through marriage to a U.S. citizen. After two years, the investor must apply to remove the conditions by demonstrating that the investment was established and in continuous operation during the two-year period. The application to remove conditions is filed within the 90-day period prior to the expiration of the conditional green card.

An application to remove conditions is as follows:

✪ *Form I-829*;

✪ filing fee of $395;

✪ a copy of a conditional green card; and,

✪ supporting documentation:

  • establishment of enterprise (i.e., tax returns);

  • required amount of investment (i.e., audited financial statement);

  • proof that the investor sustained investments throughout the conditional period;

  • bank statements;

  • invoices;

  • contracts;

  • business licenses;

  • corporate tax returns or quarterly tax statements;

  • payroll records; and,

  • *I-9 forms.*

The Form I-829 should be completed and as many supporting documents as possible should be attached. It is necessary to prove the three points set out in the above outline—namely, that the enterprise was established, the required amount of investment was made, and the investment was sustained through the two-year conditional period. This application is filed with the same service center as the original I-526 petition.

Once Form I-829 is approved and the conditions have been removed, the investment may be sold. However, it is advisable to wait until the green card actually arrives in the mail before doing so.

Cancellation of Removal

At the master calendar hearing, the immigration judge will ask what forms of relief you will be seeking. If you have been in the U.S. for ten years, you may apply for *cancellation of removal*. The immigration judge will instruct you as to the deadline and precise procedure to file the applications. You should listen carefully to the immigration judge and write down everything he or she says. The following are normally initially required:

✪ **FORM EOIR-42B**;

✪ evidence of payment of $100 filing fee;

✪ fingerprint fee of $50;

✪ **FORM G325A** (original to the USCIS attorney, copy to the court);

✪ certificate of service;

✪ proof of the qualifying relative's immigration status; and,

✪ passport-style photo.

The listing of documents in Chapter 11 is a complete list that may be used to prove a cancellation of removal case. The principal form to be completed is the **EOIR-42B**. It is a detailed seven-page form requesting seemingly every possible personal history item. Before this application is filed with the court, it must be paid for at the local USCIS office. The immigration court does not accept any filing fees. In order to pay for an application at the USCIS cashier and receive it back, you will need to complete a routing slip and place it on top of the application. After the application is filed, supporting documents will be due to the court fourteen days prior to the hearing date. Go through the list of documents and compile as many as possible for filing.

Court Rules   Bear in mind that there are local rules that need to be complied with, particularly as they relate to the filing of documents. The immigration court will supply you with these rules. If you have an attorney, as you should in immigration court, he or she will be aware of them. However, if you do not have an attorney, you will need to read and understand the court rules.

> **Example**: All documents must be two-hole-punched at the top and contain a table of contents. Most courts have a ten- or fourteen-day rule that requires all documents be filed ten or fourteen days ahead of the court hearing. If they are not, the judge can deny their admission.

The original application and supporting documents are filed with the court after the fee is paid.

A copy of any document filed with the EOIR must be served upon the trial attorneys at their office, usually called the Office of District Counsel. All documents filed with the immigration court must include a *certificate of service*. The immigration court clerk can give you the address. It is imperative that you have the court clerk stamp your copy as proof of timely filing.

Evidence   Since these removal cases are so difficult to win, it is essential that as much evidence as possible be compiled and filed with the immigration court. However, take care to only include documents that are truly beneficial to your case. Do not include documents for the sake of creating an impressively thick file. The documents should be organized in a way that aids understanding and impact.

The use of an expert witness is beneficial to assist in proving your case. Cases that turn on the country conditions in the native country require an expert to convincingly describe the conditions to the immigration judge. It is up to the trial attorneys to disprove an expert's testimony, and this is very difficult for a lay person to do. This is a dangerous path for the trial attorney if he or she tries to confront the expert. It may end up merely giving the expert another opportunity to put across his or her point of view and discuss the basis for his or her position. In a close case, having an expert will certainly tip the balance in your favor.

What to Expect   These cases are difficult to win. The legal standard of *exceptional and extremely unusual hardship* is as difficult to prove as it is to contemplate. An immigration attorney will be required to assist with developing evidence and conducting the hearing. Chapter 19 deals in detail with handling a case before the immigration court.

If your case is granted, in order to receive a green card, you must complete ADIT processing through the local USCIS office. Alien Documentation, Identification, and Telecommunication System (ADIT) processing involves completion of the card that will be made into your green card by the service center. Until this happens, a person is not a permanent resident.

14 SUPPORTING DOCUMENTS

The previous chapters have discussed the specific eligibility requirements for each adjustment category. In this chapter, issues common to all adjustment filings will be explained, especially where supporting documents are concerned.

Passport-Style Photos

An adjustment applicant is required to supply two passport-style photos. One photo will be used to make your green card. The other photo will stay in your file for identification purposes. While the photos are called *passport-style*, in fact they will be used for every immigration document you will seek to obtain, including a *naturalization certificate*.

There are certain requirements for these photos. If the studio does not recognize the term *passport-style*, then you should probably go someplace else to have the photo taken. Many places take such photos, including print shops and drugstore chains.

NOTE: *Avoid the photo places nearest the USCIS office. They often charge as much as $30 for two photos that normally cost $7.*

Whenever submitting a photo to the USCIS, write the name and *A number* on the back of each photo with a pencil or felt pen. The *A number* is the eight-digit number assigned by the USCIS that appears on your work permit, fingerprint, and interview notices.

Fingerprints

Before an applicant can adjust his or her status, he or she must have fingerprints taken so that the applicant's Federal Bureau of Investigations (FBI) criminal record can be accessed. For the vast majority of people, this is not a problem.

Not only must the prints be taken, but they must be valid at the time of the interview. That is, at the time of adjustment, the fingerprints must have been taken within fifteen months.

If you notice that your fingerprints have expired and you are still waiting for an interview or for your case to be processed, then you may want to write to your local USCIS office and ask that you be provided an *appointment letter for fingerprinting* (notice to appear for fingerprints at a specified place).

You will be asked in the appointment letter to take fingerprints at the Application Support Centers (ASC) nearest you. If you happen to move and know of a center closer to you, you can simply go there with the original notice.

Translations

Every document in a foreign language requires an English translation. If you live in an area that has a large foreign-born population, then it may be easy to find a place that will do translations at a reasonable cost. A birth certificate should not cost more than $10 or $15 to translate. If you do pay to get a translation, keep the original of the translation for your future use. The USCIS only needs a copy of the translation.

You may also translate your document yourself. (Appendix E includes an example of how to format the translation and a certification form.) It is good form to place the translation on top, followed by the certification form, and then a copy of the document in the original language.

It is not as hard as it might seem to do a translation. Do not worry too much about translating the legalistic language found on many documents such as birth certificates. The most important part of the translation is the date and place of birth and the names of the parents.

Unavailable Documents

If a birth, marriage, or death record is not available, then the following may substitute:

✪ church or baptismal record (a certificate issued by a church attesting to the birth or religious ceremony);

✪ school record (any record from a school showing the child's date of birth and the names of the parents);

✪ a census record showing the name, date, and place of birth; and,

✪ *affidavits* (sworn statements from two persons who were living at the time of the birth or marriage). The affidavit should contain the affiant's name, address, date and place of birth, relationship to the adjustment applicant, full information concerning event, and how the affiant acquired the knowledge.

In order to substitute the above documents, a *certificate of nonavailability* from the proper governmental authority in the native country may be required. Sometimes, it is possible to obtain such documents from the country's embassy in the U.S. However, these documents are not always accepted by the USCIS office. The immigration court is much more likely to use substitute records.

Medical Examination

The *medical examination* is to establish that the applicant does not carry any communicable diseases. Diseases that are tested for are HIV, tuberculosis, leprosy, sexually transmitted diseases, and so on. You cannot enter the U.S. with an active, contagious disease except with a waiver, if available, such as for HIV or TB.

The medical examination must be obtained from a certified medical provider. Each city has its own list of medical clinics. This list is not presently available on the USCIS website. The list is most easily available from either the forms line or the local USCIS office. It is also possible to call 800-375-5283 and obtain the name of the nearest doctor by entering your zip code.

Call to get a quote. The immigration exam should cost approximately $70, not including vaccinations. It may also take up to a week for the lab tests to come back. If you are in a rush, then call around. Some clinics are much faster than others.

Vaccinations   It is now a requirement that the applicant have received all appropriate vaccinations. If you have any type of vaccination record, you should bring it to your medical exam. It can save you from getting costly and perhaps unnecessary vaccinations. A full set of vaccinations can run several hundred dollars. It is possible to have vaccinations taken for a minimal charge by calling your city's health department.

Fill in Form
Completely   The biggest problem with the medical examination is that the form is not marked completely by the doctor. Remind the doctor to make certain all boxes are checked on *Form I-693* and on the vaccination form. The applicant should also double-check his or her green receipt copy of the examination to ensure that all boxes have been filled. Any X-rays received along with the sealed envelope are not submitted to the USCIS.

Timing   The medical examination is valid for only one year. If the medical exam results are filed along with the adjustment application, then it is valid no matter when the interview is scheduled. If the medical is brought to the interview, it must have been taken within the past year. Therefore, you should wait until the adjustment interview is scheduled before taking the medical exam.

Affidavit of Support

With the *Affidavit of Support* (I-864), the USCIS attempts to ensure that an intending immigrant has adequate financial support and is not likely to become a *public charge*, or financial drain on the government. This is an area that frequently causes a delay or denial of an adjustment application. Needless to say, the I-864 is extremely important to the permanent residence process, and care must be taken to carefully prepare and document.

The USCIS ensures that the rules regarding affidavits of support are met. The two things to watch for here are that the income requirement is met and that all supporting documentation is submitted, along with the forms.

By signing the affidavit of support form, the sponsor is undertaking an obligation that he or she will support the immigrant if necessary, and will reimburse any government agency or private entity that provides the sponsored immigrants with federal, state, or local means-tested public benefits.

The USCIS is seeking to ensure that you do not become a public charge. Section 212(a)(4) states that anyone who is likely to become a public charge is inadmissible. If that is not enough, Section 237(a)(5) says that any alien within five years of entry who becomes a public charge is deportable.

The income requirement may be one of the more difficult requirements to meet in completing an adjustment of status case. In order to obtain a green card, it must be demonstrated that you have sufficient income to not become a public charge.

The line had to be drawn somewhere in order to ensure this. It has been determined that an income of 125% over the poverty line is sufficient to adjust status. For 2006, the poverty guidelines are:

SPONSORS 125% POVERTY LINE			
Household Size	48 States	Alaska	Hawaii
2	$16,500	$20,625	$18,975
3	$20,750	$25,937	$23,862
4	$25,000	$31,250	$28,750
5	$29,250	$36,562	$33,637
6	$33,500	$41,875	$38,525
7	$37,750	$41,187	$43,412
8	$42,000	$52,500	$48,300
additional persons	+$4,250 per person	+$5,312 per person	+$4,887 per person

NOTE: *Military members sponsoring their spouse or child only need to have 100% of the poverty line. Multiply the above 125% level figures by .80 to get back to the 100% level.*

Other requirements are that the sponsor be over 18 years of age, have a domicile in the U.S., and be a U.S. citizen or lawful permanent resident.

Insufficient Income

First, look to assets to make up insufficient income. You must have cash assets worth five times the difference between the income requirement and your income. Attach a copy of a savings account, stocks, bonds, certificates of deposit, life insurance cash values, or real estate. You must include evidence of liens, mortgages, and liabilities for the given asset. You may also add the assets and income of the immigrant being sponsored.

You may add the income of a household member who either lives with you or is listed as a dependent on your most recent tax return. That household member then executes I-864A. Add the income to the third page of the I-864.

Joint Sponsor

You may use a *joint sponsor*. A joint sponsor is any sponsor who is not the petitioner. It is somewhat preferred that the joint sponsor be a relative or be someone who has a moral obligation to care for the beneficiary, but actually anyone can qualify. In this event, both the petitioner and joint sponsor should submit a fully documented and notarized original I-864. The joint sponsor must submit proof of U.S. citizenship or lawful permanent resident status.

Supporting Documents

The following documents are required to accompany an affidavit of support:

- ✪ Form I-864 (signed and notarized within past six months);

- ✪ Form I-864A Supplement with notarized signatures (for household member, if necessary);

- ✪ most recent federal tax return including all schedules and all W-2 forms;

- ✪ a job letter from the employer;

- ✪ proof of assets (if required to meet income requirement); and,

- ✪ proof of citizenship or LPR status for joint sponsor.

Tax returns. Each year's tax returns should be in correct order and stapled together. The W-2 forms are critically important and will be insisted upon by the USCIS officer. If any tax return or W-2 form is missing, you may simply go to the Internal Revenue Service (IRS) office and obtain the tax summary form.

NOTE: *An original signed and notarized I-864 and I-864A (if required) and one complete set of supporting documents must be submitted for each principal applicant. For other dependent family members, only a photocopy of the application is required, but not copies of the supporting documents.*

You may substitute *Letter 1722* (tax transcript) if you do not have the actual returns. You may obtain the tax letter by calling 800-829-1040 and using the automated system. It may be possible to fax it the same day, depending on the IRS service center taking your call, and if you are not going back more than three years. There is no charge. The other option is to complete *Form 4506, Request For Copy or Transcript of Tax Form*, which is available online at **www.irs.gov.**

Mail to the address indicated on the form and you should receive your transcript within two weeks.

Tax letter 1722 can also substitute for misplaced W-2 forms. If you otherwise wish to obtain duplicate copies of W-2 forms, file form 4506 and 4506-T. It may take sixty days to process the request.

If you did not have to file a tax return, then you are directed to attach a written explanation and a copy of the instructions from the Internal Revenue Service publication that shows you were not obligated to file. Check the first pages of the 1040 instructions booklet (**www.irs.gov**) on who does not have to file.

If you have not filed a tax return you were supposed to file, then you should file a late return and pay the penalty. Those who live outside the U.S. must still file an annual return. If necessary, it is often easy to rectify the missing returns by simply filing late. The penalty is not as severe as you might think.

NOTE: *You cannot substitute state income tax returns. Copies of these are not required.*

Job Letter If you cannot get a job letter, then you may substitute a pay stub. If you are self-employed, prepare a letter on your business letterhead with a description of your salary.

Exceptions An exception to the requirement for the affidavit of support is that if you already have credit for forty quarters of coverage under the Social Security Act.

The Sponsor The sponsor needs to fully understand that he or she is legally responsible for financial support of the sponsored immigrant until he or she becomes a U.S. citizen, can be credited with forty hours of work, departs the U.S. permanently, or dies.

NOTE: *A divorce does not terminate the financial obligations of the petitioner with regard to the USCIS.*

The sponsor may be asked to reimburse the government if the new lawful permanent resident receives a federal *means-tested public benefit*. The majority of the aid programs like Supplemental Security Income (SSI), food stamps, and Medicare qualify as such benefits. If unsure, you may simply ask the benefit provider whether it is a means-tested public benefit.

Address Changes There is a requirement that address changes are filed within thirty days of *Form I-865*. Strict fines are in place for failure to notify the USCIS as to an address change. However, it is doubtful that anyone will ever be asked to pay this fine.

Public Charge and Use of Public Benefits

An alien seeking adjustment of status is inadmissible if the individual is likely to be a public charge. The USCIS has moved to a *totality of the circumstances* test to make this determination. The office should consider factors such as the individual's age, health, family status, assets, resources, financial status, education, and skills.

An alien who has received certain public benefits may be determined to become a public charge. Such a person is inadmissible as a permanent resident. It can be difficult to determine which of the many assistance programs will render a person inadmissible.

In 1999, the Department of State and the USCIS issued guidance concerning this previously murky area. These regulations clarified which programs are to adversely impact an adjustment application.

The following programs may cause a public charge determination:

✪ cash welfare such as *Supplemental Security Income* (SSI);

✪ cash *Temporary Assistance for Needy Families* (TANF);

✪ *state general assistance* (the USCIS will not consider cash welfare received by an alien's children or other family members for family charge purposes, unless the cash welfare is the family's only means of support); and,

✪ *institutionalization for long-term care* (including residence in a nursing home or mental health facility at government expense).

The following programs will *not* have an adverse impact:

✪ *health care benefits* (including Medicaid, state Children's Health Insurance Program, or other health services, unless Medicaid is used for long-term institutional care);

✪ *food programs* (including food stamps, WIC (Special Supplemental Nutrition Program for Women, Infants and Children), school meals, or other food assistance);

✪ *noncash programs* (including public housing, child care, energy assistance, disaster relief, Head Start, job training, or counseling); and,

✪ *unemployment benefits*.

15 ELIGIBILITY TO ADJUST AND INADMISSIBILITY GROUNDS

An individual in the U.S. must be in valid nonimmigrant status in order to apply for adjustment, with a few important exceptions.

- ✪ If an individual is the beneficiary of any I-130 petition or labor certification filed before January 18, 1998, he or she may apply for adjustment on any available basis in the U.S. despite being out of status or even having entered the country illegally.

- ✪ If an individual is the beneficiary of any I-130 petition or labor certification filed before April 30, 2001, and was physically present in the U.S. on December 20, 2000, then he or she may apply for adjustment on any available basis in the U.S. despite being out of status or even having entered the country illegally.

- ✪ If an individual lawfully entered the U.S. on a nonimmigrant visa (other than a K-1 visa), he or she may apply for adjustment through an immediate relative petition despite overstaying the nonimmigrant visa, as long as he or she has not worked without USCIS authorization.

Essentially, exceptions one and two qualify an individual for adjustment under Section 245(i). This section lets an individual be out of status, or have violated status, and simply pay a $1,000 penalty. In other words, someone might possess a valid, unexpired tourist visa, but is working without USCIS permission. If this were discovered (and acted upon) by the USCIS officer, that person would be barred from adjustment except under this new law.

While an individual who is ineligible for adjustment in the U.S. may theoretically return to his or her home country to apply through an embassy, this is not as easy now as it once was. Under the laws that went into effect in 1996, if you are out of status for more than 180 days starting from April 1, 1997, and depart the U.S., you are barred for three years from applying for any immigration benefit. If you are out of status more than one year from April 1, 1997, and depart the U.S., you are barred for ten years. There are two important exceptions to this provision. You are not considered out of status if you are under the age of 18, or if you have had a bona fide asylum application pending with the USCIS.

There is a possible *waiver* for having accumulated unlawful presence, but it is very difficult to have approved. It requires that you have a U.S. citizen or green card-holding parent or spouse and that you can show it would be an *extreme hardship* to them if you are unable to enter the U.S. Extreme hardship is difficult to show, particularly at one of the embassies. Simply showing the emotional difficulties of being separated from family members is *not* sufficient. You will need to provide evidence that your spouse or parent requires your assistance with a medical condition, financial support, or some major reason. You will need to document these conditions by their own detailed affidavit, or a letter from a doctor.

All the grounds of inadmissibility discussed in this chapter are contained in Section 212(a) of the *Immigration and Nationality Act*. For some of them, there may be a waiver available. Just because a waiver is available does not mean it will be granted. It is critical to consult an immigration attorney to determine the appropriate course of action.

Criminal Convictions

Section 212(a) of the Immigration and Nationality Act sets forth restrictions on who may obtain a green card. Those who have committed certain types of crimes are advised to check with an immigration lawyer as to their eligibility.

If an adjustment application fails because of a criminal record, then the person may find him- or herself in removal proceedings without any relief possible in the immigration court. Filing such an application is a senseless endeavor.

The following will prevent a person from obtaining a green card:

- ✪ a conviction for a crime involving moral turpitude, if sentenced to more than six months;

- ✪ two or more convictions for a crime involving moral turpitude regardless of sentence (such as misdemeanor retail theft), or a conviction for an aggravated felony (as defined in Section 101(a)(43)). Many minor crimes are included, such as:

  - any controlled substance violation (except for possession of marijuana of less than 28 grams);

  - crime of violence where sentenced to more than one year in prison;

  - theft offense where sentenced to more than one year; and,

  - an offense involving loss to the victim of more than $10,000, etc;

- ✪ multiple criminal convictions with an aggregate sentence of more than five years;

- ✪ miscellaneous other crimes, such as unlawful use of a firearm; and,

- ✪ any aliens who may affect the security of the U.S. or engage in terrorist activity.

For some of the crimes, a waiver under Section 212(h) is available. Initial eligibility for the waiver requires a U.S. citizen or lawful permanent resident (LPR) spouse, parent, or child. Then it must be shown that it would be an extreme hardship to that qualifying relative if the applicant were to be deported. This can be a difficult showing to make, especially these days.

Health Conditions

Certain diseases may prevent you from obtaining permanent residence. These will be detected through the required medical examination. If it happens that you have such a disease, there may be a waiver available. Consult with an immigration attorney.

Public Charge

It is extremely important that the *I-864 Affidavit of Support* form be carefully completed and care taken to ensure that all financial requirements are met. This helps to ensure that no one will become a *public charge*, or financial drain for support on the government. (See Chapter 14 for instructions and more information.)

Outstanding Order of Deportation or Removal

Apart from the above, anyone who has a deportation or removal order entered against him or her is inadmissible. You may not apply for adjustment within five years of a final order of deportation or ten years after a final order of removal.

A person can have a *deportation* order even if he or she never received notice of the court hearing. If there is any doubt as to whether such an order exists, you should call the immigration court status line and possibly follow up with the specific immigration court. It is better to find out sooner rather than be informed by the USCIS officer at the interview and possibly be taken into Department of Homeland Security (DHS) custody.

In some cases, it is possible to reopen the immigration proceedings. The other option is to file a waiver on *Form I-212*, if the applicant is eligible. However, even if the waiver is approved, the alien will be required to process for adjustment at an embassy abroad, possibly causing a problem of unlawful presence in the U.S. You will really need to consult an attorney before proceeding with either of these options.

Unlawful Presence

Under Section 212(a)(9), a person may not adjust status if he or she has accumulated certain time in unlawful status. Especially at this time, the USCIS is sensitive to making sure an applicant has not been a member of any terrorist organization or convicted of any terrorist-sounding criminal charge.

If you were out of status in the U.S. for more than six months beginning April 1, 1997, and depart the U.S., you may not adjust status for three years. Similarly, if you accumulate one year of unlawful presence, you may not adjust status for ten years. Even if you are able to reenter the U.S. after the unlawful presence, you could be barred at the interview.

A waiver exists for unlawful presence, but it is difficult to obtain. The alien must have a U.S. citizen or LPR spouse or parent to qualify for the waiver. There must also be a demonstration of extreme hardship to that relative. These waivers are very difficult to obtain at an embassy. They are somewhat easier to obtain in the U.S., since the office can be face-to-face with the applicant and the qualifying relative. They might also be reviewable by an immigration judge.

NOTE: *If you have a student visa marked "duration of status" (D/S), you do not acquire unlawful presence until an USCIS officer or immigration judge finds a status violation. Thus, you are much less likely to have acquired unlawful presence.*

Other Immigration Violations

The following violations make an applicant inadmissible to the U.S. under 212(a)(6):

- ✪ being present in the U.S. without admission or parole (unless eligible under Section 245(i));

- ✪ failing to attend removal proceeding;

- ✪ fraud or willful representation;

- ✪ being a stowaway (that is, entering the U.S. illegally by travelling on a commercial transportation such as a train, bus, or boat where a fare should have been paid);

- ✪ alien smugglers;

- ✪ immigration document fraud; or,

- ✪ student visa abusers.

NSEERS Special Registration

In the fall of 2002, *National Security Entry-Exit Registration System* (NSEERS) was announced for males from eighteen primarily Middle Eastern countries. This program required that such males residing in the U.S. register with their local USCIS office by April 2003, or possibly face a bar to adjusting status in the future. Those who were out of status were arrested by the Department of Homeland Security and given notice to appear in immigration court. The annual registration requirement of the program was suspended in December 2003.

Nonetheless, those who failed to register when the program was in effect may still face a bar to adjustment unless good cause for failure to register can be shown. Many USCIS offices are willing to late register. If you must attend a late registration interview, bring the following documents and information:

- ✪ passport;

- ✪ driver's license or state-issued I.D.;

- ✪ credit cards; and,

- ✪ completed **Form G-325A**, including parents' names, dates of birth, addresses, and phone numbers.

Any nonimmigrant, particularly one subject to NSEERS, should be sure to file any address change with USCIS on **Form AR-11**. It is a criminal misdemeanor to wilfully fail to do so unless the person is a student and the address change was reported to the student system SEVIS. While it is highly unlikely to result in actual prosecution, the failure to do so may be used against you if you encounter a problem at an airport or other point of entry.

NOTE: *Consult an attorney if one of the above conditions exists.*

I6 | WORK AND TRAVEL WHILE ADJUSTMENT IS PENDING

Two important interim benefits are available to those who have an adjustment of status application pending. These are to obtain work authorization and permission to reenter the U.S. after travel outside the U.S.

Work Permit

An adjustment or asylum applicant may apply for a work permit while his or her application is pending. A *work permit* allows an alien to be lawfully employed to the same extent as a U.S. citizen. In fact, it is a violation of federal law for an employer to discriminate against an individual because he or she only has a work permit instead of a green card or a naturalization certificate.

Filing the Application

Whether the work permit is applied for at the National Benefits Center (NBC) or a service center depends on the basis for the work permit. For family-based or diversity-based visa adjustment applications, the work permit application is filed at the NBC office. For these applications, a complete filing consists simply of the following items:

✪   **FORM I-765**;

✪   filing fee of $120;

✪   a copy of the adjustment receipt notice;

✪   two passport-style photos;

✪   copy of Form I-94 (front and back), if available; and,

✪   copy of last work permit (front and back).

Mail these items to the National Benefits Center at:

U.S. Citizenship and Immigration Services
P.O. Box 805887
Chicago, IL 60680

Sometime after filing, a biometrics appointment notice will be mailed to the applicant. The entire process normally takes about three months.

Service Center Filing   For the following categories, the work permit application is mailed to the appropriate service center:

✪   employment-based adjustment applications;

✪   investor-based adjustment applications;

✪   asylum applicants, asylees, or asylee-based adjustment applications; and,

✪   refugees or refugee-based adjustment applications.

Employment- and investor-based work permit applications are mailed to the service center that has jurisdiction over the particular state. On the other hand, all asylee- and refugee-based work permit applications are filed at the Nebraska Service Center. There is no filing fee for the initial asylee- or refugee-based work permit application.

Processing   For the above categories, a work permit application consists of the **APPLICATION FOR EMPLOYMENT AUTHORIZATION (I-765)** form and several supporting documents. The following list contains all supporting documents to include with the work permit application:

- ✪ **FORM I-765**;

- ✪ filing fee of $120;

- ✪ two passport-style photos;

- ✪ a copy of adjustment receipt notice or status of asylum application (e.g., interview notice, court notice);

- ✪ a clear copy of a current work permit showing picture; and,

- ✪ a clear copy of a state-issued driver's license or ID, or the identification page of the passport showing picture.

Regardless of where the work permit application is filed, the USCIS is supposed to process it within ninety days. In the meantime, an individual with a receipt notice for a work permit application and a Social Security number is immediately authorized to work during this ninety-day period.

If the work permit is not received within ninety days, regulations permit an individual to obtain a temporary work document at his or her local USCIS office. Such persons should walk into their local office with their original work permit filing receipt notice or canceled check, and a letter from their employer stating they require immediate proof of work eligibility.

Obtaining a Social Security Number

In addition to a work permit, one must also have a Social Security number to be employed. The Social Security Administration, which is entirely separate from the USCIS, issues Social Security numbers.

An alien with an adjustment application pending is entitled to a Social Security number once he or she obtains a work permit. It is a good idea to wait ten business days before applying for the Social Security number, to allow USCIS time to update its database. After application for the Social Security card, it will take approximately one week for the card to arrive in the mail. The card will be marked "Not valid for work except with USCIS authorization." After adjustment of status to a permanent resident, a new card may be obtained without this designation.

Travel Permission—Advance Parole

In order to depart the U.S. during the time an adjustment application is pending, you must first obtain prior permission of the USCIS. This document is called *advance parole*. Upon reentry into the U.S., present this document in order to reenter the U.S. and resume the adjustment of status application.

In the past, there were restrictions that there be a personal emergency or business reasons to necessitate the granting of advance parole. Currently, any valid reason to travel is sufficient. The only restriction to obtaining advance parole is that one not have accumulated more than six months of unlawful presence in the U.S. prior to filing the adjustment application. Unlawful presence is time spent out of status in the U.S. after April 1, 1997.

NOTE: *Even if you obtain advance parole and reenter the U.S. after the unlawful presence, you could be prevented at the interview from obtaining permanent residence status.*

The following is a fully documented application for advance parole (permission to travel or reenter U.S.):

- ✪ **FORM I-131**;

- ✪ filing fee of $110;

- ✪ two passport-style photos;

- ✪ copy of driver's license or state I.D., or identification page of passport;

- ✪ **FORM I-485 RECEIPT NOTICE;**

✪ *Form I-94* arrival-departure document;

✪ proof of current status in the U.S.:

 • *Form I-797 Approval Notice* indicating current status;

 • passport of last entry;

 • *Form I-20* if in the U.S. on the F-1 visa;

 • Form *IAP-66* for a J-1 visa;

 • previous advance parole documents; and,

 • supporting letter such as medical emergency, wedding invitation, airline tickets, or itinerary (not mandatory).

(To find out more about some of the supporting documentation required, read Chapter 14. Many are explained there.)

NOTE: *If you have a student visa marked "duration of status" (D/S), you do not acquire unlawful presence until a USCIS officer or immigration judge finds a status violation. Therefore, you are eligible for advance parole when applying for adjustment.*

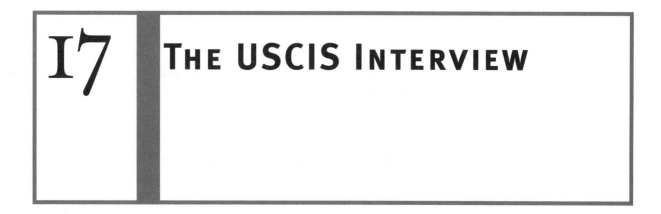

17 THE USCIS INTERVIEW

After your forms are filed, you will most likely have to face the USCIS interview. An applicant can normally only be interviewed in the district where he or she resides. Therefore, if you move out of the district office jurisdiction, you should submit **AR-11** and a separate change of address notice to the local office. Applicants should request the district office in the new place of residence to request the file from the previous office. This chapter gives you a good basis for what to expect and how to proceed.

Expediting the Interview

Making the interview happen quickly is generally difficult to do unless you fall into one of several circumstances:

✪   the petitioner is *seriously ill*;

✪   the beneficiary will *age out* (that is, turn 21 years of age and lose eligibility under the petition and is not covered under CSPA);

✪ the case is a *diversity visa case* (which has a strict deadline of September 30th for completion or else the visa expires); or,

✪ some other *verifiable emergency* affecting eligibility.

Interview Documents

Your interview notice is your ticket inside the USCIS building, especially if your interview is in the morning. There may be a long line of people outside the building. If you have an interview, you do not have to wait in this line. You should go to the front of the line and show your appointment notice to the security guard who is letting people in the building. Once inside, you will go through security.

The key to a successful interview is to be prepared with the correct documents and copies, if necessary. The following original documents should be brought to the interview even though copies may have been submitted with the application:

✪ driver's license, state-issued I.D., or passport;

✪ work permit;

✪ I-94 (if legal entry was made);

✪ original birth certificates;

✪ original marriage certificate;

✪ approval notices;

✪ if necessary, documents showing maintenance of lawful status through date of adjustment filing;

✪ naturalization certificates or green card of petitioner;

✪ adjustment of status receipt notices, including proof of payment of section 245(i);

- ✪ Social Security card;

- ✪ original job letter on company letterhead;

- ✪ three year's tax returns with W-2 forms for petitioner or sponsor; and,

- ✪ original divorce judgement.

You will need a copy of every document required in support of your application. Any document in a foreign language will require a properly certified English translation.

The petitioner is normally required to be at the interview. If the petitioner resides outside the U.S., arrangements can be made to have the petitioner report to his or her embassy or consulate in lieu of appearing at the interview. If the petitioner is ill or elderly, arrangements can be made.

Be sure that the USCIS file reflects your current address so that your green card does not get lost in the mail. You will want to bring your passport to the interview so that a green card stamp can be placed in it once the adjustment application is approved. If you do not have a passport, it is well worthwhile to make the effort to get one before the interview, both for identification purposes and to get the stamp placed in it. You may take an approval notice to the USCIS and have a stamp placed in it after the interview, but this may require making an online appointment and waiting several weeks.

USCIS Officers

While the public often has a stereotypical perception of a USCIS officer, the reality is that they differ widely. To be fair, these officers have to struggle with a difficult work environment, including interviewing fifteen or so cases each day. For the most part, you can expect the interview to be conducted in a business-like fashion.

However, there are some officers who may seem overly authoritative. If an officer strikes you as unnecessarily rude, it is appropriate to say so politely. If the behavior does not stop, then it should be reported to his or her supervisor. You should ask the officer the name of his or her direct supervisor. Ask for the supervisor to intervene at the interview or else ask to speak to the supervisor back at the reception desk. An officer does not want to frequently require the intervention of a supervisor at the interviews. Such a tendency may appear on the officer's performance appraisals.

It is easy to feel that you are at the mercy of the officer. However, this is not completely true. An officer really does not have the unfettered discretion to deny a case simply because he or she feels like it. There are too many regulations, memos, and supervisors floating around for that to be the case. They are just as concerned with acting inappropriately as you are concerned about having your case denied or delayed. Realize that a person attracted to a government job is one who is willing to follow a chain of command and who is not inclined to rock the boat. Any adverse action has to be justified to the supervisor—particularly if you ask to speak to one to explain your side. The only real concern is that processing of the case will be delayed.

At this time, there is something of a changing of the guard taking place at the USCIS. As it is increasingly becoming a high profile agency, it is attracting better qualified officers. The old guard is being replaced by officers who are better educated and more professional in demeanor.

How honest are USCIS officers? The majority are incredibly honest, especially given the stakes. While rumors always fly around about certain officers, I believe that outright fraud is actually very low.

The fact is, any officer taking an improper action would place him- or herself and his or her job at substantial risk. It is simply not worth losing one's job for a relatively small gain. Further, USCIS officers are now part of the *Department of Homeland Security* (DHS).

The biggest flaw in the system may be when cases are assigned to an officer the day before the interview. Further, in at least some offices, cases are not randomly assigned, but rather distributed to whoever wants them.

The Interview

Most adjustment of status interviews take the following form. After entering the office of the USCIS officer, you will be asked to remain standing while you take an oath. You will be asked to provide your passport, driver's license, work authorization cards, and I-94. The officer will first review Form I-485 by asking you to confirm all of the information. You will be asked some of the questions on page 3 of the application, usually whether you were ever arrested, used public benefits, were ever deported, or were a member of a terrorist organization. The applicant and the petitioner will be asked to again sign their names on page 4, indicating their presence at the interview. Then, the officer will go on to examine the underlying basis for the adjustment application, such as whether the marriage is bona fide.

Hopefully, your case will be approved at the interview. If the case is approved, the officer should stamp your passport at the interview.

If the case is not approved at the interview, a *Request for Evidence* (RFE) will be issued, asking that certain documents be submitted within a time period. Sometimes the RFE is used to prevent making a decision at the interview.

Care must be taken at the interview to ensure prompt handling of the case by the officer. Some tips to help you protect yourself include:

✪ get the name of the officer;

✪ tell the officer how long it will take to submit documents;

✪ ask how long it will take after submission of the documents to obtain a decision. Even though they may not stick to it, it is helpful to be able to later remind the officer or supervisor of the time frame promised;

✪ if the documents cannot be obtained, ask what will happen to the case;

✪ ask the officer how and when to follow up if you do not hear after thirty or sixty days (get his or her phone number and extension);

✪ if you think you have supplied enough information and the officer is not specific about why the case is not being approved, ask to see the supervisor; and,

✪ take detailed notes after the interview to the questions and answers.

Special Interview Questions   A special wrinkle is presented at an interview for a marriage-based case. If the USCIS officer is unsure whether the marriage is bona fide, then he or she may ask personal questions of the couple. The officer may even separate the couple, ask the same questions separately, and then compare answers. The following is a list of typical questions.

- ✪ Where do your in-laws live, and if deceased, since when?

- ✪ When did you last speak with them?

- ✪ What are the names of your spouse's brothers and sisters?

- ✪ What is the date of your spouse's birth and the names of his or her parents?

- ✪ Why did you come to the U.S. in the first place?

- ✪ Who invited you?

- ✪ Where did you meet your spouse?

- ✪ Who proposed and after dating for how long?

- ✪ What did you do last Valentine's Day?

- ✪ What type of marriage ceremony did you have?

- ✪ Was there a reception?

- ✪ When did you meet?

- ✪ How long did you date before becoming engaged?

- ✪ What time did you and your spouse wake up this morning?

- ✪ Who cooks which meals?

- ✪ What was eaten for breakfast today or dinner last night?

- ✪ What was the last gift you received from your spouse?

- ✪ How did you get to the interview?

✪ Did you sleep together before marriage? If so, how often?

✪ What school do your stepchildren attend?

✪ Where does your spouse work?

✪ How many bedrooms or rooms are in your apartment?

✪ What type of stove is in the kitchen (gas or electric)?

✪ Describe the headboard on your bed, curtains in the room, the dresser, other furniture, and color of the carpet?

✪ How much are rent, expenses, and salaries, and who pays the bills?

✪ Why did you get married?

NOTE: *While these are typical questions, each officer has his or her own way of questioning.*

Aftermath

At this time, the USCIS is not looking for cases to deny. It takes much longer to deny a case than to grant it. If you give them what they are looking for, chances are you will be fine.

Request for Evidence

These days, a decision should be made on the spot unless documents are missing. If your case is not approved at the interview, then you were probably issued a Request for Evidence (RFE). The RFE lists the documents required to complete the case. The RFE is your road map to getting the case approved. The RFE sets a time limit, either thirty or eighty-four days, which is difficult to extend. If an extension is needed, it may be better to turn in whatever documents you have and state what additional documents will be shortly forthcoming. Depending on the benefit, USCIS checks administrative systems to review applicant's prior immigration history, entry and exits into the U.S., student records, and immigration court records. The basic checks are the fingerprint, name, IBIS, and IDENT. Consult the glossary for a complete definition of these different checks. In a small percentage of cases, it is the name check that may be a source of delay since it is not fully automated. The response to an RFE must be sent by certified mail, return receipt requested, in order to prove mailing, should that become necessary.

A case that is pending at a USCIS office can drag on for some time. If you do not hear from the USCIS after a reasonable period of three to six months, chances are you never will. It is up to you to move the case along. Most offices have a mail-in inquiry system to start the process. This should be done and copies kept along with proof of mailing. It is also possible to make an Infopass appointment to speak in person with an immigration information officer (you may have to go online after midnight to secure an appointment slot). Be persistent. Nowhere is it more true than at a local USCIS office that the squeaky wheel gets the oil.

Also, keep track of the date of expiration of your fingerprints, which expire after fifteen months. If making an inquiry to request status of your case, also notify USCIS that a fingerprint appointment letter is required.

If the case is approved, the officer will ask that your work permit and I-94 card be turned in. According to national policy, USCIS no longer issues either an approval notice or places a green card stamp into a passport. However, if you have definite plans to travel, you could make a special request for a green card stamp for a short duration, such as sixty days.

Once the permanent resident card is received, it may be desirable to contact the Social Security Administration to obtain an unrestricted card. While the Social Security number will remain the same, there may be advantages, such as when seeking new employment.

Denial

If the denial is in error, then a *motion to reopen* should be filed pointing out the mistake along with whatever documentary evidence might be required. The motion to reopen should be followed up with a phone call to the officer or an examinations supervisor. It is good practice to first file a motion to reopen for purposes of the record.

However, the vast majority of the time, a denial results in your file being processed for initiation of deportation proceedings. A *Notice to Appear* (NTA) will likely be issued and served on the applicant. This means that the person has to appear in immigration court at a time to be set in the future. However, this is usually a slow process. In most cities, the USCIS will have a huge file room full of cases to be processed for immigration proceedings.

A further point of delay is the immigration court itself. The immigration court has a somewhat limited capacity to hear cases. There is a backlog. Once the NTA is served on the applicant and filed with the court, there is a wait for a court date. However, once the case is before an immigration judge, it will proceed quickly.

NOTE: *If your application is denied, you definitely need to speak with an attorney or person qualified in immigration law.*

Green Card Missing

If your case was approved at the interview, your green card should come in the mail within several weeks.

The biggest cause of a nonreceipt of the green card is that you change your address. Most people will file a change of address notice with the post office that is good for six months. However, the envelope with the green card contains an instruction to not forward to the new address. Sometimes, the envelope is forwarded anyway, but sometimes it is not. If you change your address, be sure to file form AR-11 immediately and also notify the service center in your jurisdiction.

If the envelope is not forwarded or otherwise cannot be delivered, it is sent back to the service center of the person's jurisdiction. It is kept there for approximately six months and then destroyed. If the card is destroyed, it will require that you go back for ADIT processing. *ADIT processing* refers to the process where the alien places his or her fingerprint and signature on a card that will eventually be made into his or her green card.

18 SERVICE CENTERS

The information in this chapter relates only to cases that are filed and pending at one of the service centers.

Once a *receipt notice* has been issued, there is typically a waiting period before the case is forwarded to an officer for *adjudication*. The length of the waiting period depends on the type of application and the particular service center. The receipt notice states a time period during which the application will be adjudicated. While this estimate is fairly accurate, the actual waiting time may vary quite widely. For example, those applying for adjustment based upon being granted asylum should expect a three- to six-year waiting period, rather than the three to six months typically stated on the receipt notice.

If the time period on the receipt notice lapses and there has been no response from USCIS, you need to contact the service center. The first step is to either call the automated phone system at 800-375-5283 or go online at **https://egov.immigration.gov/graphics/cris/jsps/index.jsp** and check the status of the case. When calling the 800 number, press "1" twice to get to the automated system. You will be asked to punch in your case number, which is found at the top left corner of the receipt notice. Include the three-letter service center designation as a number. (For example, "LIN" for the Lincoln service center is "546" on the keypad.) The same case number is also entered into the online system, which provides the same information as the phone system.

The information obtained should prove useful. For example, the recording might say that an *approval notice* or a *Request for Evidence* (RFE) has been sent. An RFE most often means that documents or certain information is missing. An RFE always allows a period of eighty-four days in which to respond. If any aspect of an RFE is confusing, you may wish to consult with an attorney.

> **Warning:** This is a very strict deadline. Any response should be returned to the USCIS by overnight mail so that proof of mailing is available should the USCIS claim it was never received. You have generally one chance to comply, so be sure you have enclosed all of the information. If it is not available, provide a detailed explanation as to why.

Usually the message will say that the case is pending. In this instance, you may want to check the processing chart for the particular service center to see if your case has been passed over. Go to the website found on page 173 and click on the "service centers" tab. Find the row containing your application, then check the date on the far right side of the chart. This is the date of cases currently being worked on.

If you filed your case before this date and there has been no response, then your case has likely been passed over. Write a short letter to the correspondence address for that service center, simply bringing this fact to their attention. Enclose a copy of the receipt notice. Keep a copy of the correspondence and proof of mailing. If after about two months there still is no response, the next step is to call 800-375-5283 to speak with an information officer. This officer will *not* be making a decision on the application—he or she does not have access to the file and may only have the same information that is in the automated system. However, the information officer may be able to unsnag a bureaucratic problem.

If the case is granted, an approval notice will be received. If *adjustment of status* was applied for, the individual will be required to appear at the local USCIS office in order to process for a green card. This is called *ADIT processing*. At that time, a *green card stamp* will be placed into a passport that has at least six months' validity remaining. This stamp serves as a green card for purposes of work and travel until the actual card arrives in the mail some three to six months later.

Normally, a case will be not be denied without allowing the alien an opportunity to respond to the legal or factual problem. Even if a case is denied, it is often possible to simply reapply if the reason for the denial can be overcome. However, the applicant will need to be *in status* at the time of the refiling unless the petition is grandfathered under Section 245(i). If not, an appeal may be filed. In the event of a denial, consult with an immigration attorney to determine the best course of action.

19 IMMIGRATION COURT

If your case is denied at the USCIS, then you may find yourself placed into *removal proceedings* before the immigration court. The most important feature of the immigration court is that it is not part of the *Department of Homeland Security* (DHS), but is a separate agency within the *Department of Justice*. The immigration judge is not bound by a decision made by the USCIS and will make a decision based upon the court record. A proceeding before the immigration court is a civil rather than criminal proceeding, although the consequences of deportation may be much more severe than in a typical civil case.

Before the law changed in 1996, proceedings before the immigration court used to be referred to as *deportation* rather than *removal proceedings*. The name was changed to reflect the substantive changes in the law and to leave behind any case law associated with the term *deportation*.

The fact that your application may have been denied by the USCIS or the asylum office is of no concern to the immigration judge. In fact, you have gained credibility before the court because you affirmatively filed an application for relief. In other words, you applied for asylum on your own, as opposed to asking for it before the immigration court for the first time in a defensive posture to avoid or delay deportation.

Other than having your application denied, there are several other ways to land in immigration court. One common way is to be apprehended by the DHS as an *illegal alien,* or as one who has been in contact with a law enforcement officer or criminal court. Even a green card holder who has committed crimes may be placed in proceedings. It is also not uncommon for a legal permanent resident who has acquired a criminal record to find him- or herself excluded from the U.S. upon reentry if his or her record is checked by the border officer.

NOTE: *The court system is so backlogged that it may be a year before a court date can be scheduled, although this varies widely by locality.*

In reality, the person who actually has a legitimate avenue for relief can fare very well in immigration court. For example, an asylum interview before the asylum office is a one-sided interview at the direction of the officer. However, before the immigration court, the same asylum applicant can not only put on a more effective case, but can also have the case decided by a more neutral and sympathetic person. Likewise, a marriage case denied by the USCIS will be treated more fairly and impartially by the immigration judge.

Immigration Judges

Naturally, as human beings, immigration judges (IJs) exhibit a wide range of personality and inclinations to grant a case. An asylum application granted by one IJ might be laughed out of court by another IJ.

The IJs are unlike most judges you will see on TV. First of all, he or she is really an administrative law judge. Immigration judges work for the Department of Justice, which is headed by the *Attorney General,* the country's top prosecutor. Thus, there is a central tension between the IJ's ultimate boss, the Attorney General, and the rights of an alien. (In contrast, a *federal judge* works for the *judiciary,* which is a separate branch of the U.S. government.)

Previously, IJs were called *special inquiry officers.* Thus, they have wide power to interrupt and conduct their own questioning. A normal judge who is part of the judiciary only runs the trial, decides questions of law, and if there is no jury, questions of fact.

Changing Judges

It pays to know your judge. It is not normally possible to request a different judge in the same city. However, if your case is assigned to a tough judge, it may be worth your while to simply move to a different city and file a motion for change of venue with the original judge. If you have indeed moved, the motion will be granted and you will be scheduled for a master calendar hearing before the new judge. IJs are likely to grant such a motion because it means the case is marked off their docket and they have saved the several hours it might have taken for a hearing.

Attorneys

Generally speaking, IJs are fair and decent people committed to upholding the law. However, the DHS is represented in court by a trial attorney who is essentially a prosecutor. The prosecutors are not part of USCIS, but fall within the *United States Immigration and Customs Enforcement* (ICE), which is also a new bureau within the Department of Homeland Security.

These trial attornies prefer to be referred to as representing DHS rather than ICE. The trial attorneys unfortunately have little discretion to make their own decisions regarding a case and therefore just oppose all but the most sympathetic cases. While they are often personally likeable people, they can be counted on to oppose the majority of cases.

Common Mistakes

The first mistake people often make regarding immigration court is that the IJ does not have absolute authority to do what is right or fair. Even if an alien is married to a U.S. citizen or has U.S. citizen children, or has lived in the U.S. for twenty years and always pays his or her taxes, these facts may not be relevant. Sometimes a certain law decisively impacts the case, and that person's personal circumstances—no matter how compelling—cannot change the outcome.

Another mistake is to think that because the IJ outwardly appears to be a likeable person, he or she will grant the case. There may be a difference between the outward demeanor of a judge and his or her leniency in rendering a decision.

Handling a Court Case

You should not be in immigration court without an immigration attorney. It is not enough that your friend had the same case and it was granted. A small fact that is different may make your case come out differently.

If you are going to proceed with your own case, you must ask at the filing window for a copy of the local rules of the court. It says how and when to file documents. You will be expected to follow these rules. You should consult an attorney so that you understand the law.

One feature of the immigration court that does make it possible to conduct your own hearing is that the *rules of evidence* are relaxed from the normal rules followed in a normal courtroom. *Hearsay* statements are allowed into evidence, or documents do not necessarily need *foundation*. Therefore, a lot of objections that the prosecutor might normally make when a lay person conducts his or her own hearing would not be appropriate before an IJ.

The principal trap is that it may seem easy to argue your case. However, the majority of what a respondent typically will say in court will be absolutely irrelevant to any form of relief, no matter how important or just it might sound.

Even attorneys who are unfamiliar with immigration law, but perhaps familiar with civil court procedure, are at a complete loss to understand the procedure, let alone figure out any avenue for relief. They, too, have a tendency to focus on the irrelevant portions of the respondent's situation.

Types of Hearings
There are two types of hearings in immigration court—the *master calendar hearing* and the *individual hearing*. It is easy to check on your hearing date and other case status information. Simply call 800-898-7180 and enter your *A number*. There are a series of five options, of which the first gives you the date of your next hearing.

Notice to Appear
An immigration case is initiated by a document called a *Notice to Appear* (NTA). If you consult with an attorney, you must be able to show this document to him or her. If you do not have it, then go to the immigration court that has your case and ask the court clerk to give you a copy. The important part of this form is that it states the grounds upon which you are removable from the U.S. and the facts that establish it.

You need to be prepared to proceed, or at least have a good excuse. You may show up to court the first time and ask for time to find an attorney. Usually in this instance, the IJ will reset your master hearing in thirty or sixty days.

The IJ will not be willing to delay the case to allow a visa petition to be approved or a labor certification or some other favorable action. Continuances are hard to come by in immigration court. The IJ wants the case off his or her crowded docket.

Master Calendar Hearing

The following are a list of items that may come up at a master calendar hearing. They are written in formal English, since this is how they will be referred to during the actual court proceeding. A respondent, through his or her attorney if he or she has one, will be asked to do at least some of the following:

- ✪ concede that he or she is the respondent named in the Notice to Appear;

- ✪ acknowledge that he or she is present in court with an attorney or acknowledge receipt of the list of free legal services programs required under the Code of Federal Regulations, Title 8, Section 242.2(d);

- ✪ acknowledge proper service of the Notice to Appear;

- ✪ agree to the admission into the record of proceedings of the Notice to Appear as Exhibit 1;

- ✪ acknowledge that he or she has been advised by an attorney as to the nature and purpose of these deportation proceedings and of the respondent's rights, and that the respondent understands this advice;

- ✪ waive a formal reading and explanation of the charges contained in the Notice to Appear;

- ✪ admit all or some of the factual allegations or deny all or some factual allegations contained in the Notice to Appear;

- ✪ concede that he or she is removable as charged in the Notice to Appear and on any *Form I-261*;

- ✪ designate a country as the country for removal purposes, if necessary;

- ✪ specify the relief from removal for which he or she is eligible from the following:

  • termination or administrative closure of proceedings;

  • adjustment of status;

- asylum or withholding of deportation;

- cancellation of removal;

- waiver of grounds of removability or excludability pursuant to section(s) of the Immigration and Nationality Act;

- voluntary departure; or,

- other;

✪ acknowledge that he or she understands that, unless otherwise ordered by the court, the respondent has thirty days from the date hereof to file application(s) for all such relief, accompanied by all required supporting documents, in accordance with all applicable regulations;

✪ understand and agree that if the respondent fails to timely file any written application(s) for relief indicated above, the court will enter a decision on the record before it without further notice or hearing, and that no voluntary departure will be granted unless otherwise stipulated by the Service on the record or in writing;

✪ estimate the time required for the hearing;

✪ state that an interpreter is not required because the respondent speaks and understands English, or request the court to order an interpreter proficient in the language for the individual calendar hearing; and,

✪ acknowledge that his or her attorney or the IJ has advised him or her of the consequences under Section 242B of the Act of failure to attend this removal proceeding, failure to depart voluntarily if the respondent has agreed or been allowed to do so, and failure to appear for removal at the time and place ordered.

The most important part of the master hearing is to determine the forms of relief for which the respondent is eligible. The IJ actually has a responsibility to see what these might be. A case will be reopened by the Board of Immigration Appeals if the IJ does not advise you as to your possible relief.

If the IJ discovers that you have an avenue for relief, then just listen to what he or she says. You must have paper with you and take very careful notes. Ask questions if you are unclear as to any instruction. Pay particular attention to which forms are required and when they should be filed. If a deadline is missed, the relief may be permanently cut off.

If you later discover that you forgot something the IJ said, you can go back to the court and listen to the tape recording of the hearing to listen again to what he or she said. Even if you still do not understand what he or she meant, the IJ would be impressed that you made that much effort to try to comply with the directions.

Individual Hearing

The individual hearing is the most critical aspect of one's immigration case, no matter how many twists and turns it has taken. Take care when preparing for the hearing. Problems and issues that might be raised by the DHS should be anticipated as much as possible.

Applications for relief and supporting documents are due to the immigration court by the *call-up date*. This is the deadline set by the immigration judge in the particular case, or if one is not specifically set, then it is either ten or fourteen days prior to the hearing, depending on the court's local operating rules. It is critical that all evidence and names of proposed witnesses be submitted to the court by this date, or else there is a risk they will not be allowed into evidence at the hearing. Any motions, such as a motion for a continuance, must also be filed prior to the call-up date.

Preparation is important. If the supporting documentation is complete and convincing and the alien is prepared to testify in detail about his or her case, then the odds of that case being approved are drastically increased. Too often it happens that a loose end to a case is not accounted for and the entire case unravels.

Direct and Cross-Examination

On the hearing date, the IJ will hear the testimony of the alien and any witnesses and consider the documents submitted. The alien will first be questioned by his or her attorney in what is called a *direct examination*. The IJ will often interrupt with his or her own questions.

At the end of the direct exam, the USCIS attorney will conduct a cross-examination. This *cross-examination* is based on the testimony of the alien and documents contained in the record. At the end of the cross-examination, the alien may conduct a *redirect* based on the cross-examination. In the same fashion, the testimony of any other witnesses will be heard.

Ending the Hearing

At the end of the hearing, the alien or his or her attorney will be allowed to make closing remarks. These remarks may be critical to summarizing the testimony and addressing any damage done by the USCIS attorney during cross-examination.

When the case is finished, the judge will issue a decision, called an *Order*. If the case is denied, the judge reads an oral decision into the record. It is important to take notes as to the basis for the denial. If the alien chooses to *appeal* the decision, it will be necessary to state the reasons for appeal on the *Notice of Appeal*.

Appeal

If an appeal is to be taken, the *Notice of Appeal* form must be received at the Board of Immigration Appeals within thirty days. This is a very strict deadline. It should be sent by overnight mail to ensure proper receipt. There is also a fee of $110 to be enclosed.

Adjustment of Status Granted

If adjustment of status is granted, in order to receive a green card, the alien must complete ADIT processing through the local USCIS office. ADIT processing is the completion of the card that will be made into a green card by the service center. Until this happens, the person has not become a permanent resident (despite language to the contrary on the order).

Family-Based Cases

There are a few special considerations that may be crucial to a family-based case. While it is possible to obtain adjustment of status through the immigration judge, you will require an approved and current I-130 petition. Unfortunately, the I-130 needs to be approved by the USCIS before the IJ can proceed with adjustment. Also, the IJ will be most impatient to finish the case and will not want to wait very long for the USCIS to complete its processing.

NOTE: *If you are married after the date the NTA is served, then you are not guaranteed a continuance. Until recently, there were long delays in processing I-130 petitions.*

A major advantage to being in immigration court is that you have the approved I-130 petition, but if you and your spouse are separated, it is still possible to go into court and have the adjustment approved. However, there cannot be a divorce. Still, since a divorce may take a substantial amount of time to complete, this scenario may work out.

Appeals and Beyond

There is often a worry on behalf of the alien that if the case is lost in the immigration court, the DHS will take the person into custody. This is a rare occurrence. You are probably more likely to be taken into custody at an adjustment interview or a citizenship interview if you have a serious criminal record.

If your case is denied by the IJ, then you have the right to appeal your case to the Board of Immigration Appeals (BIA) located in Falls Church, Virginia, just outside of Washington, D.C. (The BIA is a separate agency within the Department of Justice.)

The Notice of Appeal (Form EOIR-26) is due at the BIA within thirty days of the denial of your case. It does not matter when the documents are actually mailed. You can even mail the documents by overnight mail the day before the due date. But if the mail service makes a mistake and does not deliver through their own negligence, your appeal is terminated. Period. This is a very strict deadline, to which there are no exceptions.

Except in an unusual case, you or your attorney will not be making any appearance in front of this court. The court will make its decision based upon the briefs prepared by your attorney and the USCIS attorney and on the documents that are in the record of proceeding. The wait time is approximately six to twelve months for the transcripts to arrive in the mail, along with a briefing schedule.

An advantage of the appeals process is that if you are waiting for a preference visa, approval of your labor certificate, or approval of your I-130, it can give you a couple of years to allow all of the procedures to occur.

Removal Orders

If you are ordered removed by the immigration court, you typically cannot return to the U.S. for ten years. In the case of a removal on criminal grounds, you will be ordered to be removed for twenty years. Realistically, the same criminal ground may prevent you from ever returning to the U.S. unless you get a waiver of inadmissibility approved. That is very difficult.

A person who returns to the U.S. after removal may be criminally prosecuted and face a substantial sentence in a federal prison.

> *Warning:* Under a new operating procedure, the USCIS will be notifying the FBI of any person ordered deported for entry into the National Crime Information Center (NCIC) database. This will allow local and state police to determine if an individual is subject to a deportation order. Someone pulled over for a traffic violation like speeding can now be easily checked for an immigration violation. Such a person will likely be taken into custody and handed over to the USCIS. In such instances, a bond from immigration custody may be difficult to obtain.

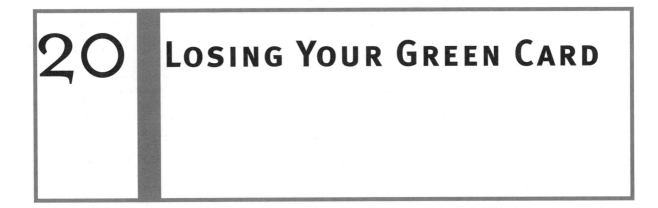

20 | LOSING YOUR GREEN CARD

This chapter discusses the different ways the green card or permanent residence status can be lost and the procedures to replace it.

Misplaced

The procedures for obtaining a new green card frequently change. It is worthwhile to check the most recent processing guidelines on the USCIS website.

The following documents should be filed to obtain a new green card:

- *Form I-90*;

- filing fee of $130;

- two passport-style photos;

- state-issued identification or foreign passport;

- copy of green card (if available);

✪   proof of name change (such as marriage certificate or divorce decree); and,

✪   fingerprint fee of $50 if now over 14 years of age (i.e., turned 14 years of age after obtaining permanent residence).

However, if the individual is eligible for naturalization, then it may be cheaper and easier to save the filing fee and hassle and simply file the *N-400* application without bothering to replace the green card. This is true if the permanent resident will not be travelling outside the U.S. or will not be needing the green card to show to his or her present or future employer. At the naturalization interview, the applicant will simply be asked to complete an affidavit saying that the green card is lost.

If you are filing because you never received a card, then file the above package with your local service center. Otherwise, mail to the following address:

U.S. Citizenship and Immigration Services
P.O. Box 54870
Los Angeles, CA 90054

Expect to receive a biometric appointment within the next ninety days, and if necessary, an appointment to appear at your local office to complete processing.

Outside U.S. for more than Six Months

A permanent resident of the U.S. is expected to permanently reside in the U.S. Generally speaking, a permanent resident reentering the U.S. after an absence of less than six months should not have any problem, except in two circumstances. The first is if the lawful permanent resident (LPR) has been convicted of a crime that makes him or her inadmissible, and second, if the fact that he or she does not actually reside in the U.S. is readily apparent.

If a permanent resident attempts to enter the U.S. after an absence of more than six months but less than one year, then he or she is really considered to be an applicant for admission. In order to be treated as a returning resident, the alien may be asked to demonstrate that he or she has not abandoned his or her permanent residence status. It is important to realize that it is possible to abandon one's status without actually knowing it. Whether an alien has abandoned permanent residence depends on the alien's continuous intent to return to the U.S. It is not sufficient that an alien merely desire to retain the benefits of permanent residence. Here is how a border officer may determine intent after an extended absence:

✪ the purpose of departure (a definite temporary reason such as family visit, education, training, liquidation of assets, etc., is best);

✪ the expectation for the visit to end shortly (a fixed termination date for the visit is best);

✪ travel to the U.S. by use of a one-way ticket or the second leg of a round-trip ticket (as opposed to the first leg of a round-trip ticket);

✪ continued filing of U.S. tax returns;

✪ whether the alien obtained a reentry permit (this does not guarantee reentry within two-year validity period but is merely one factor signalling intent) or filed *Form N-540* (to preserve naturalization eligibility);

✪ the existence of a permanent home or job based in the U.S. (as opposed to temporary, or even worse, permanent home or job abroad); and,

✪ other U.S. ties, such as family, property, memberships, bank accounts, credit cards, and driver's license.

Further, such a permanent resident may be questioned on returning about whether he or she is or will become a public charge, for which the use of welfare or long-term care may be considered.

In 2005, the *Department of Homeland Security* implemented a more sophisticated system for tracking movements of LPRs and nonimmigrants. Previously, inspectors were forced to rely on an honor system, that is the testimony of the individual. With the new system, the border official has near instantaneous access to all immigration departure records.

If it is anticipated that an absence from the U.S. will be for more than one year, then a problem may develop. The permanent resident should apply for a reentry permit, which does not guarantee reentry, but is another piece of evidence that he or she had no intention of abandoning his or her permanent residence.

Criminal Record

Lawful permanent residents need to be careful to stay away from the criminal justice system. Many types of crimes that seem to be minor charges may cause an alien to possibly lose his or her green card.

Any criminal conviction can have immigration consequences, no matter whether it is a misdemeanor, whether you have been in the U.S. for many years, or whether your spouse, children, and parents are all U.S. citizens. There are two basic categories of crimes that have an immigration consequence. One classification is *crimes involving moral turpitude* (CIMT), which include minor retail thefts. For a CIMT, an LPR can normally have a hearing before an immigration judge to show why he or she should not be deported.

The more serious type of crimes are aggravated felonies. These are listed in Section 101(a)(43) of the *Immigration and Nationality Act* (INA). When Congress first came up with the idea of the aggravated felony classification in 1988, the list consisted of a few serious crimes, such as kidnapping and murder. However, Congress has been adding to the list every year so that now most felonies are aggravated felonies. When Congress adds crimes to the list, the effect is *retroactive*. This means that even if at the time the person pled guilty the crime was not an aggravated felony, the fact that it was later added to the list meant the person now had an aggravated felony for immigration purposes.

Further, in 1996, Congress removed section 212(c) relief for a person who had an aggravated felony on his or her record. The fact that you committed the crime when it was not a deportable offense may not make a difference. LPRs with a retroactive aggravated felony now have no way to avoid deportation and are effectively barred from returning to the U.S. at any time. (Imagine having to tell a person, who now might have a family, of these harsh consequences for a crime that was committed in his or her youth.)

The following crimes make a person deportable:

- conviction of one crime involving moral turpitude (CIMT) committed within five years of entry, for which a sentence of one year may be imposed;

- conviction of two or more CIMTs, regardless of possible sentence;

- conviction of an aggravated felony (for immigration purposes);

- conviction of controlled substance violation;

- conviction of domestic violence, including misdemeanor or domestic battery;

- violation of a protection order;

- conviction of a firearms offense;

- false claim to U.S. citizenship; or,

- in very rare circumstances, use of cash welfare or long-term care within the first five years in the U.S. for an illness or disability that existed before adjustment (public charge determination).

Criminal Attorneys

Unfortunately, not every criminal attorney is aware of the immigration consequences of criminal convictions. Too many times a green card holder never knew he or she would be deportable by pleading guilty to a certain crime. Anyone who has a green card and is arrested on a criminal charge needs to consult with an immigration lawyer before proceeding with the criminal case.

Pleas

Once a *plea* is made, there is almost no going back. In many states, the only possibility of reopening your case is if your lawyer gave you wrong advice. If he or she said, "Do not worry about being deported because you are married to a U.S. citizen," then you could reopen your case. However, if the immigration consequences were never discussed, as is usually the case, you are probably stuck with a conviction and its consequences. This differs by state, so it is worth consulting with a criminal lawyer.

The best time to consult with an immigration attorney is before a guilty plea is entered so that an immigration consequence can be avoided, or at least minimized. There is an extremely fine line between a conviction that causes no problems whatsoever and one that results in deportation with no opportunity for relief.

There are many common misconceptions to be aware of. The first is that misdemeanors have only minor immigration consequences. There is no such thing as a minor immigration consequence—either the conviction makes a person deportable or it does not. Nor are misdemeanors necessarily harmless. For example, a misdemeanor, particularly almost any drug conviction, may constitute an aggravated felony for immigration purposes, with very severe consequences.

Another misconception is that someone who obtains *court supervision* as a sentence does not acquire a criminal conviction. While the state statute may specifically state that supervision is not a criminal conviction, it is a criminal conviction for immigration purposes.

Criminal attorneys and defendants often think that if the offense they are pleading guilty to is expungable, then it will have no affect on the defendant's green card or eligibility to obtain an immigration benefit. Nothing could be further from the truth. An expunged record may be removed from state records, but it is not expunged from the FBI computer off which the USCIS conducts fingerprint checks. Whether a record is expunged or not is simply immaterial with regards to eligibility for an immigration benefit.

Pardons
The only option may be to seek a *pardon* before the state governor. Most states have a prisoner review board that handles pardon applications. The review board will provide information on the pardon process. While the odds of a pardon are remote, you do have a chance. If your crime is victimless, such as possession of a small amount of drugs, then there is at least some probability of success.

Your Options
You have many more options prior to your plea. For example, it is much better to plead guilty to *simple battery*, which has no immigration effect, rather than *domestic battery*, which makes you deportable. Even if it means serving a short time in jail or longer probation, you are well advised to plead guilty rather than suffer immigration consequences in the future.

Further, there are strict provisions for mandatory custody of criminal aliens, even those with green cards. This means that if you are picked up by the DHS, you may not be eligible for a bond.

If you have picked up a conviction, you should consult with an immigration attorney before departing the country. Also, it may greatly facilitate reentry if you bring with you original certified dispositions to clarify your record.

Preventing Deportation

If an alien is in proceedings on account of a criminal record, he or she must consult with an immigration attorney to determine whether a *waiver* under INA 240(A) is available, and the likelihood of the waiver being granted.

If the crime does not involve an aggravated felony, then a waiver may be possible. While an aggravated felony conviction automatically revokes permanent residence status, those with other removable offenses, such as CIMTs, may apply for cancellation of removal.

The following is filed in immigration court at the direction of the immigration judge to initiate the *cancellation of removal* case:

- ✪ **FORM EOIR-42B, APPLICATION FOR CANCELLATION OF REMOVAL FOR CERTAIN PERMANENT RESIDENTS** filed with immigration court filing fee of $100;

- ✪ **FORM G325A** (original to DHS attorney, copy to court); and,

- ✪ certificate of service.

To qualify for cancellation, the following must be shown at the hearing:

- ✪ you have been an LPR for five years;

- ✪ after having been admitted in any status, you have resided in the U.S. continuously for seven years except during *period of residence stops* such as:

  - after service of a Notice to Appear in immigration court or

  - when you become inadmissible under section 212(a)(2) or removable under sections 237(a)(2) or (4);

- ✪ you have not been convicted of an aggravated felony;

- ✪ you were never before granted *cancellation, suspension,* or *Sec. 212(c) relief;*

- ✪ you can demonstrate positive factors:

- evidence of hardship to respondent and family if removed;

- existence of U.S. citizen spouse and children;

- other family ties within the U.S.;

- residency of long duration in the U.S.;

- history of employment;

- existence of property or business ties; or,

- existence of value and service to the community;

✪ you have proof of genuine rehabilitation:

- lack of commission of other crimes;

- attendance at rehab programs;

- statements of remorse;

- evidence attesting to good character; or,

- service in the armed forces;

✪ you can account for negative factors:

- nature and underlying circumstances of crime;

- other immigration violations;

- other criminal record; or,

- other evidence of bad character; and,

✪ if you have a drug offense or serious criminal conviction or record, you have to show *outstanding equities*.

The previous list is documentation that may be used to prove a cancellation of removal case. The principal form to be completed is the **EOIR-42A**. It is a detailed seven-page form requesting seemingly every possible personal history question. Before this application is filed with the court, it must be paid for at the local USCIS office. The immigration court does not accept any filing fees. In order to pay for an application at the USCIS cashier and receive it back, you will need to complete a routing slip and place it on top of the application. After the application is filed, supporting documents will be due to the court fourteen days prior to the hearing date. Go through the list of documents and compile as many as possible for filing.

NOTE: *The IJ can be expected to be fairly sympathetic to this type of case, particularly for a long-time permanent resident. Nonetheless, as much evidence as possible should be accumulated.*

21 NATURALIZATION

Naturalization is the process whereby a green card holder becomes a U.S. citizen through filing a *N-400* application.

It is a good idea to file for citizenship as soon as you are eligible. There are a few criteria for eligibility.

- ✪ *Residency and age.* You must be a lawful permanent resident and at least 18 years of age.

- ✪ *Time as permanent resident.* A person who has been a permanent resident for a minimum of five years (really four years and nine months) may apply for citizenship. Those who obtained their green card through marriage to a U.S. citizen can apply three years (or two years and nine months) if they are still married and residing with the U.S. citizen spouse. There are several other exceptions to the five-year rule.

- ✪ *Continuous residence in the U.S.* The time as permanent resident described above may be broken by an absence from the U.S. of six months or longer. If the absence is more than six months but less than one year, it may be possible to argue that the continuous residence was not broken.

✪ *Physical presence in the U.S.* You must spend thirty months of the sixty months prior to the filing of the naturalization application actually living in the U.S. This is only eighteen months when the green card was obtained through marriage to a U.S. citizen.

✪ *Good moral character.* You must have been a person of good moral character during the period of five years prior to filing and through the time the application is pending. *Good moral character* has been interpreted to mean character that measures up to the standards of average citizens of the community in which the applicant resides.

Not every criminal conviction breaks the good moral character requirement. A lawyer should be consulted if this is an issue. On the other hand, any person with an aggravated felony under Section 101(a)(43) must not apply for citizenship, as he or she is deportable with no possible relief in immigration court.

Grounds such as failure to pay child support, failure to file income tax returns, or false testimony on the application or at the interview may be found to constitute lack of good moral character. Failure to register with the Selective Service may be a ground, but only if the applicant *knowingly* failed to register—if a person did not know to register, then it is not a ground.

✪ *English and civic knowledge.* The applicant must be able to speak, read, and write English, as well as pass a test of U.S. history and government. The applicant must answer eight out of twelve multiple choice questions correctly out of a list of questions. Those who have been a permanent resident for more than fifteen years and are over fifty-five years of age or have been a permanent resident for more than twenty years and are over fifty may take the civics test and conduct the interview with the assistance of a translator.

NOTE: *A medical waiver on form N-648 may be submitted to waive this requirement. This form must be completed in detail by your physician.*

✪ *State residence.* You must have resided for at least three months in the state in which the petition was filed.

✪ *Dual citizenship issues.* For most countries, acquiring U.S. citizenship does not renounce the previous citizenship. The naturalized U.S. citizen simply becomes a dual citizen. However, there are numerous countries where this is not the case—for example, in Germany, Japan, and Australia. If there is any doubt, simply contact your country's embassy.

Application

The naturalization application is filed with the service center having *jurisdiction* over the person's residence. An application consists of the following:

✪ *Form N-400* application for naturalization;

✪ filing fee of $260;

✪ fingerprint fee of $50;

✪ copy of green card;

✪ two passport-style photos; and,

✪ if the applicant has been arrested or even just fingerprinted, an original certified *record of disposition* from the court's criminal clerk's office.

The above listing consists of the few items to be filed along with the N-400 application. Simply attach one check or money order in the amount of $310 ($260+$50), a copy of the green card, and two passport-style photos. If you have a criminal record, then original court dispositions obtained from the criminal clerk's office must be obtained. If the court is out of town, it is possible to simply call the court and mail in payment.

This application packet is mailed to the appropriate service center. (See Appendix B for the correct address.) The service center will process the application and then forward it to the appropriate local office for interview. To change your address prior to interview scheduling, call the National Customer Service line at 800-375-5283.

The Interview

The following documents should be brought to the interview, if applicable:

- ✪ green card;

- ✪ driver's license;

- ✪ passport;

- ✪ reentry permit or refugee travel document;

- ✪ birth certificate;

- ✪ original court dispositions;

- ✪ original police records;

- ✪ proof of spouse's citizenship;

- ✪ proof of child support payments;

- ✪ tax forms or tax summary IRS *Form 1722*;

- ✪ proof of name change; and,

- ✪ proof of residence with spouse if received green card through spouse and are applying after three years.

If the application is approved by the USCIS officer, a *swear-in date* will be received in the mail. Typically, the swear-in ceremony is held four to six weeks after the interview. At that time, the naturalization is official and a naturalization certificate will be issued.

At the ceremony, be sure to carefully review your naturalization certificate for any errors. It is much easier to have any error corrected at that time than to go through the formal process.

Finally, the individual is now fully a U.S. citizen and may now apply for a family member.

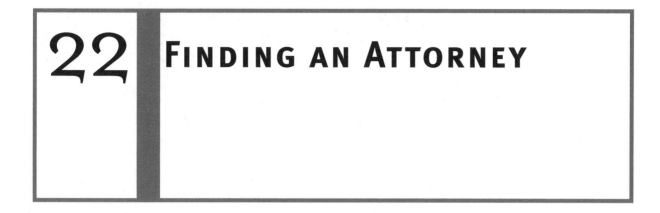

22 FINDING AN ATTORNEY

Unfortunately, there are too many instances of immigration lawyers who are not sufficiently familiar with laws and procedures. The other side of the coin are those who are experienced, but are too busy to do the work or pay close attention to the case. The problem is compounded by clients who are often desperate to get their case completed and are willing to pay whatever it takes to whoever says the case is possible. An attorney may say a case is easy only because he or she is unaware of complicating factors.

Immigration law is a particularly difficult area in which to practice. The only constant in the immigration field is change. It is almost too difficult a field for a lawyer to practice part-time and be effective. Most competent general practice attorneys know to avoid immigration cases.

The attorney who is most helpful is one who is as knowledgeable to evaluate the case as the USCIS officer or immigration judge. That is, he or she should not only know precisely the required forms, supporting documents, and procedures, but also whether the case will be approved according to statute and current national USCIS, and often more importantly, local policy. If there will be any problem with the case, this needs to be stated at the outset. There should be no surprises at the interview. If it is possible to overcome the anticipated ground of objection with documentation, then this needs to be planned for. Only in a minority of cases is the discretion of the officer or supervisor really in play. Even then, the attorney must be able to say which factors the case turns on.

Getting a Referral

It can be almost impossible to evaluate whether an attorney is competent to practice immigration law. Therefore, the same rule applies when choosing any type of service provider, whether it be a contractor, plumber, doctor, or lawyer. The only way to find an immigration lawyer is by referral from someone who is very familiar with that person and his or her work. If you have another attorney that you trust, he or she should know an immigration attorney or can get a name from a colleague.

Another excellent way to get a referral is through an ethnic association or organization. These organizations often maintain referral lists or can give the name of an attorney familiar to them. These organizations often refer many cases and therefore have gotten feedback over the years about certain attorneys. Also, if an attorney knows a case was referred by a friend or organization, he or she knows that if a problem develops the word will spread to his or her community.

Each immigration court is required to maintain a list of local nonprofit immigration service providers. You can pick this list up from the immigration court or possibly call and get a couple of phone numbers. These organizations generally provide competent legal help and are cheaper than a private attorney. If they will not take your case or if you prefer your own attorney, you should ask one of them for a referral. They should know of conscientious attorneys, particularly those who have helped out the organization on a reduced-fee basis.

Finally, if all else fails, contact the *American Immigration Lawyers Association* (AILA). This is the *only* immigration lawyer association. A referral through AILA should be fairly reliable.

In Hispanic communities, there have been too many cases of *notarios* committing outright fraud upon unsuspecting clients. Notarios must be avoided like the plague. They often charge the same or more than licensed attorneys who are more knowledgeable and who are subject to disciplinary action.

Making the Decision

When you call an attorney to make an appointment, ask if there is a consultation fee. You should expect to pay one. It is very reasonable to pay a consultation fee for the initial meeting. You could definitely call around and find an attorney who does not charge a fee, but keep in mind that you may get what you pay for.

Once you are in the attorney's office, there are certain questions you should ask.

✪   *What percentage of your practice is immigration?* Ideally, a majority of the attorney's practice should be immigration related.

✪   *Are you a member of AILA?* AILA is the only immigration lawyers' organization, through which attorneys receive critical information pertaining to all aspects of immigration law practice and developments. A conscientious attorney also attends conferences and seminars sponsored by AILA. It is difficult to be a competent practitioner without being an AILA member. You can check for yourself if the attorney is a member by calling 202-216-2400. If he or she is not a member, you should take your business elsewhere, unless you have a solid referral.

✪   *Have you done cases like mine and with what result?* He or she should be able to say what the chances of your case succeeding are and on what grounds a denial is possible.

✪   *What is the probability of my case being granted and what does it depend on?* In other words, you want to know why the case will not be granted.

✪   *Do I even need an attorney in the first place?* If the attorney is trustworthy, he or she should answer this question honestly. Your case may matter less to the attorney than you think. A busy attorney has his or her calendar filled anyway, so if he or she does not take your case, he or she will take someone else's. If the attorney recommends that you be represented, ask how he or she will assist your case apart from filling out the forms.

✪   *When are legal fees to be paid?* Under no circumstances should you pay the entire fee up front. A common fee arrangement is to pay half to start and the rest over time or when the case is complete.

✪ *How is the fee calculated?* Most immigration cases are charged on what is called a flat fee basis, meaning you will pay one fee no matter how long the case takes. This is the safest method of charging. The other billing method is by the hour. Established attorneys typically charge very substantial fees per hour—$150 per hour and up. The time necessary for an immigration case can escalate very quickly if paying by the hour. However, an attorney should have a legal staff who can do most of the legwork.

✪ *Is there any way to reduce the attorney fee without compromising my case?* For example, does the attorney recommend that his or her role is to simply put the together the filing packet and then not appear at the USCIS interview? For citizenship cases with no complicating factors, an attorney's presence is not needed.

✪ *When will the work be completed?* The flip side of finding a reputable attorney is that he or she is likely very busy. Before you entrust the attorney with the case or fee, you should get a timetable as to when the work will be done. Perhaps you can negotiate a lower fee if the work takes longer than stated. Offer to pay the attorney the first half of the payment when the case is ready to file. Then you will come back to the office to pay the filing and legal fees.

Being a Good Client

A successful attorney/client relationship is a two-way street. It is also in your best interests to be a good client.

The following are some helpful hints.

✪ Ask for a receipt that states what work will be done and the fees to be charged.

✪ Keep copies of all payment receipts.

✪ Insist on retaining a copy of everything filed and all correspondence received on your behalf. Resist the urge to be lazy and think your attorney has a copy of everything. You need to maintain your own file.

✪ Never leave original documents with your attorney. A copy of the document is all that is required to file.

✪ Make sure your attorney has your current address and phone numbers.

✪ Know under what name the attorney's office has filed the case and reference that name when calling.

✪ Designate one person from the family to be in contact with the attorney.

✪ Determine that either the attorney or the client will be in contact with the USCIS—not both.

✪ Seek as much assistance as possible from the attorney's staff rather than from the attorney. The attorney's legal staff is there to help you. You do not need to ask the attorney whether something was filed—ask the legal assistant who actually filed it.

✪ Call the attorney's office before any deadline and ensure it has been complied with.

✪ If you receive a letter from the USCIS that you do not understand, fax it to the attorney's office and ask for a call back from an assistant. The staff person will have seen the same type of letter many times and will be able to help you.

✪ Keep in touch with your attorney's office. Since some cases take years to complete, you should contact him or her at least every six months or so in case there are new legal developments. A busy attorney has many cases and cannot necessarily think of your case when a change in the law occurs.

Remember that you are completely responsible for the work your lawyer does on your behalf. If a deadline is missed or a case is improperly filed, you cannot say it was the fault of your attorney. Your only recourse is to prove that the attorney was negligent to the level of incompetence in what is called a *Matter of Lozada* filing (named after the Board of Immigration Appeals case that established a specific procedure). This does not mean that if your attorney simply made a mistake your case can be reopened or corrected. It has to be a mistake so incompetent that it falls to the level of *malpractice*. It is a tough standard to prove. You will also need to prove that he or she was actually retained to do that work. Hopefully, this is evidenced on the payment receipts.

In the end, the nature of the attorney/client relationship is such that the client inevitably must place a great deal of trust in the attorney. Adherence to a few simple guidelines at the outset can set the foundation for a successful working relationship.

GLOSSARY

A

A number. May also be referred to as an alien number, file number, green card number, or case number. Refers to the file number assigned in sequence by the USCIS or ICE to an alien who has applied for adjustment or has been apprehended by the DHS. This is the permanent file number of the alien and will eventually appear on the work permit, green card, and naturalization certificate. This number must appear on all correspondence and applications filed with the USCIS.

ADIT (Alien Documentation, Identification and Telecommunication System) processing. The process where an adjustment applicant places his or her signature and fingerprint on the I-89 card, which will be sent to a service center to be made into a green card. It is usually done at the USCIS interview.

adjudicate. This occurs when a USCIS officer makes a decision as to whether to grant or deny an application.

adjustment of status (AOS). Process where one becomes a permanent resident in the U.S. Since one has a previous status in the U.S., he or she is said to be upgrading his or her status to permanent residence.

admission. This occurs when an alien presents him- or herself for inspection to an immigration officer at a border or airport and whose entry was approved on a particular basis.

advance parole. Issued by either a local office or a service center, depending on where the adjustment application is, it is advance permission to return to the U.S. to resume processing of an adjustment application.

administrative appeal. An appeal filed at the local USCIS to the Administrative Appeals Unit in Washington, D.C. within thirty days of a petition's denial.

administrative closure. A case that is not denied but is no longer pending.

affidavit. Any type of document written by the applicant or by a third party in support of the applicant and signed in front of a notary public.

affidavit of support. Important form required in a family-based adjustment case in which the petitioner agrees to reimburse the government if the person being adjusted requires federal benefits within ten years of adjustment or the person naturalizes.

aggravated felony. In the immigration sense, this means any type of crime listed in Section 101(a)(43) of the INA, which includes many nonviolent crimes and misdemeanors.

alien. One who is not a permanent resident but is present in the U.S. on a non-immigrant visa, is out of status, or entered without inspection.

application support center (ASC). The facility that takes fingerprints of applicants.

amnesty. Time-limited benefit allowing adjustment of status that will issue out green cards based upon residence in the U.S. prior to a certain date.

approval notice. A notice from a service center stating a petition is approved. *See I-797.*

arrival/departure document. *See I-94.*

asylee. One who has been granted asylum either through the Asylum Office or by the immigration judge but who has not yet adjusted status to that of a permanent resident.

asylum. A showing that one has a well-founded fear of persecution on the basis of political opinion, religion, gender, nationality, or membership in a particular social group. (A well-founded fear can be thought of as a 10% chance of severe harm.)

asylum officer. An employee of the Department of Homeland Security who will conduct the initial administrative interview on an asylum application.

B

bag and baggage letter. A form letter (I-161) sent by the Deportation Office asking an alien to appear at the office with his or her luggage on a certain date to be deported.

beneficiary. The alien who will receive the immigration benefit from the filing of a petition on his or her behalf by either a family member who is a U.S. citizen or green card holder, or by a company making an appropriate job offer.

biographic information form. *See G-325A.*

blue passport. *See refugee travel document.*

Board of Immigration Appeals (BIA). A separate office within the Executive Office of Immigration Review that administers appeals from the Immigration Court. It is located in Falls Church, Virginia, just outside Washington, D.C.

C

call-up date. Used in the immigration court to indicate when motions or supporting documents are due to the court. It is usually ten or fourteen days before the hearing.

cancellation of removal. Procedure available to one who is before the immigration court and can demonstrate that he or she has lived for ten years in the U.S. and is a person of good moral character, and that there would be extremely unusual hardship to a U.S. citizen or lawful permanent resident parent, spouse, or child if he or she was deported.

certificate of citizenship. Document given in place of a naturalization certificate to those born abroad to U.S. citizens, adopted by U.S. citizens, or born to parents who naturalized. Normally given to those who qualify for citizenship without first becoming a permanent resident.

change of status (COS). An application made on Form I-539 by one in the U.S. to change from one nonimmigrant status to another.

change of venue. Request of the applicant or by motion of a respondent to change the jurisdiction of the USCIS office or immigration court based on a change of address.

child. Unmarried individual under 21 years of age. The Child Status Protection Act may extend child status for those applying for adjustment of status.

classification. Short code that appears on the green card and approval notice. It is the basis upon which one became a permanent resident.

clock. Generally, a running total of the number of days since an asylum application has been filed. It is used in determining when an asylum applicant may file a work permit application. The term is also used when accruing illegal presence.

Code of Federal Regulations (CFR). A multivolume detailed interpretation of federal laws, including immigration laws.

conditional resident. One who has obtained conditional permanent residence through marriage to a U.S. citizen (where the marriage is less than two years old at the time of adjustment) or through a qualifying investment.

consulate. Office run by the U.S. Department of State that is a suboffice in a larger foreign country of the main embassy office. It is responsible for the issuance of immigrant and nonimmigrant visas to aliens for entry into the U.S. May also make determinations on U.S. citizenship.

conviction. A determination in a court case that someone broke the law and a sentence is issued.

country reports. Detailed report of each foreign country published each February by the Department of State regarding human rights conditions in each country. These are heavily relied upon by immigration judges and asylum officers in deciding an asylum application.

crime involving moral turpitude (CIMT). There is no statutory definition, and it is somewhat in the eye of the beholder. A CIMT within five years of adjustment or any two CIMTs at any time may make a person removable. There is a long list of CIMTs. A retail theft, for example, is a CIMT.

current visa. A visa where the priority date on the I-130 approval notice moves past the date reflected on the visa bulletin published by the Department of State.

cutoff date. The date on the Department of State's monthly visa chart that makes people whose priority date is before it eligible to apply for permanent residence.

D

deferred admission. When a nonimmigrant or possibly lawful permanent resident has trouble reentering the U.S. and must appear at the local USCIS office to clarify his or her status. Formerly known as deferred inspection.

Department of Homeland Security (DHS). Newly formed department responsible for government functions related to security. The former INS has been split into the U.S. Citizenship and Immigration Services (USCIS), which is responsible for administering immigration services, and the Immigration and Customs Enforcement (ICE), which is responsible for immigration enforcement within the U.S.

Department of Labor (DOL). Through its oversight of the labor certification process, it is responsible for providing determinations as to the availability of qualified U.S. workers for positions offered in many of the employment-based categories.

Department of State. Runs the embassies and consulates, which decide on immigrant and nonimmigrant visa applications. Also runs the Passport Office.

deportable. State where the alien is either being asked or may be asked in the future to leave the U.S.

deportation. Occurs when a person is physically taken by a DHS deportation officer to his or her native country, usually because either a deportation order or removal order from the immigration court exists.

deportation officer. A USCIS employee whose responsibility is to apprehend and deport illegal aliens from the U.S.

derivative beneficiary. A person who obtains status on a visa petition not on account of his or her own standing but because of his or her relationship to the principal beneficiary, such as a child through his or her parent.

District Director (DD). The head official of the USCIS offices in a certain district that may include several states. The DD has considerable discretion and power over certain types of applications and waivers, such as humanitarian parole or extended voluntary departure.

diversity visa. A green card lottery run by the Department of State in which 100,000 people will be notified that they will be allowed to adjust status. However, only 50,000 visas are available.

duplicate petition. Normally filed when the original petition was lost or misplaced by the USCIS. In order to file the duplicate petition, one must have the original receipt number or a copy of the receipt notice in order to file the duplicate to the first filing.

E

embassy. The main office for the U.S. government located in a friendly foreign country.

employment authorization document (EAD). A photo identification card issued by the USCIS that evidences the holder's authorization to work in the U.S. and obtain a Social Security number.

entered without inspection (EWI, pronounced "eee-wee"). A person who entered the U.S. across the border from Mexico or Canada without being inspected by an immigration officer.

examinations section or exams. The typical name for the section of the USCIS that interviews adjustment applications.

exclusion. Occurs when a lawful permanent resident with a criminal record attempts to reenter the country and is not allowed to enter.

Executive Office for Immigration Review (EOIR). A separate agency from the USCIS within the Department of Justice that runs the immigration court.

expedited case. Adjustment cases that are time-sensitive such as diversity visas, aging out (child about to turn 21), medical reasons, or other urgent reasons.

expungement. A criminal record where the person's name has been deleted from the records of a particular state.

extension of status (EOS). Where one applies for another term of status on the same type of nonimmigrant visa.

extreme hardship. The legal standard for different types of waivers, such as for unlawful presence or entry with a false passport. The hardship must be to a qualifying relative such as U.S. citizen or lawful permanent resident parent or spouse.

F

file number. *See A number.*

filing receipt. Small yellow cash register receipt attached to the receipt letter upon filing an adjustment case.

final order of removal (deportation). An order to send a person out of the U.S. by the immigration judge that has not been appealed within the thirty-day period.

fingerprint clearance. Required fingerprint check against FBI computer records prior to adjustment of status. Fingerprints must be taken within fifteen months prior to the date of adjustment or else the fingerprints will expire and have to be retaken.

fingerprint card. Until 1997, a card having fingerprints of an alien taken on it by a law enforcement entity or a credentialed private organization. USCIS took over the fingerprinting process to avoid fraud.

fingerprint check. One of four security checks run before adjudicating any application. The Federal Bureau of Investigation's (FBI) uses an Integrated Automated Fingerprint Identification System (IAFIS), which matches criminal history records from federal, military and most state apprehensions. Also called the FBI fingerprint check.

Freedom of Information Act (FOIA). Important law allowing anyone to obtain a copy of his or her file held at a governmental agency, such as the USCIS.

Foreign Affairs Manual. The regulations that apply to consular officers in adjudicating immigrant or nonimmigrant visas.

G

G-28. Attorney appearance form. Blue form that must accompany any immigration application in order for an attorney to be officially entered as attorney of record and to receive copies of correspondence.

G-325A. Detailed biographic information form that is required with an adjustment of status application and other petitions. One of the copies is sent to the embassy in the native country and another is sent to the CIA to perform records checks. Required for all adjustment applicants fourteen years of age and over.

grandfathered. One can apply for benefits under a favorable law that is now expired, such as Section 245(i).

green card holder. *See lawful permanent resident.*

green card number. *See A number.*

green card stamp. Refers to the temporary stamp placed by a USCIS officer into a person's passport signifying his or her adjustment of status.

H

H-1B visa. The most popular temporary nonimmigrant visa, issued for a maximum of six years; most professional positions normally qualify; a job offer is required before a person can apply.

humanitarian parole. One is paroled into the U.S. for humanitarian reasons, such as for medical care or for young children to reside with parents, even if there is not a visa number available.

I

I-20. Form issued by a school when a foreign student has enrolled and paid tuition.

I-94. Small white card stapled into one's passport upon admission into the U.S. on a nonimmigrant visa. It contains the date of expiration of the nonimmigrant visa.

I-161. *See bag and baggage letter.*

I-130. Visa petition form used for a family-sponsored immediate member or preference category.

I-140. Visa petition form used for an employment-based preference category.

I-212 waiver. Form needed to waive the effect of a removal or deportation order.

I-485 Supplement A. Form filed by those eligible for *mini-amnesty.* You can only file it during certain times and you must be eligible. It is required by one who entered the country without documentation or who is out of status and is filing adjustment through a preference visa petition.

I-551 stamp. *See green card stamp.*

I-601. *See waiver.*

I-765. Work permit application.

I-797. Also called a receipt notice or approval notice of action issued by a service center in regard to an immigrant or nonimmigrant visa application.

I-864. *See affidavit of support.*

IBIS. (pronounced EYE-bis) Interagency Border Inspection System name check. One of four security checks run before adjudicating any application. Customs and Border Protection (CBP), IBIS is a database of lookouts, wants, warrants, arrests, and convictions consolidated over twenty agencies including the FBI's National Criminal Information Center.

IDENT. (pronounced EYE-dent) Automated Biometric Identification System. One of four security checks run before adjudicating any application. Managed by US-VISIT, IDENT enables agencies to screen fingerprints against databases of previous asylum applicants, criminal aliens, and repeat immigration offenders.

illegal alien. One who is in the U.S. out of status or who entered without inspection.

immediate relative. Spouse, parent, or child (under the age of 21) of a U.S. citizen. However, adopted children must have been adopted before the age of 16 and stepchildren before the age of 18 in order to qualify.

immigrant visa (IV). Used when applying for permanent residence at an embassy or consulate.

immigrant visa packet. After the alien has been approved at an embassy or consulate, he or she is given a packet to present upon arrival for inspection in the U.S. This packet must be presented to the USCIS officer for ADIT processing.

immigrant. Someone who has become a lawful permanent resident.

Immigration and Customs Enforcement (ICE). Agency that comprises the interior enforcement side of the former INS. It is part of the new Department of Homeland Security. For example, deportation officers are now part of this bureau.

immigration court (EOIR). *See Executive Office for Immigration Review.*

immigration judge (IJ). An administrative law judge who is an employee of the Department of Justice.

Immigration and Nationality Act of 1952 (INA). The starting point of current immigration law; all immigration laws passed since then are amendments to the INA.

Immigration and Naturalization Service (INS). As of March 1, 2003, the INS ceased to exist. It was split into several parts in order to separate the benefits functions (USCIS) from the enforcement (BICE), among others, all of which are now part of the new Department of Homeland Security.

inadmissible. Any one of a number of grounds, such as criminal acts or medical conditions, that cause an alien not to be admitted to the U.S.

individual hearing. Type of hearing before the immigration court in which the alien actually puts on his or her case over a one- to three-hour time period.

infopass. An online appointment made through the USCIS website to speak to an immigration information officer regarding the status of a pending case or to take certain actions in regard to it.

inspection. To be inspected by an immigration officer at an airport, or border, or on a ship. The officer will check to see that all documents are in order. The officer may admit, send the alien back, or refer the alien to deferred admission.

investigations section. Staffed by ICE officers who are allowed to carry weapons, make arrests, and do investigations on fraudulent marriages, fraudulent businesses, alien smugglers, fraudulent documents, and aliens involved in criminal and gang activities.

L

labor certification. An approved labor certification is a requirement for some employment-based adjustment applications. It is an actual recruitment of U.S. workers, under the supervision of the Department of Labor and a state employment security agency, in order to establish that there is no U.S. worker who is ready, willing, and able to take the position offered to an alien.

labor condition application (LCA). The first stage of a nonimmigrant H-1B petition; an LCA has nothing to do with a labor certification application.

late amnesty. Those illegal aliens who missed the 1988 deadline for amnesty applications and became part of several class-actions lawsuits against the USCIS such as LULAC or CSS. (Most late amnesty class members had a deadline of June 2002 to file for adjustment of status.)

lawful permanent resident (LPR). The most correct term for someone who has adjusted status through an immigrant visa.

legalization. The former process whereby aliens through the 1986 amnesty were first granted temporary residency then permanent residence.

LIFE Act. The most recent major legislation affecting immigration enacted in December 2000. Allows those who are out of status, entered without inspection, or worked in the U.S. without USCIS authorization to adjust status through a family member or a labor certification filed before April 30, 2001.

lottery. *See diversity visa.*

M

mandamus. A petition filed in federal court to have a federal judge order the USCIS to take a certain action.

master calendar hearing (MCH). As opposed to the individual hearing, usually a brief housekeeping hearing before an immigration judge at which the alien pleads to the Notice to Appear and states the relief for which he or she is applying.

medical examination. An exam done by a USCIS- or State Department-approved physician and on a special form required prior to adjustment of status or to obtaining immigrant visa at an embassy or consulate.

motion. Any type of written request, normally to the immigration court, but also to a USCIS office or service center, asking that agency to take a certain formal action.

motion to reopen. A common motion to make a previously denied or closed benefit pending again in order to obtain that benefit. There may be restrictions on the number of motions allowed, when they may be filed, and the basis for reopening.

N

name check. One of four security checks run before adjudicating any application. In response to an authorized requestor such as USCIS, information is disseminated from the FBI's Central Records System containing the FBI's administrative, personnel, and investigative files. Only partially automated, it may be the cause of a long delay in case processing. Also FBI name check or background check.

nationality. For immigration purposes, generally the same as citizenship.

National Visa Center (NVC). State Department office located in New Hampshire that stores approved visa petitions until they become current.

naturalization. Process whereby a green card holder becomes a U.S. citizen through filing a N-400 application.

naturalization certificate. A document given as evidence as having become a citizen of the U.S. by naturalization.

Nicaraguan Adjustment and Central American Relief Act (NACARA). Law that allows certain individuals from eastern European, former Soviet block countries who entered the U.S. prior to 1991 and filed for asylum at that time to apply for suspension of deportation.

nonimmigrant visa (NIV). Any one of the several dozen visa types that permit one to stay in the U.S. for a temporary period for a specific purpose.

Notice of Action. *See I-797.*

Notice to Appear (NTA). Charging document that brings a person before the immigration court.

notice of intent to deny. Issued either for an I-130 petition or asylum application (where applicant is in valid nonimmigrant status) to give the applicant an opportunity to rebut and submit additional evidence.

O

one-stop. When the I-130 and I-485 forms are filed at the same time, normally with the local USCIS office if one is the beneficiary of an immediate visa petition.

out of status (overstay). One whose nonimmigrant status as set forth on the I-94 card or a subsequent extension has ended, or the person has violated the terms of the visa; for example, by engaging in unauthorized employment.

P

parole. Generally given to an alien outside the U.S. for humanitarian reasons or to an alien in the U.S. who wishes to travel abroad and whose paperwork for adjustment is pending. Constitutes a lawful entry for purposes of applying for adjustment of status.

passport office. An office of the Department of State that issues passports, and in doing so, may make decisions on U.S. citizenship.

permanent resident. *See lawful permanent resident.*

petitioner. The U.S. citizen or legal permanent resident or U.S. corporation filing on behalf of an alien beneficiary for either an immigrant or nonimmigrant visa.

preference visa category. A family member other than an immediate relative whose petition therefore requires a waiting period between the I-130 filing and the application for adjustment.

prevailing wage. Term used in an H-1B or labor certification application where the wage offered must be at least 95% of the average of those holding that position in that city or state.

principal applicant. The lead applicant in an adjustment or asylum application.

principal beneficiary. The main beneficiary of a visa petition, as opposed to a derivative beneficiary, such as a minor child, who obtains status through the principal.

priority date (date of filing). The date used to determine when a beneficiary of a visa petition is able to apply for adjustment of status.

proceedings. *See removal proceedings.*

R

receipt number. The case number assigned by a service center to a filing. The receipt number includes the first three letters of the service center and the year in which it was filed.

record of proceedings. Formal name given to the court file in immigration court and the file upon which the immigration judge makes a decision.

reduction in recruitment (RIR). A relatively new fast-track labor certification application wherein a company has already attempted to recruit a qualified worker and therefore does not need to go through supervised recruitment by the Department of Labor.

reentry permit. A document that lets an alien stay out of the country for over a year and up to two years without abandoning his or her permanent resident status.

refugee. One who is in the U.S. having been granted refugee status abroad. May apply for adjustment of status after one year in the U.S.

refugee travel document. Blue passport that replaces the passport from one's own country and is for refugees and asylees only. Does not function as a reentry permit. Serves as advance parole for refugees and asylees.

registration (NSEERS). National Security Entry-Exit Registration System (NSEERS). The short-lived, special registration program, initiated in December 2002 and suspended one year later, that required males from 18 primarily Middle Eastern countries to report to USCIS. Failure to have registered in 2002 when the program was in effect may still be a bar to future adjustment of status unless good cause is shown.

registry. Anyone residing in the U.S. since before 1972 may be admitted as permanent residents if they can show good moral character.

regulations. *See Code of Federal Regulations or Foreign Affairs Manual.*

removable. An illegal alien or a lawful permanent resident who has violated immigration law by committing certain criminal acts or fraud and is subject to removal or deportation.

removal proceedings. One who is in proceedings is before the immigration court to determine whether he or she should be removed or deported.

remove conditions. The process by which the alien submits the proper form and evidence, generally to a service center, showing that the marriage is bona fide or the alien has completed the investment requirements.

request for evidence (RFE). Document issued by a USCIS office or service center requesting additional evidence or information to prove the alien's case.

resident alien. A permanent resident or someone on an extended nonimmigrant visa, but not a tourist visa.

respondent. The name given to an alien who is in removal proceedings before the immigration court; similar to a defendant in a criminal proceeding.

routing slip. Form required in conjunction with an immigration court proceeding where an application must be paid for at the USCIS cashier prior to filing with the court. Form allows the USCIS cashier to return the paid application to the applicant so that it may be filed with the immigration court at the instruction of the immigration judge.

S

section 212(c) relief. Where a lawful permanent resident who has committed crimes involving moral turpitude but not an aggravated felony may seek to stop removal before an immigration judge upon a sufficient demonstration of the existence of certain positive factors or equities on his behalf.

section 245(i) eligible. A person who is eligible to file the I-485A Supplement and pay the $1,000 penalty and adjust status.

self-petition. An alien of extraordinary ability, a battered spouse, or the widow or widower of a U.S. citizen who had been married to that citizen for at least two years.

service center. One of the several remote processing facilities. Each service center accepts certain petitions and application from people who live in the states within its jurisdiction.

signature card. Small card used for thumbprint in conjunction with an application for employment authorization at some service centers or possibly the I-89 card used in ADIT processing.

special registration. *See registration.*

sponsor. An individual or company who is filing a petition on behalf of a relative or employee, or a joint sponsor who is filing an affidavit of support.

state employment security agency (SESA). Agency that operates with the Department of Labor to ensure that there is no available U.S. worker for a particular position that is sought by an immigrant.

stay of deportation. An application made on Form I-246 and filed with the Deportation Office to request that a scheduled deportation be delayed for extenuating circumstances.

stowaway. Person who entered illegally by traveling on a commercial transportation such as a train, bus, or boat where a fare should have been paid.

T

temporary protected status (TPS). Status given to aliens of certain countries where there is war, famine, or natural disaster, such as hurricanes, that allows the alien to work and obtain a Social Security number.

temporary resident alien. The correct term for someone granted the initial stage of the legalization process from the 1986 amnesty.

trial attorney. A prosecutor employed by the Department of Homeland Security to represent it in immigration court, among other duties.

U

undocumented alien. Someone who entered the U.S. illegally across a border without a visa.

unlawful presence. Time that an alien is in the U.S. illegally or out of status since April 1, 1997.

U.S. citizen (USC). Someone born in the U.S., someone born outside the U.S. to a U.S. citizen parent, or someone who has naturalized or obtained a certificate of citizenship.

United States Citizenship and Immigration Services (USCIS). Agency that comprises the benefits side of the former INS. It is part of the new Department of Homeland Security.

V

visa. Used by itself, it refers to one of the nonimmigrant temporary visas, of which the most common is the tourist B-2 Visa.

visa bulletin. Information updated monthly by the Department of State available by mail, Internet, or phone showing which preference categories are currently available.

visa lottery. *See diversity visa.*

visa petition. Either the alien relative I-130 petition or the employment-based I-140 petition filed on behalf of a beneficiary.

visa waiver. Entry into the U.S. without a visa from a changing list of approximately twenty countries whose citizens are known to respect U.S. immigration laws.

V visa. New benefit from LIFE Act that allows spouses or minor unmarried children of green card holders after three years wait on the I-130 petition to obtain lawful nonimmigrant status in the U.S. or enter the U.S. if abroad in order to wait the remaining years on their visa petition.

voluntary departure. Granted by an immigration judge or a USCIS officer wherein the alien agrees to leave the U.S. at his or her own expense by a certain date in lieu of deportation and the effects of a deportation order.

W

waiver. Generally, one of the several forms, such as I-212, I-601, I-602 or I-612, used to waive or negate a condition of inadmissibility such as entry on a false passport or criminal record.

white card. *See I-94.*

white passport. *See reentry passport.*

withholding of removal. Requires a showing that it is more likely than not that one faces persecution on the basis of political opinion, religion, gender, nationality, or membership in a particular social group.

work permit. *See employment authorization document.*

Appendix A:
USCIS Field Offices

The following is a state-by-state list of USCIS Field Offices.

Alabama:
USCIS Atlanta District Office
Martin Luther King Jr. Federal Building
77 Forsyth Street SW
Atlanta, GA 30303
404-331-0253

Alaska:
USCIS Anchorage District Office
620 East 10th Avenue
Suite 102
Anchorage, Alaska 99501
907-271-3521

Arizona:
USCIS Phoenix District Office
2035 North Central Avenue
Phoenix, AZ 85004
602-514-7799

USCIS Tucson Sub Office
6431 South Country Club Road
Tucson, AZ 85706
520-670-4624

Arkansas:
USCIS Sub Office
4977 Old Greenwood Road
Fort Smith, AR 72903
501-646-4721

California:
USCIS Los Angeles District Office
300 North Los Angeles Street
Room 1001
Los Angeles, CA 90012
213-830-4940

USCIS San Diego District Office
U.S. Federal Building
880 Front Street
Suite 1234
San Diego, CA 92101
619-557-5645

USCIS San Francisco District Office
630 Sansome Street
San Francisco, CA 94111
415-844-5200

USCIS Sub Office
34 Civic Center Plaza
Room 520
Santa Ana, CA 92701
714-972-6600

USCIS Sub Office
655 West Rialto Avenue
San Bernadino, CA 94210

USCIS Fresno Sub Office
1177 Fulton Mall
Fresno, CA 93721
559-487-5132

USCIS Sacramento Sub Office
650 Capitol Mall
Sacramento, CA 95814
916-498-6480

USCIS San Jose Sub Office
1887 Monterey Road
San Jose, CA 95112
408-918-4000

Colorado:
USCIS Denver District Office
4730 Paris Street
Denver, CO 80239
303-371-0986

Connecticut:
USCIS Hartford Sub Office
450 Main Street, 4th Floor
Hartford, CT 06103
860-240-3050

Delaware:
USCIS Dover Satellite Office
1305 McD Drive
Dover, DE 19901
302-730-9311

District of Columbia:
USCIS Washington District Office
2675 Prosperity Avenue
Fairfax, VA 222031
202-307-1642

Florida:
USCIS Miami District Office
7880 Biscayne Boulevard
Miami, FL 33138
305-762-3680

USCIS Jacksonville Sub Office
4121 Southpoint Boulevard
Jacksonville, FL 32216
904-232-2164

USCIS Orlando Sub Office
9403 Tradeport Drive
Orlando, FL 32827
407-855-1241

USCIS Tampa Sub Office
5524 West Cypress Street
Tampa, FL 33607
813-637-3010

USCIS West Palm Beach Satellite Office
326 Fern Street
West Palm Beach, FL 33401
561-841-0498

Georgia:
USCIS Atlanta District
Martin Luther King Jr. Federal Building
77 Forsyth Street SW
Atlanta, GA 30303
404-331-0253

Guam:
USCIS Agana Sub Office
108 Hernan Cortez Avenue
Sirena Plaza
Suite 100
Hagatna, Guam 96910
671-472-7466

Hawaii:
USCIS Honolulu District Office
595 Ala Moana Boulevard
Honolulu, HI 96813
808-532-3746

Idaho:
USCIS Boise Sub Office
1185 South Vinnell Way
Boise, ID 83709

Illinois:
USCIS Chicago District Office
10 West Jackson Boulevard
Chicago, IL 60604
312-385-1820 or 312-385-1500

USCIS Chicago Adjudications Office
230 South Dearborn
23rd floor
Chicago, IL 60604

USCIS Chicago Citizenship Office
539 South Clark Street
Chicago, IL 60605
312-353-5440

Indiana:
USCIS Indianapolis Sub Office
950 North Meridian Street
Room 400
Indianapolis, IN 46204

Iowa:
USCIS Des Moine Sub Office
210 Walnut Street
Room 369
Federal Building
Des Moine, IA 50309

Kansas:
USCIS Wichita Satellite Office
271 West 3rd Street N
Suite 1050
Wichita, KS 67202

Kentucky:
USCIS Louisville ASC
601 West Broadway
Room 22
Louisville, KY 40202
502-582-6526

Louisiana:
USCIS Louisiana District Office
701 Loyola Avenue
Room T-8011
New Orleans, LA 70113
504-589-6521

Maine:
USCIS Portland District Office
176 Gannett Drive
South Portland, ME 04106
207-780-3399

Maryland:
USCIS Baltimore District Office
Fallon Federal Building
31 Hopkins Plaza
Baltimore, MD 21201
410-962-2010

Massachusetts:
USCIS Boston District Office
John F. Kennedy Federal Building
Government Center
Boston, MA 02203
617-565-4274

Michigan:
USCIS Detroit District Office
333 Mt. Elliot
Detroit, MI 48207
313-568-6000

Minnesota:
USCIS St. Paul District Office
2901 Metro Drive
Suite 100
Bloomington, MN 55425
612-313-9020

Mississippi:
USCIS Jackson Sub Office
Dr. A. H. McCoy Federal Building
100 West Capitol Street
Suite 727
Jackson, MS 39269

Missouri:
USCIS Kansas City District Office
9747 Northwest Conant Avenue
Kansas City, MO 64153
816-891-7422

USCIS St. Louis Sub Office
Robert A. Young Federal Building
1222 Spruce Street
Room 1.100
St. Louis, MO 63103
314-539-2516

Montana:
USCIS Helena District Office
2800 Skyway Drive
Helena, MT 59602
406-449-5220

Nebraska:
USCIS Omaha District Office
1717 Avenue HE
Omaha, NE 68110
402-697-1129

Nevada:
USCIS Las Vegas Sub Office
3373 Pepper Lane
Las Vegas, NV 89120
702-451-3597

USCIS Reno Sub Office
1351 Corporate Boulevard
Reno, NV 89502
775-784-5427

New Hampshire:
USCIS Manchester Office
803 Canal Street
Manchester, NH 03101
603-625-5276

New Jersey:
USCIS Newark District Office
Peter Rodino, Jr. Federal Building
970 Broad Street
Newark, NJ 07102
973-645-4421

USCIS Cherry Hill Sub Office
1886 Greentree Road
Cherry Hill, NJ 08003
609-424-7712

New Mexico:
USCIS Albuquerque Sub Office
1720 Randolph Road SE
Albuquerque, NM 87106
505-241-0450

New York:
USCIS Buffalo District Office
130 Delaware Avenue
Buffalo, NY 14202
716-849-6760

USCIS New York City District Office
26 Federal Plaza
New York City, NY 10278
212-264-5891

USCIS Albany Sub Office
1086 Troy-Schenectady Road
Latham, NY 12110
518-220-2100

North Carolina:
USCIS Charlotte Sub Office
6130 Tyvola Centre Drive
Charlotte, NC 28217
704-672-6990

North Dakota:
USCIS St. Paul District
2901 Metro Drive
Suite 100
Bloomington, MN 55425
612-313-9020

Ohio:
USCIS Cleveland District
A.J.C. Federal Building
1240 East Ninth Street
Room 501
Cleveland, OH 44199
216-522-4766

USCIS Cincinnati Sub Office
J.W. Peck Federal Building
550 Main Street
Room 4001
Cincinnati, OH 45202
513-684-2412

USCIS Columbus Sub Office
50 West Broad Street
Suite 306
Columbus, OH 43215
614-469-2900

Oklahoma:
USCIS Oklahoma City Sub Office
4400 SW 44th Street
Suite A
Oklahoma City, OK 73119
405-231-5944

Oregon:
USCIS Portland District Office
511 NW Broadway
Portland, OR 97209
503-326-7585

Pennsylvania:
USCIS Philadelphia District Office
1600 Callowhill Street
Philadelphia, PA 19130
215-656-7150

USCIS Pittsburgh Sub Office
3000 Sidney Street
Pittsburgh, PA 15203
412-395-4460

Puerto Rico and U.S. Virgin Islands:
(Street address:)
USCIS San Juan District Office
San Patricio Office Center
7 Tabonuco Street
Suite 100
Guaynabo, Puerto Rico 00968
787-706-2343

(Mailing address:)
USCIS San Juan District Office
P.O. Box 365068
San Juan, PR 00936

USCIS Charlotte Amalie Sub Office
8000 Nisky Center
Suite 1A
First Floor South
Charlotte Amalie, St. Thomas
U. S. Virgin Islands 00802
340-774-1390

USCIS Sub Office
Sunny Isle Shopping Center
Christiansted, St. Croix
U. S. Virgin Islands 00823

Rhode Island:
USCIS Providence Sub Office
200 Dyer Street
Providence, RI 02903
401-528-5528

South Carolina:
USCIS Charleston Office
1 Poston Road
Suite 130
Charleston, SC 29407
843-727-4422

South Dakota:
USCIS St. Paul District
2901 Metro Drive
Suite 100
Bloomington, MN 55425
612-313-9020

Tennessee:
USCIS Memphis Sub Office
842 Virginia Run Cove
Memphis, TN 38122
901-544-0256

Texas:
USCIS District Office
8101 North Stemmons Freeway
Dallas, TX 75247
214-905-5800

USCIS El Paso District Office
1545 Hawkins Boulevard Suite 167
El Paso, TX 79925
915-225-1750

USCIS Harlingen District
1717 Zoy Street
Harlingen, TX 78552
956-427-8592

USCIS Houston District Office
126 Northpoint
Houston, Texas 77060
281-774-4629

USCIS San Antonio District Office
8940 Fourwinds Drive
San Antonio, TX 78239
210-967-7109

Utah:
USCIS Salt Lake City Sub Office
5272 South College Drive, #100
Murray, UT 84123
801-265-0109

Vermont:
USCIS St. Albans Office
64 Gricebrook Road
St. Albans, VT 05478

Virginia:
USCIS Norfolk Sub Office
5280 Henneman Drive
Norfolk, VA 23513
757-858-7519

Washington:
USCIS Seattle District Office
12500 Tukwila International Boulevard
Seattle, WA 98168
206-553-1332

USCIS Spokane Sub Office
U.S. Courthouse
920 West Riverside
Room 691
Spokane, WA 99201
509-353-2761

USCIS Yakima Sub Office
415 North 3rd Street
Yakima, WA 98901

West Virginia:
USCIS Charleston Sub Office
210 Kanawha Boulevard West
Charleston, WV 25302

Wisconsin:
USCIS Milwaukee Sub Office
310 East Knapp Street
Milwaukee, WI 53202
414-287-6387

Wyoming:
USCIS Denver District Office
4730 Paris Street
Denver, CO 80239
303-371-0986

APPENDIX B:
USCIS SERVICE CENTERS

This appendix contains contact information for the USCIS service centers. Four of these service centers are identical in that they each process all USCIS applications and differ by processing applications only from persons residing in their particular region of the U.S.

The fifth and newest center, the National Benefits Center, is unique in that it is not responsible for any particular region or state but only processes the three new types of applications arising from the 2000 LIFE Act. The National Benefits Center was originally created as the Missouri Service Center and was set up to process the three types of new applications associated with the LIFE Act. Now called the National Benefits Center, it serves the additional role as the hub and conduit for all USCIS field offices by completing pre-interview processing of forms generally requiring an interview, particularly family-based cases.

When filing an application at a service center, care must be taken to address the envelope to the correct street address or post office box.

California Service Center

Jurisdiction over Arizona, California, Guam, Hawaii, and Nevada.

General Correspondence:
U.S. Department of Homeland Security
United States Citizenship and
Immigration Services
P.O. Box 30111
Laguna Niguel, CA 92607

Courier:
California Service Center
24000 Avila Road
2ⁿᵈ Floor
Room 2302
Laguna Niguel, CA 92677

U.S. Department of Homeland Security
United States Citizenship and
Immigration Services
California Service Center
P.O. Box *(insert correct box number listed below)*
Laguna Niguel, CA *(insert correct zip code listed below)*

I-90:
P.O. Box 10090
Laguna Niguel, CA 92607-1009

I-90A (SAW):
P.O. Box 10190
Laguna Niguel, CA 92607-1019

I-129 (& related I-539s):
P.O. Box 10129
Laguna Niguel, CA 92607-1012

I-130/I-129F & EOIR-29:
P.O. Box 10130
Laguna Niguel, CA 92607-1013

I-140:
P.O. Box 10140
Laguna Niguel, CA 92607-1014

I-290A and I-290B:
P.O. Box 10290
Laguna Niguel, CA 92607-1029

I-360:
P.O. Box 10360
Laguna Niguel, CA 92607-1036

I-485:
P.O. Box 10485
Laguna Niguel, CA 92607-1048

I-526:
P.O. Box 10526
Laguna Niguel, CA 92607-1052

I-539:
P.O. Box 10539
Laguna Niguel, CA 92607-1053

I-589:
P.O. Box 10589
Laguna Niguel, CA 92607-1058

I-690:
P.O. Box 10690
Laguna Niguel, CA 92607-1069

I-694:
P.O. Box 10694
Laguna Niguel, CA 92607-1094

I-695:
P.O. Box 10695
Laguna Niguel, CA 92607-1095

I-698:
P.O. Box 10698
Laguna Niguel, CA 92607-1098

I-751:
P.O. Box 10751
Laguna Niguel, CA 92607-1075

I-765:
P.O. Box 10765
Laguna Niguel, CA 92607-1076

I-817:
P.O. Box 10817
Laguna Niguel, CA 92607-1081

I-821:
P.O. Box 10821
Laguna Niguel, CA 92607-1082

I-824:
Use the P.O. Box number for the type of approved application or petition for which action is being requested.

I-829:
P.O. Box 10526
Laguna Niguel, CA 92607-1052

N-400:
P.O. Box 10400
Laguna Niguel, CA 92607-1040

Walk-in Information Counter:
Chet Holifeld Federal Building
24000 Avila Road
2nd Floor
Laguna Niguel, CA
Open Monday through Friday
(9:00 AM to 2:30 PM) excluding holidays
800-375-5283

Special information:

- If fingerprints have not been scheduled within 120 days after filing, fax an inquiry to 949-389-3055.

- For status inquiries, do not send an inquiry letter. Instead, call Customer Service at 1-800-375-5283.

National Benefits Center

Courier:
United States Citizenship and
Immigration Services
1907–1909 S Blue Island Avenue
Chicago, IL 60608

V visa:
United States Citizenship and
Immigration Services
P.O. Box 7216
Chicago, IL 60680-7216

K visa:
United States Citizenship and
Immigration Services
P.O. Box 7218
Chicago, IL 60680-7218

Legalization and Family Unity:
United States Citizenship and
Immigration Services
P.O. Box 7219
Chicago, IL 60680-7219

Special information:

- The national customer service telephone number is 800-375-5283. It is
  best to call for case status information.

- Since all applications are scanned, there
  should be no staples in any forms. Use
  paperclips and binder clips.

- Write full name and *A number* on the
  back of the photo with pencil or felt
  marker, as there is greater chance of

photos becoming separated during
scanning process.

- The above addresses are for initial filings only. All other correspondence
  should be mailed to:

  USCIS—NBC
  P.O. Box 648005
  Lee's Summit, MO 64064

- Changes of address: applicants and
  petitioners who have filed for benefits
  with the NBC should file a Form AR-
  11 with the USCIS address listed on the
  form and notify the NBC of the address
  change by either calling the National
  Customer Service Center toll-free at
  800-375-5283, or by writing the NBC
  at the address above.

Nebraska Service Center

Jurisdiction over Alaska, Colorado, Idaho, Illinois, Indiana, Iowa, Kansas, Michigan, Minnesota, Missouri, Montana, Nebraska, North Dakota, Ohio, Oregon, South Dakota, Utah, Washington, Wisconsin, and Wyoming.

Courier Delivery:
USCIS Nebraska Service Center
850 S Street (P.O. Box *insert correct box number*)
Lincoln, NE 68508 + 4 digit zip code

All applications should be sent to:
U.S. Department of Homeland Security
United States Citizenship and
Immigration Services
Nebraska Service Center
P.O. Box (*insert correct box number*)
Lincoln, NE (*insert correct zip code*)

General Correspondence:
P.O. Box 82521
Lincoln, NE 68501-2521

I-102:
P.O. Box 87102
Lincoln, NE 68501-7102

I-129:
P.O. Box 87129
Lincoln, NE 68501-7129

I-129 (Premium Processing):
P.O. Box 87103
Lincoln, NE 68501-7103

I-129F:
P.O. Box 87130
Lincoln, NE 68501-7130

I-130:
P.O. Box 87130
Lincoln, NE 68501-7130

I-131:
P.O. Box 87131
Lincoln, NE 68501-7131

I-140:
P.O. Box 87140
Lincoln, NE 68501-7140

I-290 (Appeals and Motions):
P.O. Box 87290
Lincoln, NE 68501-7290

I-360:
P.O. Box 87360
Lincoln, NE 68501-7360

N-400:
P.O. Box 87400
Lincoln, NE 68501-7400

I-485:
P.O. Box 87485
Lincoln, NE 68501-7485

I-539:
P.O. Box 87539
Lincoln, NE 68501-7539

I-589:
P.O. Box 87589
Lincoln, NE 68501-7589

I-694:
P.O. Box 87698
Lincoln, NE 68501-7698

I-730:
P.O. Box 87730
Lincoln, NE 68501-7730

I-751:
P.O. Box 87751
Lincoln, NE 68501-7751

I-765:
P.O. Box 87765
Lincoln, NE 68501-7765

I-817:
P.O. Box 87817
Lincoln, NE 68501-7817

I-821:
(ONLY for applicants from El Salvador,
Honduras, and Nicaragua; all other TPS
applicants file with the local USCIS offices)
P.O. Box 87821
Lincoln, NE 68501-7821

I-824:
P.O. Box 87824
Lincoln, NE 68501-7824
402-323-7830

Texas Service Center

Jurisdiction over Alabama, Arkansas, Florida,
Georgia, Kentucky, Louisiana, Mississippi,
New Mexico, North Carolina, Oklahoma,
South Carolina, Tennessee, and Texas.

General Correspondence:
USCIS TSC
P.O. Box 851488
Mesquite, TX 75185-1488

Courier Delivery:
USCIS TSC
4141 N. St. Augustine Rd.
Dallas, TX 75227

I-102, I-131, I-539, I-824:
USCIS TSC
P.O. Box 851182
Mesquite, TX 75185-1182

I-765:
USCIS TSC
P.O. Box 851041
Mesquite, TX 75185-1041

I-485:
USCIS TSC
P.O. Box 851804
Mesquite, TX 75185-1804

I-129:
USCIS TSC
P.O. Box 852211
Mesquite, TX 75185-2211

I-130:
USCIS TSC
P.O. Box 850919
Mesquite, TX 75185-0919

I-589:
USCIS TSC
P.O. Box 851892
Mesquite, TX 75185-1892

I-140, I-290 A&B, I-360, I-526, I-829:
USCIS TSC
P.O. Box 852135
Mesquite, TX 75185-2135

I-212, I-612, I-751:
USCIS TSC
P.O. Box 850965
Mesquite, TX 75185-0965

N-400:
USCIS TSC
P.O. Box 851204
Mesquite, TX 75185-1204

Attorney/Address Change:
USCUS TSC
P.O. Box 850891
Mesquite,TX 75185-0891

Motions & Appeals:
USCIS TSC
P.O. Box 852841
Mesquite,TX 75185-0891

Vermont Service Center

Jurisdiction over Connecticut, Delaware, District of Columbia, Maine,Maryland, Massachusetts, New Hampshire, New Jersey, New York, Pennsylvania, Puerto Rico, Rhode Island, Vermont, Virgin Islands,Virginia, and West Virginia.

All applications other than N-400s:
U.S. Department of Homeland Security
United States Citizenship and
Immigration Services
Vermont Service Center
75 Lower Welden Street
Saint Albans, VT 05479

N-400:
U.S. Department of Homeland Security
United States Citizenship and
Immigration Services
Vermont Service Center
75 Lower Welden Street
Saint Albans, VT 05479-9400
802-527-4913

APPENDIX C:
WEBSITES AND
CONTACT INFORMATION

United States Citizenship and Immigration Services (USCIS)

✪ *National Customer Service Center:* 800-375-5283

✪ *USCIS Forms Line:* 800-870-3676

✪ *FOIA inquiry (National Records Center):* 816-350-5570

✪ *Websites:*

www.uscis.gov
(home page)

www.uscis.gov/graphics/formsfee/forms
(forms, fees)

www.uscis.gov/graphics/fieldoffices/alphaa.htm
(local offices and service centers)

www.uscis.gov/graphics/services/factsheet/index.htm#eH
(helpful "How do I" series)

www.uscis.gov/graphics/howdoi/affsupp.htm#poverty
(poverty guidelines for affidavit of support form)

www.uscis.gov/graphics/lawsregs/handbook
(USCIS manuals)

https://egov.immigration.gov/graphics/cris/jsps
(processing times for service centers and local USCIS offices)

www.cdc.gov/ncidod/dq/pdf/ti-civil.pdf
(medical examination guidelines)

www.uscis.gov/graphics/exec/cs
(civil surgeon locator)

www.customs.ustreas.gov/xp/cgov/toolbox/contacts/deferred_
inspection/overview_deferred_inspection.xml
(deferred inspection overview)

www.sss.gov
(Selective Service info: 847-688-6888)

www.choicepoint.com
(obtain available personal background information)

www.fbi.gov/hq/cjisd/fprequest.htm
(request federal fingerprint record)

www.immigrationwatch.com
(useful case processing information)

Immigration Court (EOIR)

✪   *EOIR status line:* 800-898-7180

✪   *BIA:* 703-605-1007

✪   *Websites:*

www.usdoj.gov/eoir
(home page)

www.usdoj.gov/eoir/vll/libindex.html
(BIA Practice Manual, BIA decisions)

http://trac.syr.edu/immigration/reports
(asylum denial rates of each immigration judge)

www.usdoj.gov/eoir/efoia/foiafreq.htm
(asylum grant rates by country)

www.uscourts.gov
(links to federal courts, forms)

www.findlaw.com
(links to federal and state statutes)

Department of State (DOS)

✪ *Visa Bulletin* (recording): 202-663-1541

✪ *Websites:*

www.state.gov
(home page)

www.foia.state.gov
(reading room)

http://usembassy.state.gov
(links to all embassies and consulates)

http://travel.state.gov/visa/temp/wait/tempvisitors_wait.php
(nonimmigrant visa wait times for all embassies)

http://travel.state.gov/visa/visa_1750.html
(visa policy and procedures)

www.state.gov/g/drl/hr
(country reports)

www.dvlottery.state.gov
(diversity visa online registration)

Department of Labor (DOL)

✪ *Websites:*

http://workforcesecurity.doleta.gov/foreign/
(home page for foreign worker information)

www.flcdatacenter.com
(prevailing wage information)

www.onetcenter.org
(replacement for Dictionary of Occupational Titles)

www.cgfns.org
(credential evaluation for health workers)

www.bls.gov/oco
(Occupational Outlook Handbook)

www.bls.gov/soc/socguide.htm
(Standard Occupational Classification)

www.naics.com
(to obtain NAICS code for I-140)

http://www.sba.gov/starting_business/planning/
writingplan.html
(business plan models)

U.S. Congress

✪ *Websites:*

www.house.gov/judiciary/privimmpro.pdf
(rules on private bills)

www.senate.gov

Canadian Immigration

✪ *Websites:*

www.ci.gc.ca
(Canadian government's immigration site)

www.ci.gc.ca/english/skilled/assess/index.html
(qualification test)

Legal Assistance Organizations

✪ *Websites:*

www.usdoj.gov/eoir/probono/states.htm
(accredited legal assistance organizations)

www.nationalimmigrationproject.org
(National Immigration Project: referrals, domestic violence info,
useful links)

www.nationalimmigrationreform.org
(LIFE Act amnesty information)

http://nilc.org
(National Immigration Law Center)

Asylum Assistance

✪ *Websites:*

http://www.mihrc.org/probonoinfo.asp
(well-documented guide to asylum procedure)

www.state.gov/g/drl/hr
(State Department country reports)

www.state.gov/g/drl/rls/irf
(International Religious Freedom reports)

www.ind.homeoffice.gov.uk
(country reports)

www.unhchr.ch
(United Nations Human Rights Commission)

www.asylumlaw.org
(information for asylum seekers)

www.rferl.org
(Radio Free Europe)

www.amnesty.org
(Amnesty International)

www.hrw.org
(Human Rights Watch)

Government Benefit Programs

✪ *Food Stamps:* 800-221-5689

✪ *Asylee Benefits:* 800-354-0365

✪ *Websites:*

www.acf.hhs.gov
(Department of Health and Human Services—assistance programs)

www.servicelocator.org
(job assistance)

www.ssa.gov
(Social Security Administration)

www.fns.usda.gov
(WIC)

www.govspot.com
(links to state, federal, and foreign government sites)

APPENDIX D:
FEE CHART

NOTE: *The fees listed in the chart below became effective on October 26, 2005, and replace fees printed on applications, petitions, or any other printed material.*

Make checks or money orders payable to U.S. Citizenship and Immigration Services. Applications or petitions mailed, postmarked, or otherwise filed on or after this date require the new fee. If you fail to include the correct fee, your application or petition will be rejected by USCIS and you will not be accorded a filing date.

I-17............$230	**I-290B**.........$385	**I-829**.................$475
I-90............$190*	**I-360** $190	**N-300** $120
I-102..........$160	**1-485**.................**	**N-336** $265
I-129..........$190	**I-526** $408	**N-400** $330*
I-129F........$170	**I-539** $200	**N-410** $50
I-130..........$190	**I-600** $545*	**N-455** $90
I-131..........$170	**I-600A**........$545*	**N-470** $155
I-140..........$195	**I-601** $265	**N-565** $220
I-191..........$265	**I-612** $265	**N-600** $255
I-192..........$265	**1-751**..........$205	**N-644** $80
I-193..........$265	**I-765** $180	
I-212..........$265	**I-817** $200*	
I-246..........$155	**I-824** $200	

**I-485   under the age of 14 ......$225
            age 14 and older...........$325
            refugees............................no fee

Listed filing fee does not include the $70 biometric service fee.

APPENDIX E:
BLANK FORMS

You may tear out these forms and use them, but it will be best if you make copies first, in case you make a mistake. For additional information on these forms, go to the USCIS website at **www.uscis.gov.**

Table of Forms

Department of Homeland Security
U.S. Citizenship and Immigration Services

OMB #1615-0012; Expires 01/31/07

I-130, Petition for Alien Relative

DO NOT WRITE IN THIS BLOCK - FOR USCIS OFFICE ONLY

A#	Action Stamp	Fee Stamp

Section of Law/Visa Category
- ☐ 201(b) Spouse - IR-1/CR-1
- ☐ 201(b) Child - IR-2/CR-2
- ☐ 201(b) Parent - IR-5
- ☐ 203(a)(1) Unm. S or D - F1-1
- ☐ 203(a)(2)(A)Spouse - F2-1
- ☐ 203(a)(2)(A) Child - F2-2
- ☐ 203(a)(2)(B) Unm. S or D - F2-4
- ☐ 203(a)(3) Married S or D - F3-1
- ☐ 203(a)(4) Brother/Sister - F4-1

Petition was filed on: _____ (priority date)
- ☐ Personal Interview
- ☐ Pet. ☐ Ben. " A" File Reviewed
- ☐ Field Investigation
- ☐ 203(a)(2)(A) Resolved
- ☐ Previously Forwarded
- ☐ I-485 Filed Simultaneously
- ☐ 204(g) Resolved
- ☐ 203(g) Resolved

Remarks:

A. Relationship   You are the petitioner.   Your relative is the beneficiary.

1. I am filing this petition for my:	2. Are you related by adoption?	3. Did you gain permanent residence through adoption?
☐ Husband/Wife ☐ Parent ☐ Brother/Sister ☐ Child	☐ Yes ☐ No	☐ Yes ☐ No

B. Information about you

1. Name (Family name in CAPS)   (First)   (Middle)

2. Address (Number and Street)   **(Apt.No.)**

(Town or City)   (State/Country)   (Zip/Postal Code)

3. Place of Birth (Town or City)   (State/Country)

4. Date of Birth (mm/dd/yyyy)

5. Gender
☐ Male
☐ Female

6. Marital Status
☐ Married ☐ Single
☐ Widowed ☐ Divorced

7. Other Names Used (including maiden name)

8. Date and Place of Present Marriage (if married)

9. U.S. Social Security Number (if any)   **10. Alien Registration Number**

11. Name(s) of Prior Husband(s)/Wive(s)   **12. Date(s) Marriage(s) Ended**

13. If you are a U.S. citizen, complete the following:
My citizenship was acquired through (check one):
- ☐ Birth in the U.S.
- ☐ Naturalization. Give certificate number and date and place of issuance.

_____

- ☐ Parents. Have you obtained a certificate of citizenship in your own name?
  - ☐ Yes. Give certificate number, date and place of issuance. ☐ No

14a. If you are a lawful permanent resident alien, complete the
following: Date and place of admission for or adjustment to lawful
permanent residence and class of admission.

14b. Did you gain permanent resident status through marriage to a
U.S. citizen or lawful permanent resident?
☐ Yes   ☐ No

C. Information about your relative

1. Name (Family name in CAPS)   (First)   (Middle)

2. Address (Number and Street)   **(Apt. No.)**

(Town or City)   (State/Country)   (Zip/Postal Code)

3. Place of Birth (Town or City)   (State/Country)

4. Date of Birth (mm/dd/yyyy)

5. Gender
☐ Male
☐ Female

6. Marital Status
☐ Married ☐ Single
☐ Widowed ☐ Divorced

7. Other Names Used (including maiden name)

8. Date and Place of Present Marriage (if married)

9. U. S. Social Security Number (if any)   **10. Alien Registration Number**

11. Name(s) of Prior Husband(s)/Wive(s)   **12. Date(s) Marriage(s) Ended**

13. Has your relative ever been in the U.S.?   ☐ Yes   ☐ No

14. If your relative is currently in the U.S., complete the following:
He or she arrived as a::
(visitor, student, stowaway, without inspection, etc.)

Arrival/Departure Record (I-94)   **Date arrived** (mm/dd/yyyy)

| | | | ▬ | | | | | | | |

Date authorized stay expired, or will expire,
as shown on Form I-94 or I-95

15. Name and address of present employer (if any)

Date this employment began (mm/dd/yyyy)

16. Has your relative ever been under immigration proceedings?
☐ No ☐ Yes Where _____ When _____
☐ Removal ☐ Exclusion/Deportation ☐ Recission ☐ Judicial Proceedings

INITIAL RECEIPT   RESUBMITTED   RELOCATED: Rec'd _____   Sent _____   COMPLETED: Appv'd _____   Denied _____   Ret'd _____

C. Information about your alien relative (continued)

17. List husband/wife and all children of your relative.

(Name)	(Relationship)	(Date of Birth)	(Country of Birth)

18. Address in the United States where your relative intends to live.
(Street Address)　　　　　　　　　　(Town or City)　　　　　　　(State)

19. Your relative's address abroad. (Include street, city, province and country)

Phone Number (if any)

20. If your relative's native alphabet is other than Roman letters, write his or her name and foreign address in the native alphabet.
(Name)　　　　　　　Address (Include street, city, province and country):

21. If filing for your husband/wife, give last address at which you lived together. (Include street, city, province, if any, and country):

From: (Month) (Year)　　To: (Month) (Year)

22. Complete the information below if your relative is in the United States and will apply for adjustment of status.
Your relative is in the United States and will apply for adjustment of status to that of a lawful permanent resident at the USCIS office in:
_____. If your relative is not eligible for adjustment of status, he or she
(City)　　(State)
will apply for a visa abroad at the American consular post in _____
(City)　　　　　(Country)

NOTE: Designation of an American embassy or consulate outside the country of your relative's last residence does not guarantee acceptance for processing by that post. Acceptance is at the discretion of the designated embassy or consulate.

D. Other information

1. If separate petitions are also being submitted for other relatives, give names of each and relationship.

2. Have you ever before filed a petition for this or any other alien? ☐ Yes ☐ No
If "Yes," give name, place and date of filing and result.

WARNING: USCIS investigates claimed relationships and verifies the validity of documents. USCIS seeks criminal prosecutions when family relationships are falsified to obtain visas.

PENALTIES: By law, you may be imprisoned for not more than five years or fined $250,000, or both, for entering into a marriage contract for the purpose of evading any provision of the immigration laws. In addition, you may be fined up to $10,000 and imprisoned for up to five years, or both, for knowingly and willfully falsifying or concealing a material fact or using any false document in submitting this petition.

YOUR CERTIFICATION: I certify, under penalty of perjury under the laws of the United States of America, that the foregoing is true and correct. Furthermore, I authorize the release of any information from my records that the U.S. Citizenship and Immigration Services needs to determine eligibility for the benefit that I am seeking.

E. Signature of petitioner.

Date　　Phone Number ( )

F. Signature of person preparing this form, if other than the petitioner.

I declare that I prepared this document at the request of the person above and that it is based on all information of which I have any knowledge.

Print Name _____　　Signature _____　　Date _____

Address _____　　G-28 ID or VOLAG Number, if any. _____

Department of Homeland Security
U. S. Citizenship and Immigration Services

OMB No. 1615-0013; Expires 11/30/07

I-131, Application for Travel Document

DO NOT WRITE IN THIS BLOCK	FOR USCIS USE ONLY (except G-28 block below)

Document Issued
☐ Reentry Permit
☐ Refugee Travel Document
☐ Single Advance Parole
☐ Multiple Advance Parole
  Valid to: _____

If Reentry Permit or Refugee Travel Document, mail to:
☐ Address in Part 1
☐ American embassy/consulate
  at: _____
☐ Overseas DHS office
  at: _____

Action Block

Receipt

☐ Document Hand Delivered
  On _____ By _____

To be completed by Attorney/Representative, if any.
Attorney State License # _____
☐ Check box if G-28 is attached.

Part 1.   Information about you. *(Please type or print in black ink.)*

1. A #

2. Date of Birth *(mm/dd/yyyy)*

3. Class of Admission

4. Gender
Male ☐   Female ☐

5. Name *(Family name in capital letters)*   *(First)*   *(Middle)*

6. Address *(Number and Street)*   Apt. #

City   State or Province   Zip/Postal Code   Country

7. Country of Birth

8. Country of Citizenship

9. Social Security # *(if any.)*

Part 2.   Application type *(check one).*

a. ☐ I am a permanent resident or conditional resident of the United States and I am applying for a reentry permit.

b. ☐ I now hold U.S. refugee or asylee status and I am applying for a refugee travel document.

c. ☐ I am a permanent resident as a direct result of refugee or asylee status and I am applying for a refugee travel document.

d. ☐ I am applying for an advance parole document to allow me to return to the United States after temporary foreign travel.

e. ☐ I am outside the United States and I am applying for an advance parole document.

f. ☐ I am applying for an advance parole document for a person who is outside the United States. *If you checked box "f", provide the following information about that person:*

1. Name *(Family name in capital letters)*   *(First)*   *(Middle)*

2. Date of Birth *(mm/dd/yyyy)*

3. Country of Birth

4. Country of Citizenship

5. Address *(Number and Street)*   Apt. #   Daytime Telephone # *(area/country code)*

City   State or Province   Zip/Postal Code   Country

INITIAL RECEIPT _____ RESUBMITTED _____ RELOCATED: Rec'd. _____ Sent _____ COMPLETED: Appv'd. _____ Denied _____ Ret'd. _____

Form I-131 (Rev. 10/26/05) Y

Part 3. Processing information.

1. Date of Intended Departure *(mm/dd/yyyy)*

2. Expected Length of Trip

3. Are you, or any person included in this application, now in exclusion, deportation, removal or recission proceedings?   ☐ No   ☐ Yes *(Name of DHS office)*:

If you are applying for an Advance Parole Document, skip to Part 7.

4. Have you ever before been issued a reentry permit or refugee travel *for the last document issued to you)*:   ☐ No   ☐ Yes *(Give the following information*

Date Issued *(mm/dd/yyyy)*:   Disposition *(attached, lost, etc.)*:

5. Where do you want this travel document sent? *(Check one)*

a. ☐ To the U.S. address shown in **Part 1** on the first page of this form.

b. ☐ To an American embassy or consulate at: City: Country:

c. ☐ To a DHS office overseas at: City: Country:

d. If you checked "b" or "c", where should the notice to pick up the travel document be sent?

☐ To the address shown in **Part 2** on the first page of this form.

☐ To the address shown below:

Address *(Number and Street)*   Apt. #   Daytime Telephone # *(area/country code)*

City   State or Province   Zip/Postal Code   Country

Part 4. Information about your proposed travel.

Purpose of trip. *If you need more room, continue on a seperate sheet(s) of paper.*	List the countries you intend to visit.

Part 5. Complete only if applying for a reentry permit.

Since becoming a permanent resident of the United States (or during the past five years, whichever is less) how much total time have you spent outside the United States?

☐ less than six months   ☐ two to three years
☐ six months to one year   ☐ three to four years
☐ one to two years   ☐ more than four years

Since you became a permanent resident of the United States, have you ever filed a federal income tax return as a nonresident, or failed to file a federal income tax return because you considered yourself to be a nonresident? *(If "Yes," give details on a separate sheet(s) of paper.)*   ☐ Yes   ☐ No

Part 6. Complete only if applying for a refugee travel document.

1. Country from which you are a refugee or asylee:

If you answer "Yes" to any of the following questions, you must explain on a separate sheet(s) of paper.

2. Do you plan to travel to the above named country?   ☐ Yes   ☐ No

3. Since you were accorded refugee/asylee status, have you ever:

a. returned to the above named country?   ☐ Yes   ☐ No

b. applied for and/or obtained a national passport, passport renewal or entry permit of that country?   ☐ Yes   ☐ No

c. applied for and/or received any benefit from such country (for example, health insurance benefits).   ☐ Yes   ☐ No

4. Since you were accorded refugee/asylee status, have you, by any legal procedure or voluntary act:

a. reacquired the nationality of the above named country?   ☐ Yes   ☐ No

b. acquired a new nationality?   ☐ Yes   ☐ No

c. been granted refugee or asylee status in any other country?   ☐ Yes   ☐ No

Form I-131 (Rev. 10/26/05) Y Page 2

Part 7. Complete only if applying for advance parole.

On a separate sheet(s) of paper, please explain how you qualify for an advance parole document and what circumstances warrant issuance of advance parole. Include copies of any documents you wish considered. *(See instructions.)*

1. For how many trips do you intend to use this document? ☐ One trip ☐ More than one trip

2. If the person intended to receive an advance parole document is outside the United States, provide the location (city and country) of the American embassy or consulate or the DHS overseas office that you want us to notify.

City

Country

3. If the travel document will be delivered to an overseas office, where should the notice to pick up the document be sent:

☐ To the address shown in **Part 2** on the first page of this form.

☐ To the address shown below:

Address *(Number and Street)*

Apt. #

Daytime Telephone # *(area/country code)*

City

State or Province

Zip/Postal Code

Country

Part 8. Signature. *Read the information on penalties in the instructions before completing this section. If you are filing for a reentry permit or refugee travel document, you must be in the United States to file this application.*

I certify, under penalty of perjury under the laws of the United States of America, that this application and the evidence submitted with it are all true and correct. I authorize the release of any information from my records that the U.S. Citizenship and Immigration Services needs to determine eligibility for the benefit I am seeking.

Signature

Date *(mm/dd/yyyy)*

Daytime Telephone Number *(with area code)*

Please Note: If you do not completely fill out this form or fail to submit required documents listed in the instructions, you may not be found eligible for the requested document and this application may be denied.

Part 9. Signature of person preparing form, if other than the applicant. *(Sign below.)*

I declare that I prepared this application at the request of the applicant and it is based on all information of which I have knowledge.

Signature

Print or Type Your Name

Firm Name and Address

Daytime Telephone Number *(with area code)*

Fax Number *(if any.)*

Date *(mm/dd/yyyy)*

This page intentionally left blank.

Department of Homeland Security
U.S. Citizenship and Immigration Services

OMB No. 1615-0015; Exp. 06-30-06

I-140, Immigrant Petition for Alien Worker

START HERE - Please type or print in black ink.

Part 1. **Information about the person or organization filing this petition.** If an individual is filing, use the top name line. Organizations should use the second line.

Family Name (Last Name)

Given Name (First Name)

Full Middle Name

Company or Organization Name

Address: (Street Number and Name)

Suite #

Attn:

City

State/Province

Country

Zip/Postal Code

IRS Tax #

U.S. Social Security # *(if any)*

E-Mail Address *(if any)*

For USCIS Use Only	
Returned	Receipt
Date	
Date	
Resubmitted	
Date	
Date	
Reloc Sent	
Date	
Date	
Reloc Rec'd	
Date	
Date	

Part 2. Petition type.

This petition is being filed for: *(Check one.)*

a. ☐ An alien of extraordinary ability.

b. ☐ An outstanding professor or researcher.

c. ☐ A multinational executive or manager.

d. ☐ A member of the professions holding an advanced degree or an alien of exceptional ability (who is NOT seeking a National Interest Waiver).

e. ☐ A professional (at a minimum, possessing a bachelor's degree or a foreign degree equivalent to a U.S. bachelor's degree) or a skilled worker (requiring at least two years of specialized training or experience).

f. ☐ (Reserved.)

g. ☐ Any other worker (requiring less than two years of training or experience).

h. ☐ Soviet Scientist.

i. ☐ An alien applying for a National Interest Waiver (who **IS** a member of the professions holding an advanced degree or an alien of exceptional ability).

Classification:
☐ 203(b)(1)(A) Alien of Extraordinary Ability
☐ 203(b)(1)(B) Outstanding Professor or Researcher
☐ 203(b)(1)(C) Multi-National Executive or Manager
☐ 203(b)(2) Member of Professions w/Adv. Degree or Exceptional Ability
☐ 203(b)(3)(A)(i) Skilled Worker
☐ 203(b)(3)(A)(ii) Professional
☐ 203(b)(3)(A)(iii) Other Worker

Certification:
☐ National Interest Waiver (NIW)
☐ Schedule A, Group I
☐ Schedule A, Group II

Priority Date	Consulate

Concurrent Filing:

☐ **I-485 filed concurrently.**

Remarks

Action Block

Part 3. Information about the person you are filing for.

Family Name (Last Name)

Given Name (First Name)

Full Middle Name

Address: (Street Number and Name)

Apt. #

C/O: (In Care Of)

City

State/Province

Country

Zip/Postal Code

E-Mail Address *(if any)*

Daytime Phone # *(with area/country codes)*

Date of Birth *(mm/dd/yyyy)*

City/Town/Village of Birth

State/Province of Birth

Country of Birth

Country of Nationality/Citizenship

A # *(if any)*

U.S. Social Security # *(if any)*

If in the U.S.

Date of Arrival *(mm/dd/yyyy)*

I-94 # *(Arrival/Departure Document)*

Current Nonimmigrant Status

Date Status Expires *(mm/dd/yyyy)*

To Be Completed by
Attorney or Representative, if any.
☐ Fill in box if G-28 is attached to represent the applicant.

ATTY State License #

Form I-140 (Rev. 04/01/06)Y

Part 4.   Processing Information.

1. Please complete the following for the person named in **Part 3**: *(Check one)*

☐ Alien will apply for a visa abroad at the American Embassy or Consulate at:

City | Foreign Country

☐ Alien is in the United States and will apply for adjustment of status to that of lawful permanent resident.
Alien's country of current residence or, if now in the U.S., last permanent residence abroad.

2. If you provided a U.S. address in **Part 3**, print the person's foreign address:

3. If the person's native alphabet is other than Roman letters, write the person's foreign name and address in the native alphabet:

4. Are any other petition(s) or application(s) being filed with this Form I-140?

☐ No   ☐ Yes-(check all that apply)   ☐ Form I-485   ☐ Form I-765
☐ Form I-131   ☐ Other - Attach an explanation.

5. Is the person you are filing for in removal proceedings?   ☐ No   ☐ Yes-Attach an explanation.

6. Has any immigrant visa petition ever been filed by or on behalf of this person?   ☐ No   ☐ Yes-Attach an explanation.

If you answered yes to any of these questions, please provide the case number, office location, date of decision and disposition of the decision on a separate sheet(s) of paper.

Part 5.   Additional information about the petitioner.

1. Type of petitioner *(Check one.)*

☐ Employer   ☐ Self   ☐ Other (Explain, e.g., Permanent Resident, U.S. citizen or any other person filing on behalf of the alien.)

2. If a company, give the following:

Type of Business | Date Established *(mm/dd/yyyy)* | Current Number of Employees

Gross Annual Income | Net Annual Income | NAICS Code

DOL/ETA Case Number

3. If an individual, give the following:

Occupation | Annual Income

Part 6.   Basic information about the proposed employment.

1. Job Title | **2.** SOC Code

3. Nontechnical Description of Job

4. Address where the person will work if different from address in **Part 1**.

5. Is this a full-time position?   ☐ Yes ☐ No | **6.** If the answer to **Number 5** is "No," how many hours per week for the position?

7. Is this a permanent position?   ☐ Yes ☐ No | **8.** Is this a new position?   ☐ Yes ☐ No | **9.** Wages per week $

Part 7. Information on spouse and all children of the person for whom you are filing.

List husband/wife and all children related to the individual for whom the petition is being filed. Provide an attachment of additional family members, if needed.

Name *(First/Middle/Last)*	Relationship	Date of Birth *(mm/dd/yyyy)*	Country of Birth

Part 8. Signature.
*Read the information on penalties in the instructions before completing this section. If someone helped you prepare this petition, he or she must complete **Part 9**.*

I certify, under penalty of perjury under the laws of the United States of America, that this petition and the evidence submitted with it are all true and correct. I authorize U.S. Citizenship and Immigration Services to release to other government agencies any information from my USCIS (or former INS) records, if USCIS determines that such action is necessary to determine eligibility for the benefit sought.

Petitioner's Signature   **Daytime Phone Number** *(Area/Country Codes)*   **E-Mail Address**

Print Name   **Date** *(mm/dd/yyyy)*

NOTE: *If you do not fully complete this form or fail to submit the required documents listed in the instructions, a final decision on your petition may be delayed or the petition may be denied.*

Part 9. Signature of person preparing form, if other than above. *(Sign below.)*

I declare that I prepared this petition at the request of the above person and it is based on all information of which I have knowledge.

Attorney or Representative: In the event of a Request for Evidence (RFE), may the USCIS contact you by Fax or E-mail? ☐ Yes ☐ No

Signature   **Print Name**   **Date** *(mm/dd/yyyy)*

Firm Name and Address

Daytime Phone Number *(Area/Country Codes)*   **Fax Number** *(Area/Country Codes)*   **E-Mail Address**

This page intentionally left blank.

Department of Homeland Security
U.S. Citizenship and Immigration Services

OMB No. 1615-0008

G-325A, Biographic Information

(Family name)	(First name)	(Middle name)	☐ Male ☐ Female	Birthdate (mm/dd/yyyy)	Citizenship/Nationality	File Number A

All Other Names Used (Including names by previous marriages)	City and Country of Birth	U.S. Social Security # *(If any)*

	Family Name	First Name	Date, City and Country of Birth (If Known)	City and Country of Residence
Father				
Mother (Maiden name)				

Husband (If none, so state) or Wife	Family Name (For wife, give maiden name)	First Name	Birthdate	City and Country of Birth	Date of Marriage	Place of Marriage

Former Husbands or Wives(if none, so state) Family Name (For wife, give maiden name)	First Name	Birthdate	Date and Place of Marriage	Date and Place of Termination of Marriage

Applicant's residence last five years. List present address first.

Street and Number	City	Province or State	Country	From Month	From Year	To Month	To Year
						Present Time	

Applicant's last address outside the United States of more than one year.

Street and Number	City	Province or State	Country	From Month	From Year	To Month	To Year

Applicant's employment last five years. (If none, so state.) List present employment first.

Full Name and Address of Employer	Occupation (Specify)	From Month	From Year	To Month	To Year
				Present Time	

Show below last occupation abroad if not shown above. (Include all information requested above.)

This form is submitted in connection with application for: ☐ Naturalization ☐ Status as Permanent Resident ☐ Other (Specify):	Signature of Applicant	Date

Submit all copies of this form.	If your native alphabet is in other than Roman letters, write your name in your native alphabet below:

Penalties: Severe penalties are provided by law for knowingly and willfully falsifying or concealing a material fact.

Applicant: Be sure to put your name and Alien Registration Number in the box outlined by heavy border below.

Complete This Box (Family Name)	(Given Name)	(Middle Name)	(Alien Registration Number)

(1) Ident.

Form G-325A (Rev. 05/31/05)N (Prior editions may be used until 12/31/05)

This page intentionally left blank.

OMB No. 1615-0020; Expires 06/30/06

I-360, Petition for Amerasian, Widow(er) or Special Immigrant

Department of Homeland Security
U.S. Citizenship and Immigration Services

START HERE - Please type or print in black ink.	For USCIS Use Only

Part 1. Information about person or organization filing this petition.

(Individuals should use the top name line; organizations should use the second line.) If you are a self-petitioning spouse or child and do not want USCIS to send notices about this petition to your home, you may show an alternate mailing address here. If you are filing for yourself and do not want to use an alternate mailing address, skip to part 2.

For USCIS Use Only:
- Returned
- Receipt
- Resubmitted
- Reloc Sent
- Reloc Rec'd
- Petitioner/Applicant Interviewed
- Beneficiary Interviewed
- I-485 Filed Concurrently
- Bene "A" File Reviewed
- Classification
- Consulate
- Priority Date
- Remarks:

Family Name / Given Name / Middle Name

Company or Organization Name

Address - C/O

Street Number and Name / Apt. #

City / State or Province

Country / Zip/Postal Code

U.S. Social Security # / A # / IRS Tax # (if any)

Part 2. Classification Requested (check one):

a. ☐ Amerasian
b. ☐ Widow(er) of a U.S. citizen who died within the past two (2) years
c. ☐ Special Immigrant Juvenile
d. ☐ Special Immigrant Religious Worker
e. ☐ Special Immigrant based on employment with the Panama Canal Company, Canal Zone Government or U.S. Government in the Canal Zone
f. ☐ Special Immigrant Physician
g. ☐ Special Immigrant International Organization Employee or family member
h. ☐ Special Immigrant Armed Forces Member
i. ☐ Self-Petitioning Spouse of Abusive U.S. Citizen or Lawful Permanent Resident
j. ☐ Self-Petitioning Child of Abusive U.S. Citizen or Lawful Permanent Resident
k. ☐ Other, explain: _____

Part 3. Information about the person this petition is for.

Family Name / Given Name / Middle Name

Address - C/O

Street Number and Name / Apt. #

City / State or Province

Country / Zip/Postal Code

Date of Birth (mm/dd/yyyy) / Country of Birth

U.S. Social Security # / A # (if any)

Marital Status: ☐ Single ☐ Married ☐ Divorced ☐ Widowed

Complete the items below if this person is in the United States:

Date of Arrival (mm/dd/yyyy) / I-94#

Current Nonimmigrant Status / Expires on (mm/dd/yyyy)

Action Block

To Be Completed by
☐ *Attorney or Representative,* if any
Fill in box if G-28 is attached to represent the applicant

VOLAG#

ATTY State License #

Part 4. Processing Information.

Below give information on U.S. Consulate you want notified if this petition is approved and if any requested adjustment of status cannot be granted.

American Consulate: City	Country

If you gave a United States address in **Part 3**, print the person's foreign address below. If his or her native alphabet does not use Roman letters, print his or her name and foreign address in the native alphabet.

Name	Address

Gender of the person this petition is for.	☐ Male	☐ Female
Are you filing any other petitions or applications with this one?	☐ No	☐ Yes (How many? _____)
Is the person this petition is for in deportation or removal proceedings?	☐ No	☐ Yes (Explain on a separate sheet of paper)
Has the person this petition is for ever worked in the U.S. without permission?	☐ No	☐ Yes (Explain on a separate sheet of paper)
Is an application for adjustment of status attached to this petition?	☐ No	☐ Yes

Part 5. Complete only if filing for an Amerasian.

Section A. Information about the mother of the Amerasian

Family Name	Given Name	Middle Name

Living? ☐ No (Give date of death _____) ☐ Yes (complete address line below) ☐ Unknown (attach a full explanation)

Address

Section B. Information about the father of the Amerasian: If possible, attach a notarized statement from the father regarding parentage. Explain on separate paper any question you cannot fully answer in the space provided on this form.

Family Name	Given Name	Middle Name
Date of Birth *(mm/dd/yyyy)*	Country of Birth	

Living? ☐ No (give date of death _____) ☐ Yes (complete address line below) ☐ Unknown (attach a full explanation)

Home Address

Home Phone # ( )	Work Phone # ( )

At the time the Amerasian was conceived:

The father was in the military (indicate branch of service below - and give service number here): _____

☐ Army ☐ Air Force ☐ Navy ☐ Marine Corps ☐ Coast Guard

☐ The father was a civilian employed abroad. Attach a list of names and addresses of organizations which employed him at that time.

☐ The father was not in the military, and was not a civilian employed abroad. (Attach a full explanation of the circumstances.)

Part 6. Complete only if filing for a Special Immigrant Juvenile Court Dependent.

Section A. Information about the Juvenile

List any other names used.

Answer the following questions regarding the person this petition is for. If you answer "No," explain on a separate sheet of paper.

Is he or she still dependent upon the juvenile court or still legally committed to or under the custody of an agency or department of a state? ☐ No ☐ Yes

Does he or she continue to be eligible for long term foster care? ☐ No ☐ Yes

Part 7. Complete only if filing as a Widow/Widower, a Self-petitioning Spouse of an Abuser, or as a Self-petitioning Child of an Abuser.

Section A. Information about the U.S. citizen husband or wife who died or about the U.S. citizen or lawful permanent resident abuser.

Family Name	Given Name	Middle Name

Date of Birth *(mm/dd/yyyy)*	Country of Birth	Date of Death *(mm/dd/yyyy)*

He or she is now, or was at time of death a (check one):

☐ U.S. citizen through Naturalization *(Show A #)* _____

☐ U.S. citizen born in the United States.

☐ U.S. lawful permanent resident (Show A #) _____

☐ U.S. citizen born abroad to U.S. citizen parents.

☐ Other, explain _____

Section B. Additional Information about you.

How many times have you been married?	How many times was the person in Section A married?	Give the date and place where you and the person in Section A were married. *(If you are a self-petitioning child, write: "N/A")*

When did you live with the person named in **Section A**? From *(Month/Year)* _____ until *(Month/Year)* _____

If you are filing as a widow/widower, were you legally separated at the time of the U.S citizens's death? ☐ No ☐ Yes, *(attach explanation).*

Give the last address at which you lived together with the person named in **Section A**, and show the last date that you lived together with that person at that address:

If you are filing as a self-petitioning spouse, have any of your children filed separate self-petitions? ☐ No ☐ Yes *(show child(ren)'s full names):*

Part 8. Information about the spouse and children of the person this petition is for.

A widow/widower or a self-petitioning spouse of an abusive citizen or lawful permanent resident should also list the children of the deceased spouse or of the abuser.

A. Family Name	Given Name	Middle Name	Date of Birth *(mm/dd/yyyy)*
Country of Birth	Relationship ☐ Spouse ☐ Child		A #
B. Family Name	Given Name	Middle Name	Date of Birth *(mm/dd/yyyy)*
Country of Birth	Relationship ☐ Child		A #
C. Family Name	Given Name	Middle Name	Date of Birth *(mm/dd/yyyy)*
Country of Birth	Relationship ☐ Child		A #
D. Family Name	Given Name	Middle Name	Date of Birth *(mm/dd/yyyy)*
Country of Birth	Relationship ☐ Child		A #
E. Family Name	Given Name	Middle Name	Date of Birth *(mm/dd/yyyy)*
Country of Birth	Relationship ☐ Child		A #
F. Family Name	Given Name	Middle Name	Date of Birth *(mm/dd/yyyy)*
Country of Birth	Relationship ☐ Child		A #

Part 8. Information about the spouse and children of the person this petition is for. (Continued.)

G. Family Name	Given Name	Middle Name	Date of Birth *(mm/dd/yyyy)*
Country of Birth	Relationship ☐ Child		A #
H. Family Name	Given Name	Middle Name	Date of Birth *(mm/dd/yyyy)*
Country of Birth	Relationship ☐ Child		A #

Part 9. Signature.

Read the information on penalties in the instructions before completing this part. If you are going to file this petition at a USCIS office in the United States, sign below. If you are going to file it at a U.S. consulate or USCIS office overseas, sign in front of a USCIS or consular official.

I certify, or, if outside the United States, I swear or affirm, under penalty of perjury under the laws of the United States of America, that this petition and the evidence submitted with it is all true and correct. If filing this on behalf at an organization, I certify that I am empowered to do so by that organization. I authorize the release of any information from my records, or from the petitioning organization's records, that the U.S. Citizenship and Immigration Services needs to determine eligibility for the benefit being sought.

Signature	Date

Signature of USCIS or Consular Official	Print Name	Date

NOTE: If you do not completely fill out this petition or fail to submit required documents listed in the instructions, the person(s) filed for may not be found eligible for a requested benefit and the petition may be denied.

Part 10. Signature of person preparing form, if other than above. (Sign below.)

I declare that I prepared this application at the request of the above person and it is based on all information of which I have knowledge.

Signature	Print Your Name	Date

Firm Name
and Address

OMB No. 1615-0023; Expires 09/30/08

Department of Homeland Security
U.S. Citizenship and Immigration Services

I-485, Application to Register
Permanent Residence or Adjust Status

START HERE - Please type or print in black ink.

Part 1.   Information about you.

Family Name	Given Name	Middle Name

Address- C/O

Street Number and Name		Apt. #

City

State	Zip Code

Date of Birth *(mm/dd/yyyy)*	Country of Birth:
	Country of Citizenship/Nationality:

U.S. Social Security #	A # *(if any)*

Date of Last Arrival *(mm/dd/yyyy)*	I-94 #

Current USCIS Status	Expires on *(mm/dd/yyyy)*

For USCIS Use Only

Returned	Receipt
Resubmitted	
Reloc Sent	
Reloc Rec'd	
Applicant Interviewed	

Section of Law
- [ ] Sec. 209(b), INA
- [ ] Sec. 13, Act of 9/11/57
- [ ] Sec. 245, INA
- [ ] Sec. 249, INA
- [ ] Sec. 1 Act of 11/2/66
- [ ] Sec. 2 Act of 11/2/66
- [ ] Other

Country Chargeable

Eligibility Under Sec. 245
- [ ] Approved Visa Petition
- [ ] Dependent of Principal Alien
- [ ] Special Immigrant
- [ ] Other

Preference

Action Block

Part 2.   Application type. *(Check one.)*

I am applying for an adjustment to permanent resident status because:

a. [ ] an immigrant petition giving me an immediately available immigrant visa number has been approved. (Attach a copy of the approval notice, or a relative, special immigrant juvenile or special immigrant military visa petition filed with this application that will give you an immediately available visa number, if approved.)

b. [ ] my spouse or parent applied for adjustment of status or was granted lawful permanent residence in an immigrant visa category that allows derivative status for spouses and children.

c. [ ] I entered as a K-1 fiancé(e) of a United States citizen whom I married within 90 days of entry, or I am the K-2 child of such a fiancé(e). (Attach a copy of the fiancé(e) petition approval notice and the marriage certificate).

d. [ ] I was granted asylum or derivative asylum status as the spouse or child of a person granted asylum and am eligible for adjustment.

e. [ ] I am a native or citizen of Cuba admitted or paroled into the United States after January 1, 1959, and thereafter have been physically present in the United States for at least one year.

f. [ ] I am the husband, wife or minor unmarried child of a Cuban described above in (e) and I am residing with that person, and was admitted or paroled into the United States after January 1, 1959, and thereafter have been physically present in the United States for at least one year.

g. [ ] I have continuously resided in the United States since before January 1, 1972.

h. [ ] Other basis of eligibility. Explain. If additional space is needed, use a separate piece of paper.

I am already a permanent resident and am applying to have the date I was granted permanent residence adjusted to the date I originally arrived in the United States as a nonimmigrant or parolee, or as of May 2, 1964, whichever date is later, and: *(Check one.)*

i. [ ] I am a native or citizen of Cuba and meet the description in (e) above.

j. [ ] I am the husband, wife or minor unmarried child of a Cuban, and meet the description in (f) above.

To be Completed by
***Attorney or Representative*, if any**
[ ] Fill in box if G-28 is attached to represent the applicant.

VOLAG #

ATTY State License #

Form I-485 (Rev. 04/01/06)Y

Part 3. Processing information.

A. City/Town/Village of Birth | Current Occupation

Your Mother's First Name | Your Father's First Name

Give your name exactly as it appears on your Arrival/Departure Record (Form I-94)

Place of Last Entry Into the United States *(City/State)* | In what status did you last enter? *(Visitor, student, exchange alien, crewman, temporary worker, without inspection, etc.)*

Were you inspected by a U.S. Immigration Officer? ☐ Yes ☐ No

Nonimmigrant Visa Number | Consulate Where Visa Was Issued

Date Visa Was Issued (mm/dd/yyyy) | Gender: ☐ Male ☐ Female | Marital Status: ☐ Married ☐ Single ☐ Divorced ☐ Widowed

Have you ever before applied for permanent resident status in the U.S.? ☐ No ☐ Yes. If you checked "Yes," give date and place of filing and final disposition.

B. List your present husband/wife, all of your sons and daughters (If you have none, write "none." If additional space is needed, use separate paper).

Family Name	Given Name	Middle Initial	Date of Birth *(mm/dd/yyyy)*
Country of Birth	Relationship	A #	Applying with you? ☐ Yes ☐ No
Family Name	Given Name	Middle Initial	Date of Birth *(mm/dd/yyyy)*
Country of Birth	Relationship	A #	Applying with you? ☐ Yes ☐ No
Family Name	Given Name	Middle Initial	Date of Birth *(mm/dd/yyyy)*
Country of Birth	Relationship	A #	Applying with you? ☐ Yes ☐ No
Family Name	Given Name	Middle Initial	Date of Birth *(mm/dd/yyyy)*
Country of Birth	Relationship	A #	Applying with you? ☐ Yes ☐ No
Family Name	Given Name	Middle Initial	Date of Birth *(mm/dd/yyyy)*
Country of Birth	Relationship	A #	Applying with you? ☐ Yes ☐ No

C. List your present and past membership in or affiliation with every organization, association, fund, foundation, party, club, society or similar group in the United States or in other places since your 16th birthday. Include any foreign military service in this part. If none, write "none." Include the name(s) of organization(s), location(s), dates of membership, from and to, and the nature of the organization(s). If additional space is needed, use a separate piece of paper.

Part 3. Processing information. *(Continued)*

Please answer the following questions. (If your answer is **"Yes"** on any one of these questions, explain on a separate piece of paper. Answering **"Yes"** does not necessarily mean that you are not entitled to adjust status or register for permanent residence.)

1. Have you ever, in or outside the United States:

    a. knowingly committed any crime of moral turpitude or a drug-related offense for which you have not been arrested? ☐ Yes ☐ No

    b. been arrested, cited, charged, indicted, fined or imprisoned for breaking or violating any law or ordinance, excluding traffic violations? ☐ Yes ☐ No

    c. been the beneficiary of a pardon, amnesty, rehabilitation decree, other act of clemency or similar action? ☐ Yes ☐ No

    d. exercised diplomatic immunity to avoid prosecution for a criminal offense in the United States? ☐ Yes ☐ No

2. Have you received public assistance in the United States from any source, including the United States government or any state, county, city or municipality (other than emergency medical treatment), or are you likely to receive public assistance in the future? ☐ Yes ☐ No

3. Have you ever:

    a. within the past ten years been a prostitute or procured anyone for prostitution, or intend to engage in such activities in the future? ☐ Yes ☐ No

    b. engaged in any unlawful commercialized vice, including, but not limited to, illegal gambling? ☐ Yes ☐ No

    c. knowingly encouraged, induced, assisted, abetted or aided any alien to try to enter the United States illegally? ☐ Yes ☐ No

    d. illicitly trafficked in any controlled substance, or knowingly assisted, abetted or colluded in the illicit trafficking of any controlled substance? ☐ Yes ☐ No

4. Have you ever engaged in, conspired to engage in, or do you intend to engage in, or have you ever solicited membership or funds for, or have you through any means ever assisted or provided any type of material support to any person or organization that has ever engaged or conspired to engage in sabotage, kidnapping, political assassination, hijacking or any other form of terrorist activity? ☐ Yes ☐ No

5. Do you intend to engage in the United States in:

    a. espionage? ☐ Yes ☐ No

    b. any activity a purpose of which is opposition to, or the control or overthrow of, the government of the United States, by force, violence or other unlawful means? ☐ Yes ☐ No

    c. any activity to violate or evade any law prohibiting the export from the United States of goods, technology or sensitive information? ☐ Yes ☐ No

6. Have you ever been a member of, or in any way affiliated with, the Communist Party or any other totalitarian party? ☐ Yes ☐ No

7. Did you, during the period from March 23, 1933 to May 8, 1945, in association with either the Nazi Government of Germany or any organization or government associated or allied with the Nazi Government of Germany, ever order, incite, assist or otherwise participate in the persecution of any person because of race, religion, national orgin or political opinion? ☐ Yes ☐ No

8. Have you ever engaged in genocide, or otherwise ordered, incited, assisted or otherwise participated in the killing of any person because of race, religion, nationality, ethnic origin or political opinion? ☐ Yes ☐ No

9. Have you ever been deported from the United States, or removed from the United States at government expense, excluded within the past year, or are you now in exclusion, deportation, removal or recission proceedings? ☐ Yes ☐ No

10. Are you under a final order of civil penalty for violating section 274C of the Immigration and Nationality Act for use of fraudulent documents or have you, by fraud or willful misrepresentation of a material fact, ever sought to procure, or procured, a visa, other documentation, entry into the United States or any immigration benefit? ☐ Yes ☐ No

11. Have you ever left the United States to avoid being drafted into the U.S. Armed Forces? ☐ Yes ☐ No

12. Have you ever been a J nonimmigrant exchange visitor who was subject to the two-year foreign residence requirement and have not yet complied with that requirement or obtained a waiver? ☐ Yes ☐ No

13. Are you now withholding custody of a U.S. citizen child outside the United States from a person granted custody of the child? ☐ Yes ☐ No

14. Do you plan to practice polygamy in the United States? ☐ Yes ☐ No

Part 4. Signature.

(Read the information on penalties in the instructions before completing this section. You must file this application while in the United States.)

Your registration with U.S. Citizenship and Immigration Services.

"I understand and acknowledge that, under section 262 of the Immigration and Nationality Act (Act), as an alien who has been or will be in the United States for more than 30 days, I am required to register with U.S. Citizenship and Immigration Services. I understand and acknowledge that, under section 265 of the Act, I am required to provide USCIS with my current address and written notice of any change of address within **ten** days of the change. I understand and acknowledge that USCIS will use the most recent address that I provide to USCIS, on any form containing these acknowledgements, for all purposes, including the service of a Notice to Appear should it be necessary for USCIS to initiate removal proceedings against me. I understand and acknowledge that if I change my address without providing written notice to USCIS, I will be held responsible for any communications sent to me at the most recent address that I provided to USCIS. I further understand and acknowledge that, if removal proceedings are initiated against me and I fail to attend any hearing, including an initial hearing based on service of the Notice to Appear at the most recent address that I provided to USCIS or as otherwise provided by law, I may be ordered removed in my absence, arrested and removed from the United States."

Selective Service Registration.

The following applies to you if you are a male at least 18 years old, but not yet 26 years old, who is required to register with the Selective Service System: "I understand that my filing this adjustment of status application with U.S. Citizenship and Immigration Services authorizes USCIS to provide certain registration information to the Selective Service System in accordance with the Military Selective Service Act. Upon USCIS acceptance of my application, I authorize USCIS to transmit to the Selective Service System my name, current address, Social Security Number, date of birth and the date I filed the application for the purpose of recording my Selective Service registration as of the filing date. If, however, USCIS does not accept my application, I further understand that, if so required, I am responsible for registering with the Selective Service by other means, provided I have not yet reached age 26."

Applicant's Certification.

I certify, under penalty of perjury under the laws of the United States of America, that this application and the evidence submitted with it is all true and correct. I authorize the release of any information from my records that U.S. Citizenship and Immigration Services (USCIS) needs to determine eligibility for the benefit I am seeking.

Signature	*Print Your Name*	*Date*	*Daytime Phone Number*
			( )

NOTE: *If you do not completely fill out this form or fail to submit required documents listed in the instructions, you may not be found eligible for the requested document and this application may be denied.*

Part 5. Signature of person preparing form, if other than above. (sign below)

I declare that I prepared this application at the request of the above person and it is based on all information of which I have knowledge.

Signature	*Print Your Full Name*	*Date*	**Phone Number** *(Include Area Code)*
			( )

Firm Name and Address   *E-Mail Address (if any)*

OMB No. 1615-0023; Expires 09/30/08

Department of Homeland Security
U.S. Citizenship Immigration and Service

Supplement A to Form I-485
Adjustment of Status Under Section 245(i)

NOTE: Use this form only if you are applying to adjust status to that of a lawful permanent resident under section 245(i) of the Immigration and Nationality Act.

Part A. Information about you.	For USCIS Use Only

Last Name | First Name | Middle Name

Action Block

Address: In Care Of

Street Number and Name   Apt. #

City   State   Zip Code

Alien Registration Number (A #) if any   Date of Birth *(mm/dd/yyyy)*

Country of Birth   Country of Citizenship/Nationality

Telephone Number   E-Mail Address, if any

( )

Part B. Eligibility. *(Check the correct response.)*

1. I am filing Supplement A to Form I-485 because:

 a. ☐ I am the beneficiary of a visa petition filed on or before January 14, 1998.

 b. ☐ I am the beneficiary of a visa petition filed on or after January 15, 1998, and on or before April 30, 2001.

 c. ☐ I am the beneficiary of an application for a labor certification filed on or before January 14, 1998.

 d. ☐ I am the beneficiary of an application for a labor certification filed on or after January 15, 1998, and on or before April 30, 2001.

 If you checked box b or d in Question 1, you must submit evidence demonstrating that you were physically present in the United States on December 21, 2000.

2. And I fall into one or more of these categories: *(Check all that apply to you.)*

 a. ☐ I entered the United States as an alien crewman;

 b. ☐ I have accepted employment without authorization;

 c. ☐ I am in unlawful immigration status because I entered the United States without inspection or I remained in the United States past the expiration of the period of my lawful admission;

 d. ☐ I have failed (except through no fault of my own or for technical reasons) to maintain, continuously, lawful status;

 e. ☐ I was admitted to the United States in transit without a visa;

 f. ☐ I was admitted as a nonimmigrant visitor without a visa;

 g. ☐ I was admitted to the United States as a nonimmigrant in the S classification; or

 h. ☐ I am seeking employment-based adjustment of status and am not in lawful nonimmigrant status.

Part C. Additional eligibility information.

1. Are you applying to adjust status based on any of the below reasons?

 a. You were granted asylum in the United States;

 b. You have continuously resided in the United States since January 1, 1972;

 c. You entered as a K-1 fiancé(e) of a U.S. citizen;

 d. You have an approved Form I-360, Petition for Amerasian, Widow(er), Battered or Abused Spouse or Child, or Special Immigrant, and are applying for adjustment as a special immigrant juvenile court dependent or a special immigrant who has served in the U.S. armed forces, or a battered or abused spouse or child;

 e. You are a native or citizen of Cuba, or the spouse or child of such alien, who was not lawfully inspected or admitted to the United States;

 f. You are a special immigrant retired international organization employee or family member;

 g. You are a special immigrant physician;

  Form I-485 Supplement A (Rev. 10/26/05) Y

Part C. Additional eligibility information. *(Continued.)*

h. You are a public interest parolee, who was denied refugee status, and are from the former Soviet Union, Vietnam, Laos or Cambodia (a "Lautenberg Parolee" under Public Law 101-167); or

i. You are eligible under the Immigration Nursing Relief Act.

☐ **No.** I am not applying for adjustment of status for any of these reasons. *(Go to next question.)*

☐ **Yes.** I am applying for adjustment of status for any one of these reasons. **(If you answered "Yes," do not file this form.)**

2. Do any of the following conditions describe you?

    a. You are already a lawful permanent resident of the United States.

    b. You have continuously maintained lawful immigration status in the United States since November 5, 1986.

    c. You are applying to adjust status as the spouse or unmarried minor child of a U.S. citizen or the parent of a U.S. citizen child at least 21 years of age, and you were inspected and lawfully admitted to the United States.

    ☐ **No.** None of these conditions describe me. *(Go to next question.)*

    ☐ **Yes.** If you answered "Yes," do not file this form.

Part D. Signature. *Read the information on penalties in the instructions before completing this section.*

I certify, under penalty of perjury under the laws of the United States of America, that this application and the evidence submitted with it is all true and correct. I authorize the release of any information from my records that the U.S. Citizenship and Immigration Services needs to determine eligibility for the benefit being sought.

Signature	Print Name	Date

Part E. Signature of person preparing form, if other than above. *Read the information on penalties in the instructions before completing this section.*

I certify, under penalty of perjury under the laws of the United States of America, that I prepared this form at the request of the above person and that to the best of my knowledge the contents of this application are all true and correct.

Signature	Print Name	Date

Firm Name and Address

Daytime Phone Number *(Area Code and Number)*

(   )

E-Mail Address, if any

U.S. Department of Homeland Security
Bureau of Citizenship and Immigration Services

U.S. Department of Justice
Executive Office for Immigration Review

OMB No. 1615-0067; Expires 11/30/06

Application for Asylum and for Withholding of Removal

Start Here - Please Type or Print. **USE BLACK INK. SEE THE SEPARATE INSTRUCTION PAMPHLET FOR INFORMATION ABOUT ELIGIBILITY AND HOW TO COMPLETE AND FILE THIS APPLICATION.** (Note: There is NO filing fee for this application.)

Please check the box if you also want to apply for withholding of removal under the Convention Against Torture. ☐

PART A. I. INFORMATION ABOUT YOU

1. Alien Registration Number(s)(A#'s)*(If any)*	2. Social Security No. *(If any)*
3. Complete Last Name	4. First Name	5. Middle Name

6. What other names have you used? *(Include maiden name and aliases.)*

7. Residence in the U.S. C/O	Telephone Number
Street Number and Name	Apt. No.
City State	ZIP Code

8. Mailing Address in the U.S., if other than above	Telephone Number
Street Number and Name	Apt. No.
City State	ZIP Code

9. Sex ☐ Male ☐ Female   10. Marital Status: ☐ Single ☐ Married ☐ Divorced ☐ Widowed

11. Date of Birth *(Mo/Day/Yr)*   12. City and Country of Birth

13. Present Nationality *(Citizenship)*   14. Nationality at Birth   15. Race, Ethnic or Tribal Group   16. Religion

17. *Check the box, a through c that applies:*   a. ☐ I have never been in immigration court proceedings.
b. ☐ I am now in immigration court proceedings.   c. ☐ I am **not** now in immigration court proceedings, but I have been in the past.

18. *Complete 18 a through c.*
a. When did you last leave your country? *(Mo/Day/Yr)* _____   b. What is your current I-94 Number, if any? _____

c. Please list each entry to the U.S. beginning with your most recent entry.
List date (Mo/Day/Yr), place, and your status for each entry. (Attach additional sheets as needed.)

Date _____ Place _____ Status _____ Date Status Expires _____
Date _____ Place _____ Status _____
Date _____ Place _____ Status _____
Date _____ Place _____ Status _____

19. What country issued your last passport or travel document?	20. Passport # Travel Document #	21. Expiration Date *(Mo/Day/Yr)*
22. What is your native language?	23. Are you fluent in English? ☐ Yes ☐ No	24. What other languages do you speak fluently?

FOR EOIR USE ONLY	**FOR BCIS USE**
	Action: Interview Date: _____ **Decision:** __ Approval Date: _____ — Denial Date: _____ — Referral Date: _____ Asylum Officer ID# _____

Form I-589 (Rev. 07/03/03)Y

PART A. II. **INFORMATION ABOUT YOUR SPOUSE AND CHILDREN**

Your Spouse. ☐ I am not married. (Skip to *Your Children*, *below.*)

1. Alien Registration Number (A#) *(If any)*	2. Passport/ID Card No. *(If any)*	3. Date of Birth *(Mo/Day/Yr)*	4. Social Security No. *(If any)*
5. Complete Last Name	6. First Name	7. Middle Name	8. Maiden Name
9. Date of Marriage *(Mo/Day/Yr)*	10. Place of Marriage	11. City and Country of Birth	
12. Nationality *(Citizenship)*	13. Race, Ethnic or Tribal Group	14. Sex ☐ Male ☐ Female	

15. Is this person in the U.S.? ☐ Yes *(Complete blocks 16 to 24.)* ☐ No *(Specify location)*

16. Place of last entry in the U.S. ?	17. Date of last entry in the U.S. *(Mo/Day/Yr)*	18. I-94 No. *(If any)*	19. Status when last admitted *(Visa type, if any)*
20. What is your spouse's current status?	21. What is the expiration date of his/her authorized stay, if any? *(Mo/Day/Yr)*	22. Is your spouse in immigration court proceedings? ☐ Yes ☐ No	23. If previously in the U.S., date of previous arrival *(Mo/Day/Yr)*

24. If in the U.S., is your spouse to be included in this application? *(Check the appropriate box.)*

☐ Yes *(Attach one (1) photograph of your spouse in the upper right hand corner of page 9 on the extra copy of the application submitted for this person.)*
☐ No

Your Children. Please list **ALL** of your children, regardless of age, location, or marital status.

☐ I do not have any children. *(Skip to Part A. III., **Information about Your Background.**)*
☐ I do have children. Total number of children _____

(Use Supplement A Form I-589 or attach additional pages and documentation if you have more than four (4) children.)

1. Alien Registration Number (A#) *(If any)*	2. Passport/ID Card No. *(If any)*	3. Marital Status *(Married, Single, Divorced, Widowed)*	4. Social Security No. *(If any)*
5. Complete Last Name	6. First Name	7. Middle Name	8. Date of Birth *(Mo/Day/Yr)*
9. City and Country of Birth	10. Nationality *(Citizenship)*	11. Race, Ethnic or Tribal Group	12. Sex ☐ Male ☐ Female

13. Is this child in the U.S.? ☐ Yes *(Complete blocks 14 to 21.)* ☐ No *(Specify Location)*

14. Place of last entry in the U.S.?	15. Date of last entry in the U.S.? *(Mo/Day/Yr)*	16. I-94 No. *(If any)*	17. Status when last admitted *(Visa type, if any)*
18. What is your child's current status?	19. What is the expiration date of his/her authorized stay, if any? *(Mo/Day/Yr)*	20. Is your child in immigration court proceedings? ☐ Yes ☐ No	

21. If in the U.S., is this child to be included in this application? *(Check the appropriate box.)*

☐ Yes *(Attach one (1) photograph of your child in the upper right hand corner of page 9 on the extra copy of the application submitted for this person.)*
☐ No

PART A. II. INFORMATION ABOUT YOUR SPOUSE AND CHILDREN Continued

1. Alien Registration Number (A#) *(If any)*	2. Passport/IDCard No. *(If any)*	3. Marital Status *(Married, Single, Divorced, Widowed)*	4. Social Security No. *(If any)*
5. Complete Last Name	6. First Name	7. Middle Name	8. Date of Birth *(Mo/Day/Yr)*
9. City and Country of Birth	10. Nationality *(Citizenship)*	11. Race, Ethnic or Tribal Group	12. Sex ☐ Male ☐ Female

13. Is this child in the U.S.? ☐ Yes *(Complete blocks 14 to 21.)* ☐ No *(Specify Location)*

14. Place of last entry in the U.S.?	15. Date of last entry in the U.S.? *(Mo/Day/Yr)*	16. I-94 No. *(If any)*	17. Status when last admitted *(Visa type, if any)*
18. What is your child's current status?	19. What is the expiration date of his/her authorized stay, *(if any)?* *(Mo/Day/Yr)*	20. Is your child in immigration court proceedings? ☐ Yes ☐ No	

21. If in the U.S., is this child to be included in this application? *(Check the appropriate box.)*
☐ Yes *(Attach one (1) photograph of your child in the upper right hand corner of page 9 on the extra copy of the application submitted for this person.)*
☐ No

1. Alien Registration Number (A#) *(If any)*	2. Passport/ID Card No.*(If any)*	3. Marital Status *(Married, Single, Divorced, Widowed)*	4. Social Security No. *(If any)*
5. Complete Last Name	6. First Name	7. Middle Name	8. Date of Birth *(Mo/Day/Yr)*
9. City and Country of Birth	10. Nationality *(Citizenship)*	11. Race, Ethnic or Tribal Group	12. Sex ☐ Male ☐ Female

13. Is this child in the U.S. ? ☐ Yes *(Complete blocks 14 to 21.)* ☐ No *(Specify Location)*

14. Place of last entry in the U.S.?	15. Date of last entry in the U.S.? *(Mo/Day/Yr)*	16. I-94 No. *(If any)*	17. Status when last admitted *(Visa type, if any)*
18. What is your child's current status?	19. What is the expiration date of his/her authorized stay, if any? *(Mo/Day/Yr)*	20. Is your child in immigration court proceedings? ☐ Yes ☐ No	

21. If in the U.S., is this child to be included in this application? *(Check the appropriate box.)*
☐ Yes *(Attach one (1) photograph of your child in the upper right hand corner of page 9 on the extra copy of the application submitted for this person.)*
☐ No

1. Alien Registration Number (A#) *(If any)*	2. Passport/ID Card No. *(If any)*	3. Marital Status *(Married, Single, Divorced, Widowed)*	4. Social Security No. *(If any)*
5. Complete Last Name	6. First Name	7. Middle Name	8. Date of Birth *(Mo/Day/Yr)*
9. City and Country of Birth	10. Nationality *(Citizenship)*	11. Race, Ethnic or Tribal Group	12. Sex ☐ Male ☐ Female

13. Is this child in the U.S.? ☐ Yes *(Complete blocks 14 to 21.)* ☐ No *(Specify Location)*

14. Place of last entry in the U.S.?	15. Date of last entry in the U.S.? *(Mo/Day/Yr)*	16. I-94 No. *(If any)*	17. Status when last admitted *(Visa type, if any)*
18. What is your child's current status?	19. What is the expiration date of his/her authorized stay, if any? *(Mo/Day/Yr)*	20. Is your child in immigration court proceedings? ☐ Yes ☐ No	

21. If in the U.S., is this child to be included in this application? *(Check the appropriate box.)*
☐ Yes *(Attach one (1) photograph of your child in the upper right hand corner of page 9 on the extra copy of the application submitted for this person.)*
☐ No

PART A. III.   INFORMATION ABOUT YOUR BACKGROUND

1. Please list your last address where you lived before coming to the U.S. If this is not the country where you fear persecution, also list the last address in the country where you fear persecution. *(List Address, City/Town, Department, Province, or State, and Country.) (Use Supplement B Form I-589 or additional sheets of paper if necessary.)*

Number and Street *(Provide if available)*	City/Town	Department, Province or State	Country	Dates From *(Mo/Yr)* To *(Mo/Yr)*

2. Provide the following information about your residences during the last five years. List your present address first. *(Use Supplement Form B or additional sheets of paper if necessary.)*

Number and Street	City/Town	Department, Province or State	Country	Dates From *(Mo/Yr)* To *(Mo/Yr)*

3. Provide the following information about your education, beginning with the most recent. *(Use Supplement B Form I-589 or additional sheets of paper if necessary.)*

Name of School	Type of School	Location (Address)	Attended From *(Mo/Yr)* To *(Mo/Yr)*

4. Provide the following information about your employment during the last five years. List your present employment first. *(Use Supplement Form B or additional sheets of paper if necessary.)*

Name and Address of Employer	Your Occupation	Dates From *(Mo/Yr)* To *(Mo/Yr)*

5. Provide the following information about your parents and siblings (brother and sisters). Check box if the person is deceased. *(Use Supplement B Form I-589 or additional sheets of paper if necessary.)*

Name	City/Town and Country of Birth	Current Location
Mother		☐ Deceased
Father		☐ Deceased
Siblings		☐ Deceased
		☐ Deceased

PART B.   INFORMATION ABOUT YOUR APPLICATION

(Use Supplement B Form I-589 or attach additional sheets of paper as needed to complete your responses to the questions contained in PART B.)

When answering the following questions about your asylum or other protection claim (withholding of removal under 241(b)(3) of the Act or withholding of removal under the Convention Against Torture) you should provide a detailed and specific account of the basis of your claim to asylum or other protection. To the best of your ability, provide specific dates, places, and descriptions about each event or action described. You should attach documents evidencing the general conditions in the country from which you are seeking asylum or other protection and the specific facts on which you are relying to support your claim. If this documentation is unavailable or you are not providing this documentation with your application, please explain why in your responses to the following questions. Refer to Instructions, Part 1: Filing Instructions, Section II, "Basis of Eligibility," Parts A - D, Section V, "Completing the Form," Part B, and Section VII, "Additional Documents that You Should Submit" for more information on completing this section of the form.

1.   Why are you applying for asylum or withholding of removal under section 241(b)(3) of the Act, or for withholding of removal under the Convention Against Torture? Check the appropriate box (es) below and then provide detailed answers to questions A and B below:

I am seeking asylum or withholding of removal based on

- ☐ Race
- ☐ Religion
- ☐ Nationality
- ☐ Political opinion
- ☐ Membership in a particular social group
- ☐ Torture Convention

A.   Have you, your family, or close friends or colleagues ever experienced harm or mistreatment or threats in the past by anyone?

☐ No ☐ Yes If your answer is "Yes," explain in detail:

1) What happened;
2) When the harm or mistreatment or threats occurred;
3) Who caused the harm or mistreatment or threats; and
4) Why you believe the harm or mistreatment or threats occurred.

B.   Do you fear harm or mistreatment if you return to your home country?

☐ No   ☐ Yes If your answer is "Yes," explain in detail:

1) What harm or mistreatment you fear;
2) Who you believe would harm or mistreat you; and
3) Why you believe you would or could be harmed or mistreated.

PART B.   INFORMATION ABOUT YOUR APPLICATION Continued

---

2. Have you or your family members ever been accused, charged, arrested, detained, interrogated, convicted and sentenced, or imprisoned in any country other than the United States?

☐ No   ☐ Yes If "Yes," explain the circumstances and reasons for the action.

3. A.   Have you or your family members ever belonged to or been associated with any organizations or groups in your home country, such as, but not limited to, a political party, student group, labor union, religious organization, military or paramilitary group, civil patrol, guerrilla organization, ethnic group, human rights group, or the press or media?

☐ No   ☐ Yes If "Yes," describe for each person the level of participation, any leadership or other positions held, and the length of time you or your family members were involved in each organization or activity.

B.   Do you or your family members continue to participate in any way in these organizations or groups?

☐ No   ☐ Yes If "Yes," describe for each person, your or your family members' current level of participation, any leadership or other positions currently held, and the length of time you or your family members have been involved in each organization or group.

4. Are you afraid of being subjected to torture in your home country or any other country to which you may be returned?

☐ No   ☐ Yes If "Yes," explain why you are afraid and describe the nature of the torture you fear, by whom, and why it would be inflicted.

PART C.   ADDITIONAL INFORMATION ABOUT YOUR APPLICATION

(Use Supplement B Form I-589 or attach additional sheets of paper as needed to complete your responses to the questions contained in Part C.)

1. Have you, your spouse, your child(ren), your parents, or your siblings ever applied to the United States Government for refugee status, asylum, or withholding of removal?   ☐ No ☐ Yes

    If "Yes" explain the decision and what happened to any status you, your spouse, your child(ren), your parents, or your siblings received as a result of that decision. Please indicate whether or not you were included in a parent or spouse's application. If so, please include your parent or spouse's A- number in your response. If you have been denied asylum by an Immigration Judge or the Board of Immigration Appeals, please describe any change(s) in conditions in your country or your own personal circumstances since the date of the denial that may affect your eligibility for asylum.

2. A. After leaving the country from which you are claiming asylum, did you or your spouse or child(ren), who are now in the United States, travel through or reside in any other country before entering the United States?   ☐ No   ☐ Yes

    B. Have you, your spouse, your child(ren), or other family members such as your parents or siblings ever applied for or received any lawful status in any country other than the one from which you are now claiming asylum?   ☐ No   ☐ Yes

    If "Yes" to either or both questions (2A and/or 2B), provide for each person the following: the name of each country and the length of stay; the person's status while there; the reasons for leaving; whether the person is entitled to return for lawful residence purposes; and whether the person applied for refugee status or for asylum while there, and, if not, why he or she did not do so.

3. Have you, your spouse, or child(ren) ever ordered, incited, assisted, or otherwise participated in causing harm or suffering to any person because of his or her race, religion, nationality, membership in a particular social group or belief in a particular political opinion?

    ☐ No   ☐ Yes If "Yes," describe in detail each such incident and your own or your spouse's or child(ren)'s involvement.

274 ◆

PART C.   ADDITIONAL INFORMATION ABOUT YOUR APPLICATION Continued

4.   After you left the country where you were harmed or fear harm, did you return to that country?

☐ No   ☐ Yes   If "Yes," describe in detail the circumstances of your visit (for example, the date(s) of the trip(s), the purpose(s) of the trip(s), and the length of time you remained in that country for the visit(s)).

5.   Are you filing the application more than one year after your last arrival in the United States?

☐No   ☐ Yes   If "Yes," explain why you did not file within the first year after you arrived.   You should be prepared to explain at your interview or hearing why you did not file your asylum application within the first year after you arrived. For guidance in answering this question, see Instructions, Part 1: Filing Instructions, Section V. "Completing the Form," Part C.

6.   Have you or any member of your family included in the application ever committed any crime and/or been arrested, charged, convicted and sentenced for any crimes in the United States?

☐   No   ☐   Yes If "Yes," for each instance, specify in your response what occurred and the circumstances; dates; length of sentence received; location; the duration of the detention or imprisonment; the reason(s) for the detention or conviction; any formal charges that were lodged against you or your relatives included in your application; the reason(s) for release. Attach documents referring to these incidents, if they are available, or an explanation of why documents are not available.

PART D.   YOUR SIGNATURE

After reading the information regarding penalties in the instructions, complete and sign below. If someone helped you prepare this application, he or she must complete Part E.

I certify, under penalty of perjury under the laws of the United States of America, that this application and the evidence submitted with it are all true and correct. Title 18, United States Code, Section 1546, provides in part: "Whoever knowingly makes under oath, or as permitted under penalty of perjury under Section 1746 of Title 28, United States Code, knowingly subscribes as true, any false statement with respect to a material fact in any application, affidavit, or knowingly presents any such application, affidavit, or other document required by the immigration laws or regulations prescribed thereunder, or knowingly presents any such application, affidavit, or other document containing any such false statement or which fails to contain any reasonable basis in law or fact - shall be fined in accordance with this title or imprisoned not more than five years, or both." I authorize the release of any information from my record which the Bureau of Citizenship and Immigration Services needs to determine eligibility for the benefit I am seeking.

Staple your photograph here or the photograph of the family member to be included on the extra copy of the application submitted for that person.

WARNING: **Applicants who are in the United States illegally are subject to removal if their asylum or withholding claims are not granted by an Asylum Officer or an Immigration Judge. Any information provided in completing this application may be used as a basis for the institution of, or as evidence in, removal proceedings even if the application is later withdrawn. Applicants determined to have knowingly made a frivolous application for asylum will be permanently ineligible for any benefits under the Immigration and Nationality Act. See 208(d)(6) of the Act and 8 CFR 208.20.**

Print Complete Name	Write your name in your native alphabet

Did your spouse, parent, or child(ren) assist you in completing this application? ☐ No ☐ Yes *(If "Yes," list the name and relationship.)*

_____   _____   _____   _____
(Name)   *(Relationship)*   *(Name)*   *(Relationship)*

Did someone other than your spouse, parent, or child(ren) prepare this application? ☐ No ☐ Yes *(If "Yes," complete Part E)*

Asylum applicants may be represented by counsel. Have you been provided with a list of persons who may be available to assist you, at little or no cost, with your asylum claim?   ☐ No   ☐ Yes

Signature of Applicant *(The person in Part A. I.)*

[_____]   _____
Sign your name so it all appears within the brackets   Date *(Mo/Day/Yr)*

PART E.   DECLARATION OF PERSON PREPARING FORM IF OTHER THAN APPLICANT, SPOUSE, PARENT OR CHILD

I declare that I have prepared this application at the request of the person named in Part D, that the responses provided are based on all information of which I have knowledge, or which was provided to me by the applicant and that the completed application was read to the applicant in his or her native language or a language he or she understands for verification before he or she signed the application in my presence. I am aware that the knowing placement of false information on the Form I-589 may also subject me to civil penalties under 8 U.S.C. 1324(c).

Signature of Preparer	Print Complete Name		
Daytime Telephone Number ( )	Address of Preparer: Street Number and Name		
Apt. No.	City	State	ZIP Code

PART F.   TO BE COMPLETED AT INTERVIEW OR HEARING

You will be asked to complete this Part when you appear before an Asylum Officer of the U.S. Department of Homeland Security, Bureau of Citizenship and Immigration Services (BCIS), or an Immigration Judge of the U.S. Department of Justice, Executive Office for Immigration Review (EOIR) for examination.

I swear (affirm) that I know the contents of this application that I am signing, including the attached documents and supplements, that they are all true to the best of my knowledge taking into account correction(s) numbered _____ to _____ that were made by me or at my request.

Signed and sworn to before me by the above named applicant on:

_____   _____
Signature of Applicant   Date *(Mo/Day/Yr)*

_____   _____
Write Your Name in Your Native Alphabet   Signature of Asylum Officer or Immigration Judge

This page intentionally left blank.

OMB No. 1615-0040; Expires 08/31/08

Department of Homeland Security
U.S. Citizenship and Immigration Services

I-765, Application for
Employment Authorization

Instructions

U.S. Citizenship and Immigration Services (USCIS) recommends that you retain a copy of your completed application for your records.
NOTE: USCIS is comprised of offices of the former Immigration and Naturalization Service (INS).

Index

Part 1. General.

Purpose of the Application. Certain aliens who are temporarily in the United States may file a Form I-765, Application for Employment Authorization, to request an Employment Authorization Document (EAD). Other aliens who are authorized to work in the United States without restrictions should also use this form to apply to USCIS for a document evidencing such authorization. Please review **Part 2: Eligibility Categories** to determine whether you should use this form.

If you are a Lawful Permanent Resident, a Conditional Resident, or a nonimmigrant authorized to be employed with a specific employer under 8 CFR 274a.12(b), please do **not** use this form.

Definitions

Employment Authorization Document (EAD): Form I-688, Form I-688A, Form I-688B, Form I-766, or any successor document issued by USCIS as evidence that the holder is authorized to work in the United States.

Renewal EAD: an EAD issued to an eligible applicant at or after the expiration of a previous EAD issued under the same category.

Replacement EAD: an EAD issued to an eligible applicant when the previously issued EAD has been lost, stolen, mutilated, or contains erroneous information, such as a misspelled name.

Interim EAD: an EAD issued to an eligible applicant when USCIS has failed to adjudicate an application within 90 days of receipt of a properly filed EAD application or within 30 days of a properly filed initial EAD application based on an asylum application filed on or after January 4, 1995. The interim EAD will be granted for a period not to exceed 240 days and is subject to the conditions noted on the document.

Part 2. Eligibility Categories.

The USCIS adjudicates a request for employment authorization by determining whether an applicant has submitted the required information and documentation, and whether the applicant is eligible. In order to determine your eligibility, you must identify the category in which you are eligible and fill in that category in **Question 16** on the Form I-765. Enter only **one** of the following category numbers on the application form. For example, if you are a refugee applying for an EAD, you should write **"(a)(3)"** at **Question 16**.

For easier reference, the categories are subdivided as follows:

Asylee/Refugee Categories.

Refugee--(a)(3). File your EAD application with either a copy of your Form I-590, Registration for Classification as Refugee, approval letter or a copy of a Form I-730, Refugee/Asylee Relative Petition, approval notice.

Paroled as a Refugee--(a)(4). File your EAD application with a copy of your Form I-94, Departure Record.

Asylee (granted asylum)--(a)(5). File your EAD application with a copy of the INS letter, or judge's decision, granting you asylum. It is not necessary to apply for an EAD as an asylee until 90 days before the expiration of your current EAD.

Asylum Applicant (with a pending asylum application) who Filed for Asylum on or after January 4, 1995--(c)(8). (For specific instructions for applicants with pending asylum claims, see page 5).

278 ◆

Nationality Categories.

Citizen of Micronesia, the Marshall Islands or Palau--(a)(8). File your EAD application if you were admitted to the United States as a citizen of the Federated States of Micronesia (CFA/FSM), the Marshall Islands (CFA/MIS), or Palau, pursuant to agreements between the United States and the former trust territories.

Deferred Enforced Departure (DED) / Extended Voluntary Departure--(a)(11). File your EAD application with evidence of your identity and nationality.

Temporary Protected Status (TPS)--(a)(12). File your EAD application with Form I-821, Application for Temporary Protected Status. If you are filing for an initial EAD based on your TPS status, include evidence of identity and nationality as required by the Form I-821 instructions.

Temporary treatment benefits --(c)(19). For an EAD based on 8 CFR 244.5. Include evidence of nationality and identity as required by the Form I-821 instructions.

* Extension of TPS status: Include a copy (front and back) of your last available TPS document: EAD, Form I-94 or approval notice.

* Registration for TPS only without employment authorization : File the Form I-765, Form I-821, and a letter indicating that this form is for registration purposes only. No fee is required for the Form I-765 filed as part of TPS registration. (Form I-821 has separate fee requirements.)

NACARA Section 203 Applicants who are eligible to apply for NACARA relief with INS--(c)(10). See the instructions to Form I-881, Application for Suspension of Deportation or Special Rule Cancellation of Removal, to determine if you are eligible to apply for NACARA 203 relief with USCIS.

If you are eligible, follow the instructions below and submit your Form I-765 at the same time you file your Form I-881 application with USCIS:

* If you are filing a Form I-881 with USCIS, file your EAD application at the same time and at the same filing location. Your response to **Question 16** on the Form I-765 should be **"(c)(10)."**

* If you have already filed your I-881 application at the service center specified on the Form I-881, and now wish to apply for employment authorization, your response to **Question 16** on Form I-765 should be **"(c)(10)."** You should file your EAD application at the Service Center designated in Part 5 of these instructions.

* If you are a NACARA Section 203 applicant who previously filed a Form I-881 with USCIS, and the application is still pending, you may renew your EAD. Your response to **Question 16** on Form I-765 should be **"(c)(10)."** Submit the required fee and the EAD application to the service center designated in Part 5 of these instructions.

Dependent of TECRO E-1 Nonimmigrant--(c)(2). File your EAD application with the required certification from the American Institute in Taiwan if you are the spouse, or unmarried dependent son or daughter of an E-1 employee of

Foreign Students.

F-1 Student Seeking Optional Practical Training in an Occupation Directly Related to Studies--(c)(3)(i). File your EAD application with a Certificate of Eligibility of Nonimmigrant (F-1) Student Status (Form I-20 A-B/I-20 ID) endorsed by a Designated School Official within the past 30 days.

F-1 Student Offered Off-Campus Employment under the Sponsorship of a Qualifying International Organization-- (c)(3)(ii). File your EAD application with the international organization's letter of certification that the proposed employment is within the scope of its sponsorship, and a Certificate of Eligibility of Nonimmigrant (F-1) Student Status--For Academic and Language Students (Form I-20 A-B/I-20 ID) endorsed by the Designated School Official within the past 30 days.

F-1 Student Seeking Off-Campus Employment Due to Severe Economic Hardship--(c)(3)(iii). File your EAD application with Form I-20 A-B/I-20 ID, Certificate of Eligibility of Nonimmigrant (F-1) Student Status--For Academic and Language Students, and any evidence you wish to submit, such as affidavits, that detail the unforeseen economic circumstances that cause your request, and evidence you have tried to find off-campus employment with an employer who has filed a labor and wage attestation.

J-2 Spouse or Minor Child of an Exchange Visitor--(c)(5). File your EAD application with a copy of your J-1's (principal alien's) Certificate of Eligibility for Exchange Visitor (J-1) Status (Form IAP-66). You must submit a written statement, with any supporting evidence showing, that your employment is not necessary to support the J-1 but is for other purposes.

M-1 Student Seeking Practical Training after Completing Studies--(c)(6). File your EAD application with a completed Form I-539, Application to Change/Extend Nonimmigrant Status. Form I-20 M-N, Certificate of Eligibility for Nonimmigrant (M-1) Student Status--For Vocational Students endorsed by the Designated School Official within the past 30 days.

Eligible Dependents of Employees of Diplomatic Missions, International Organizations or NATO.

Dependent of A-1 or A-2 Foreign Government Officials--(c)(1).

Submit your EAD application with Form I-566, Inter-Agency Record of Individual Requesting Change/Adjustment to, or from, A or G Status; or Requesting A, G, or NATO Dependent Employment Authorization, through your diplomatic mission to the Department of State (DOS). The DOS will forward all favorably endorsed applications directly to the Nebraska Service Center for adjudication.

Dependent of G-1, G-3 or G-4 Nonimmigrant--(c)(4).

Submit your EAD application with a Form I-566, Inter-Agency Record of Individual Requesting Change/Adjustment to or from A or G Status; or Requesting A, G, or NATO Dependent Employment Authorization, through your international organization to the Department of State (DOS). [In New York City, the United Nations (UN) and UN missions should submit such applications to the United States Mission to the UN (USUN).] The DOS or USUN will forward all favorably endorsed applications directly to the Nebraska Service Center for adjudication.

Dependent of NATO-1 through NATO-6--(c)(7).

Submit your EAD application with Form I-566, Inter-Agency Record of Individual Requesting Change/Adjustment to, or from, A or G Status; or Requesting A, G or NATO Dependent Employment Authorization, to NATO SACLANT, 7857 Blandy Road, C-027, Suite 100, Norfolk, VA 23551-2490. NATO/SACLANT will forward all favorably endorsed applications directly to the Nebraska Service Center for adjudication.

Employment-Based Nonimmigrant Categories.

B-1 Nonimmigrant who is the personal or domestic servant of a nonimmigrant employer--(c)(17)(i).

File your EAD application with:

- Evidence from your employer that he or she is a B, E, F, H, I, J, L, M, O, P, R, or TN nonimmigrant and you were employed for at least one year by the employer before the employer entered the United States or your employer regularly employs personal and domestic servants and has done so for a period of years before coming to the United States; and
- Evidence that you have either worked for this employer as a personal or domestic servant for at least one year or, evidence that you have at least one year's experience as a personal or domestic servant; and
- Evidence establishing that you have a residence abroad which you have no intention of abandoning.

B-1 Nonimmigrant Domestic Servant of a U.S. Citizen-- (c)(17)(ii).

File your EAD application with:

- Evidence from your employer that he or she is a U.S. citizen; and
- Evidence that your employer has a permanent home abroad or is stationed outside the United States and is temporarily visiting the United States or the citizen's current assignment in the United States will not be longer than four 4 years; and
- Evidence that he or she has employed you as a domestic servant abroad for at least six 6 months prior to your admission to the United States.

B-1 Nonimmigrant Employed by a Foreign Airline--(c)(17)(iii).

File your EAD application with a letter from the airline fully describing your duties and indicating that your position would entitle you to E nonimmigrant status except for the fact that you are not a national of the same country as the airline or because there is no treaty of commerce and navigation in effect between the United States and that country.

Spouse of an E-1/E-2 Treaty Trader or Investor--(a)(17).

File your EAD application with evidence of your lawful status and evidence you are a **spouse** of a principal E-1/E-2, such as your I-94. (Other relatives or dependents of E-1/E-2 aliens who are in E status are not eligible for employment authorization and may not file under this category.)

Spouse of an L-1 Intracompany Transferee--(a)(18).

File your EAD application with evidence of your lawful status and evidence you are a **spouse** of a principal L-1, such as your I-94. (Other relatives or dependents of L-1 aliens who are in L status are not eligible for employment authorization and may not file under this category.)

Family-Based Nonimmigrant Categories.

K-1 Nonimmigrant Fiance(e) of U.S. Citizen or K-2 Dependent--(a)(6).

File your EAD application if you are filing within 90 days from the date of entry. This EAD cannot be renewed. Any EAD application other than for a replacement must be based on your pending application for family-based adjustment under (c)(9).

K-3 Nonimmigrant Spouse of U.S. Citizen or K-4 Dependent--(a)(9).

File your EAD application along with evidence of your admission such as copies of your Form I-94, passport, and K visa.

Family Unity Program--(a)(13). File your EAD application with a copy of the approval notice, if you have been granted status under this program. You may choose to file your EAD application concurrently with your Form I-817, Application for Voluntary Departure under the Family Unity Program. USCIS may take up to 90 days from the date upon which you are granted status under the Family Unity Program to adjudicate your EAD application. If you were denied Family Unity status solely because your legalized spouse or parent first applied under the Legalization/SAW programs after May 5, 1988, file your EAD application with a new Form I-817 application and a copy of the original denial. However, if your EAD application is based on continuing eligibility under (c)(12), please refer to **Deportable Alien Granted Voluntary Departure.**

LIFE Family Unity--(a)(14). If you are applying for initial employment authorization pursuant to the Family Unity provisions of section 1504 of the LIFE Act Amendments, or an extension of such authorization, you should not be using this form. Please obtain and complete a Form I-817, Application for Family Unity Benefits. If you are applying for a replacement EAD that was issued pursuant to the LIFE Act Amendments Family Unity provisions, file your EAD application with the required evidence listed in **Part 3**.

V-1, V-2 or V-3 Nonimmigrant--(a)(15). If you have been inspected and admitted to the United States with a valid V visa, file this application along with evidence of your admission, such as copies of your Form I-94, passport, and K visa. If you have been granted V status while in the United States, file this application along with evidence of your V status, such as an approval notice. If you are in the United States but you have not yet filed an application for V status, you may file this application at the same time as you file your application for V status. USCIS will adjudicate this application after adjudicating your application for V status.

EAD Applicants Who Have Filed for Adjustment of Status.

Employment-Based Adjustment Applicant--(c)(9). File your EAD application with a copy of the receipt notice or other evidence that your Form I-485, application for permanent residence, is pending. If you have not yet filed your Form I-485, you may submit Form I-765 together with your Form I-485.

Family-Based Adjustment Application --(c)(9). File your EAD application with a clpy of the receipt notice other evidence that your Form I-485, application for permanent residence, is pending. You may file Form I-765 together with your Form I-485 is.

Adjustment Applicant Based on Continuous Residence Since January 1, 1972--(c)(16). File your EAD application with your Form I-485, Application for Permanent Residence; a copy of your receipt notice; or other evidence that the Form I-485 is pending.

Others.

N-8 or N-9 Nonimmigrant--(a)(7). File your EAD application with the required evidence listed in **Part 3**.

Granted Withholding of Deportation or Removal --(a)(10). File your EAD application with a copy of the Immigration Judge's order. It is not necessary to apply for a new EAD until 90 days before the expiration of your current EAD.

Applicant for Suspension of Deportation--(c)(10). File your EAD application with evidence that your Form I-881, Application for Suspension of Deportation, or EOIR-40, is pending

Paroled in the Public Interest--(c)(11). File your EAD application if you were paroled into the United States for emergent reasons or reasons strictly in the public interest.

Deferred Action--(c)(14). File your EAD application with a copy of the order, notice or document placing you in deferred action and evidence establishing economic necessity for an EAD.

Final Order of Deportation--(c)(18). File your EAD application with a copy of the order of supervision and a request for employment authorization which may be based on, but not limited to the following:
- Existence of a dependent spouse and/or children in the United States who rely on you for support; and
- Existence of economic necessity to be employed;
- Anticipated length of time before you can be removed from the United States.

LIFE Legalization applicant--(c)(24). We encourage you to file your EAD application together with your Form I-485, Application to Regsiter Permanent Residence or Adjust Status, to facilitate processing. However, you may file Form I-765 at a later date with evidence that you were a CSS, LULAC, or Zambrano class member applicant before October 1, 2000 and with a copy of the receipt notice or other evidence that your Form I-485 is pending.

T-1 Nonimmigrant--(a)(16). If you are applying for initial employment authorization as a T-1 nonimmigrant, file this form only if you did not request an employment authorization document when you applied for T nonimmigrant status. If you have been granted T status and this is a request for a renewal or replacement of an employment authorization document, file this application along with evidence of your T status, such as an approval notice.

T-2, T-3, or T-4 Nonimmigrant--(c)(25). File this form with a copy of your T-1's (principal alien's) approval notice and proof of your relationship to the T-1 principal.

Part 3. Required Documentation.

All applications must be filed with the documents required below, in addition to the particular evidence required for the category listed in **Part 2, Eligibility Categories**, with fee, if required.

If you are required to show economic necessity for your category (See **Part 2**), submit a list of your assets, income and expenses.

Please assemble the documents in the following order:

Your application with the filing fee. See **Part 4, Fee** for details.

If you are mailing your application to the USCIS, you must also submit:

- A copy of Form I-94 Departure Record (front and back), if available.

- A copy of your last EAD (front and back).

- Two passport-style color photos with a white background taken no earlier than 30 days before submission to USCIS. They should be unmounted, glossy and unretouched. The photos should show a full-frontal facial position. Your head should be bare unless you are wearing a headdress as required by a religious order to which you belong. The photo should not be larger than 2 x 2 inches, with the distance from the top of the head to just below the chin about 1 1/4 inches. Lightly print our name and your A#, if known, on the back of each photo with a pencil.

Special Filing Instructions for Those With Pending Asylum Applications (c)(8).

Asylum applicant (with a pending asylum application) who filed for asylum on or after January 4, 1995. *You must wait at leat 150 days following the filing of your asylum claim before you are eligible to apply for an EAD. If you file your EAD application early, it will be denied. File your EAD application with:*

- A copy of the USCIS acknowledgement mailer which was mailed to you; or

- Other evidence that your Form I-589 was filed with USCIS; or

- Evidence that your Form I-589 was filed with an Immigration Judge at the Executive Office for Immigration Review (EOIR); or

- Evidence that your asylum application remains under administrative or judicial review.

Asylum applicant (with a pending asylum application) who filed for asylum and for withholding of deportation prior to January 4, 1995 and is *NOT* in exclusion or deportation proceedings. You may file your EAD application at any time; however, it will only be granted if USCIS finds that your asylum application is not frivolous. File your EAD application with:

- A complete copy of your previously filed Form I-589;
  AND

- A copy of your USCIS receipt notice; or

- A copy of the USCIS acknowledgement mailer; or

- Evidence that your Form I-589 was filed with EOIR; or

- Evidence that your asylum application remains under administrative or judicial review; or

- Other evidence that you filed an asylum application.

Asylum applicant (with a pending asylum application) who filed an initial request for asylum prior to January 4, 1995, and IS IN exclusion or deportation proceedings. If you filed your Request for Asylum and Withholding of Deportation (Form I-589) prior to January 4, 1995 and you ARE IN exclusion or deportation proceedings, file your EAD application with:

- A date-stamped copy of your previously filed Form I-589; or

- A copy of Form I-221, Order to Show Cause and Notice of Hearing, or Form I-122, Notice to Applicant for Admission Detained for Hearing Before Immigration Judge; or

- A copy of EOIR-26, Notice of Appeal, date stamped by the Office of the Immigration Judge; or

- A date-stamped copy of a petition for judicial review or for *habeas corpus* issued to the asylum applicant; or

- Other evidence that you filed an asylum application with EOIR.

Asylum Application Under the ABC Settlement Agreement--(c)(8). If you are a Salvadoran or Guatemalan national eligible for benefits under the ABC settlement agreement, American Baptist Churches v. Thornburgh , 760 F. Supp. 976 (N.D. Cal. 1991), please follow the instructions contained in this section when filing your Form I-765.

You must have asylum application (Form I-589) on file either with USCIS or with an immigration judge in order to receive work authorization. Therefore, please submit evidence that you have previously filed an asylum application when you submit your EAD application. You are not required to submit this evidence when you apply, but it will help USCIS process your request efficiently.

If you are renewing or replacing your EAD, you must pay the filing fee.

Mark your application as follows:

- Write "ABC" in the top right corner of your EAD application. You must identify yourself as an ABC class member if you are applying for an EAD under the ABC settlement agreement.

- Write "(c)(8)" in **Section 16** of the application.

You are entitled to an EAD without regard to the merits of your asylum claim. Your application for an EAD will be decided within 60 days if: (1) you pay the filing fee, (2) you have a complete, pending asylum application on file, and (3) write "ABC" in the top right corner of your EAD application. If you do not pay the filing fee for an initial EAD request, your request may be denied if USCIS finds that your asylum application is frivolous. However, if you cannot pay the filing fee for an EAD, you may qualify for a fee waiver under 8 CFR 103.7(c). See **Part 4** concerning fee waivers.

Part 4. Fee.

What Is the Fee? Applicants must pay a fee of **$180.00** unless noted below.

If a fee is required, it will not be refunded. Pay in the exact amount. Checks and money orders must be payable in U.S. currency. Make check or money order payable to the **"Department of Homeland Security,"** unless:

If you live in Guam make your check or money order payable to "**Treasurer, Guam**." If you live in the U.S. Virgin Islands make your check or money order payable to **"Commissioner of Finance of the Virgin Islands."**

A charge of $30.00 will be imposed if a check in payment of a fee is not honored by the bank on which it is drawn. Please do **not** send cash in the mail.

Initial EAD: If this is your initial application and you are applying under one of the following categories, a filing fee is **not** required:

- (a)(3) Refugee;
- (a)(4) Paroled as Refugee;
- (a)(5) Asylee;
- (a)(7) N-8 or N-9 nonimmigrant;
- (a)(8) Citizen of Micronesia, Marshall Islands or Palau;
- (a)(10) Granted Withholding of Deportation;
- (a)(11) Deferred Enforced Departure;
- (a)(16) Victim of Severe Form of Trafficking (T-1);
- (c)(1), (c)(4), or (c)(7) Dependent of certain foreign government, international organization, or NATO personnel; or
- (c)(8) Applicant for asylum [an applicant filing under the special ABC procedures must pay the fee].

Renewal EAD: If this is a renewal application and you are applying under one of the following categories, a filing fee is **not** required:

- (a)(8) Citizen of Micronesia, Marshall Islands, or Palau;
- (a)(10) Granted Withholding of Deportation;
- (a)(11) Deferred Enforced Departure; or
- (c)(1), (c)(4), or (c)(7) Dependent of certain foreign government, international organization, or NATO personnel.

Replacement EAD: If this is your replacement application and you are applying under one of the following categories, *a* filing fee is **not** required:

- (c)(1), (c)(4), or (c)(7) Dependent of certain foreign government, international organization, or NATO personnel.

You may be eligible for a fee waiver under 8 CFR 103.7(c).

USCIS will use the Poverty Guidelines published annually by the Department of Health and Human Services as the basic criteria in determining the applicant's eligibility when economic necessity is identified as a factor.

The Poverty Guidelines will be used as a guide, but not as a conclusive standard, in adjudicating fee waiver requests for employment authorization applications requiring a fee.

How to Check If the Fee Is Correct: The fee on this form is current as of the edition date appearing in the lower right corner of this page. However, because USCIS fees change periodically, you can verify if the fee is correct by following one of the steps below:

- Visit our website at **www.uscis.gov** and scroll down to "Forms and E-Filing" to check the appropriate fee, or

- Review the Fee Schedule included in your form package, if you called us to request the form, or

- Telephone our National Customer Service Center at **1-800-375-5283** and ask for the fee information.

NOTE: If your application requires a biometric services fee for USCIS to take your fingerprints, photograph or signature, you can use the same procedure above to confirm the biometrics fee.

Part 5. Where to File.

If your response to **Question 16** is: **(a)(3), (a)(4), (a)(5), (a)(7)** or **(a)(8)** mail your application to:

USCIS Service Center
P.O. Box 87765
Lincoln, NE 68501-7765

If your response to **Question 16** is **(a)(9)**, mail your application to:

USCIS
P.O. Box 7218
Chicago, IL 60680-7218

If your response to **Question 16** is **(a)(15)**, mail your application to:

USCIS
P.O. Box 7216
Chicago, IL 60680-7216

If your response to **Question 16** is **(a)(14)** or **(c)(24)**, mail your application to:

USCIS
P.O. Box 7219
Chicago, IL 60680-7219

If your response to **Question 16** is: **(a)(16)** or **(c)(25)** mail your application to:

USCIS Service Center
75 Lower Welden St.
St. Albans, VT 05479-0001

If your response to **Question 16** is: **(a)(10), (c)(11), (c)(12), (c)(14), (c)(16)** or **(c)(18),** apply at the local USCIS office having jurisdiction over your place of residence.

If your response to **Question 16** is: **(a)(12)** or **(c)(19)**, file your EAD application according to the instructions in the Federal Register notice for your particular country's TPS designation.

If your response to **Question 16** is **(c)(1), (c)(4)** or **(c)(7)**, submit your application through your principal's sponsoring organization . Your application will be reviewed and forwarded by the DOS, USUN or NATO/SACLANT to the Nebraska Service Center following certification of your eligibility for an EAD.

If your response to **Question 16** is **(c)(8)** under the special ABC filing instructions and you are filing your asylum and EAD applications together, mail your application to the office where you are filing your asylum application.

If your response to **Question 16** is **(c)(9), employment-based adjustment**, file your application as follows:

Concurrent Forms I-765/I-140/I-485 Filings:

* If you are filing your Form I-765 together with a Forms I-140 (Petition for Alien Worker)/I-485 package, submit the entire package of the three forms to:

> **USCIS Service Center**
> P.O. Box 87485
> Lincoln, NE 68501-7485

Concurrent Forms I-765/I-485 Fillings:

* If your Form I-140 petition is pending or has already been approved, file your Forms I-485/I-765 package with the service center where the Form I-140 is pending or approved. Include the Form I-140 receipt or approval notice.

Form I-765 Filed Alone:

* If your employment-based Form I-485 is pending, file your Form I-765 at the same Service Center currently processing your Form I-485. Include a copy of your receipt notice.

* In all other cases if your response to **Question 16** is **(c)(9)**, file your Form I-765 according to the instructions noted on the "Direct Mail Instructions for Persons Filing Form I-765" that are included with the Form I-765 on our website at **www. uscis.gov** under "Forms and E-Filing."

If your response to **Question 16** is:
(a)(6), (a)(11), (a)(13), (a)(17), (a)(18), (c)(2), (c)(3)(i), (c)(3)(ii), (c)(3)(iii), (c)(5), (c)(6), (c)(8),(c)(17)(i), (c)(17)(ii) or (c)(17)(iii): mail your application based on your address to the appropriate **Service Center**. The correct **Service Center** is based on the state or territory in which you live.

If you live in:		Mail your application to:
Connecticut D.C. Maryland New Hampshire New York Puerto Rico Vermont West Virginia	Delaware Maine Massachusetts New Jersey Pennsylvania Rhode Island Virginia U.S.V.I.	**USCIS Service Center** 75 Lower Welden Street St. Albans, VT 05479-0001
Arizona Guam Nevada	California Hawaii	**USCIS Service Center** P.O. Box 10765 Laguna Niguel, CA 92067-1076
Alabama Florida Kentucky Mississippi North Carolina South Carolina Texas	Arkansas Georgia Lousiana New Mexico Oklahoma Tennessee	**USCIS Service Center** P.O. Box 851041 Mesquite, TX 75185-1041
Alaska Idaho Indiana Kansas Minnesota Montana North Dakota Oregon Utah Wisconsin	Colorado Illinois Iowa Michigan Missouri Nebraska Ohio South Dakota Washington Wyoming	**USCIS Service Center** P.O. Box 87765 Lincoln, NE 68501-7765

* If your response to **Question 16** is **(c)(10)**, and you are a NACARA 203 applicant eligible to apply for relief with USCIS, or if your Form I-881 application is still pending with USCIS and you wish to renew your EAD, mail your EAD application with the required fee to the appropriate USCIS service center below:

If you live in Alabama, Arkansas, Colorado, Connecticut, Delaware, the District of Columbia, Florida, Georgia, Louisiana, Maine, Maryland, Massachusetts, Mississippi, New Hampshire, New Jersey, New Mexico, New York, North Carolina, Oklahoma, Pennsylvania, Puerto Rico, Rhode Island, South Carolina, Tennessee, Texas, Utah, the U.S. Virgin Islands, Vermont, Virginia, West Virginia or Wyoming, mail your application to:

> **USCIS Service Center**
> 75 Lower Welden St.
> St. Albans, VT 05479-0001

• If you live in Alaska, Arizona, California, the Commonwealth of Guam, Hawaii, Idaho, Illinois, Indiana, Iowa, Kansas, Kentucky, Michigan, Minnesota, Missouri, Montana, Nebraska, Nevada, North Dakota, Oregon, Ohio, South Dakota, Washington, or Wisconsin, mail your application to:

USCIS Service Center
P.O. Box 10765
Laguna Niguel, CA 92067-1076

You should submit the fee for the EAD application on a separate check or money order. Do not combine your check or money order with the fee for the Form I-881.

If your response to **Question 16 is (c)(10) and you are not eligible to apply for NACARA 203 relief with USCIS,** but you are eligible for other deportation or removal relief, apply at the local USCIS office having jurisdiction over your place of residence.

Part 6. Processing Information.

Acceptance. If your application is complete and filed at a USCIS Service Center, you will be mailed a Form I-797 receipt notice. However, an application filed without the required fee, evidence, signature or photographs (if required) will be returned to you as incomplete. You may correct the deficiency and resubmit the application; however, an application is not considered properly filed until USCIS accepts it.

Approval. If approved, your EAD will either be mailed to you or you may be required to appear at your local USCIS office to pick it up.

Request for Evidence. If additional information or documentation is required, a written request will be sent to you specifying the information or advising you of an interview.

Denial. If your application cannot be granted, you will receive a written notice explaining the basis of your denial.

Interim EAD. If you have not received a decision within 90 days of receipt by USCIS of a properly filed EAD application or within 30 days of a properly filed initial EAD application based on an asylum application filed on or after January 4, 1995, you may obtain interim work authorization by appearing in person at your local USCIS district office. You must bring proof of identity and any notices that you have received from USCIS in connection with your application for employment authorization.

Part 7. Other Information.

Penalties for Perjury. All statements contained in response to questions in this application are declared to be true and correct under penalty of perjury. Title 18, United States Code, Section 1546, provides in part:

. . . Whoever knowingly makes under oath, or as permitted under penalty of perjury under 1746 of Title 28, United States Code, knowingly subscribes as true, any false statement with respect to a material fact in any application, affidavit, or other document required by the immigration laws or regulations prescribed thereunder, or knowingly presents any such application, affidavit, or other document containing any such false statement-shall be fined in accordance with this title or imprisoned not more than five years, or both.

The knowing placement of false information on this application may subject you and/or the preparer of this application to criminal penalties under Title 18 of the United States Code. The knowing placement of false information on this application may also subject you and/or the preparer to civil penalties under Section 274C of the Immigration and Nationality Act (INA), 8 U.S.C. 1324c. Under 8 U.S.C. 1324c, a person subject to a final order for civil document fraud is deportable from the United States and may be subject to fines.

Authority for Collecting This Information. The authority to require you to file Form I-765, Application for Employment Authorization, when applying for employment authorization is found at sections 103(a) and 274A(h)(3) of the Immigration and Nationality Act. Information you provide on your Form I-765 is used to determine whether you are eligible for employment authorization and for the preparation of your Employment Authorization Document if you are found eligible. Failure to provide all information as requested may result in the denial or rejection of this application. The information you provide may also be disclosed to other federal, state, local and foreign law enforcement and regulatory agencies during the course of the USCIS investigations.

USCIS Forms and Information. To order USCIS forms, call our toll-free number at **1-800-870-3676.** You can also get USCIS forms and information on immigration laws, regulations and procedures by telephoning our **National Customer Service Center** at 1-800-375-5283 or visiting our internet website at **www.uscis.gov.**

Use InfoPass for an Appointments. As an alternative to waiting in line for assistance at your local USCIS office, you can now schedule an appointment through our internet-based system, **InfoPass.** To access the system, visit our website at **www.uscis. gov.** Use the **InfoPass** appointment scheduler and follow the screen prompts to set up your appoinment. **InfoPass** generates an electronic appointment notice that appears on the screen. Print the notice and take it with you to your appointment. The notice gives the time and date or your appoinment, along with the address of the USCIS office.

Paperwork Reduction Act. An agency may not conduct or sponsor an information collection and a person is not required to respond to a collection of information unless it displays a currently valid OMB control number.

Department of Homeland Security
U.S. Citizenship and Immigration Services

OMB No. 1615-0040; Expires 08/31/08

I-765, Application for Employment Authorization

Do not write in this block.

Remarks	Action Block	Fee Stamp
A#		
Applicant is filing under §274a.12 _____		

☐ Application Approved. Employment Authorized / Extended *(Circle One)* until _____ (Date).
_____ (Date).

Subject to the following conditions: _____

☐ Application Denied.
  ☐ Failed to establish eligibility under 8 CFR 274a.12 (a) or (c).
  ☐ Failed to establish economic necessity as required in 8 CFR 274a.12(c)(14), (18) and 8 CFR 214.2(f)

I am applying for: ☐ Permission to accept employment.
  ☐ Replacement of lost Employment Authorization Document.
  ☐ Renewal of my permission to accept employment *(attach previous Employment Authorization Document)*.

1. Name (Family Name in CAPS)   (First)   (Middle)

2. Other Names Used (Include Maiden Name)

3. Address in the United States (Number and Street)   (Apt. Number)

(Town or City)   (State/Country)   (ZIP Code)

4. Country of Citizenship/Nationality

5. Place of Birth (Town or City)   (State/Province)   (Country)

6. Date of Birth   (mm/dd/yyyy)   7. Gender   ☐ Male   ☐ Female

8. Marital Status   ☐ Married   ☐ Single   ☐ Widowed   ☐ Divorced

9. U.S. Social Security Number (Include all numbers you have ever used, if any)

10. Alien Registration Number (A-Number) or I-94 Number (if any)

11. Have you ever before applied for employment authorization from USCIS?
☐ Yes (If yes, complete below)   ☐ No
Which USCIS Office?   Date(s)

Results (Granted or Denied - attach all documentation)

12. Date of Last Entry into the U.S.   (mm/dd/yyyy)

13. Place of Last Entry into the U.S.

14. Manner of Last Entry (Visitor, Student, etc.)

15. Current Immigration Status (Visitor, Student, etc.)

16. Go to **Part 2** of the Instructions, Eligibility Categories. In the space below place the letter and number of the category you selected from the instructions. (For example, (a)(8); (c)(17)(iii); etc.)

Eligibility under 8 CFR 274a.12

( ) ( ) ( )

Certification.

Your Certification: I certify, under penalty of perjury under the laws of the United States of America, that the foregoing is true and correct. Furthermore, I authorize the release of any information that U.S. Citizenship and Immigration Services needs to determine eligibility for the benefit I am seeking. I have read the Instructions in **Part 2** and have identified the appropriate eligibility category in **Block 16**.

Signature   Telephone Number   Date

Signature of person preparing form, if other than above:
I declare that this document was prepared by me at the request of the applicant and is based on all information of which I have any knowledge.

Print Name   Address   Signature   Date

Remarks	Initial Receipt	Resubmitted	Relocated		Completed		
			Rec'd	Sent	Approved	Denied	Returned

f

Form I-765 (Rev. 04/01/06)Y

This page intentionally left blank.

OMB Approval: 1205-0451
Expiration Date: 03/31/2008

Application for Permanent Employment Certification
ETA Form 9089
U.S. Department of Labor

Please read and review the filing instructions before completing this form. A copy of the instructions can be found at http://workforcesecurity.doleta.gov/foreign/ .

Employing or continuing to employ an alien unauthorized to work in the United States is illegal and may subject the employer to criminal prosecution, civil money penalties, or both.

A. Refiling Instructions

1. Are you seeking to utilize the filing date from a previously submitted Application for Alien Employment Certification (ETA 750)?	❏ Yes ❏ No

1-A. If Yes, enter the previous filing date

1-B. Indicate the previous SWA or local office case number OR if not available, specify state where case was originally filed:

B. Schedule A or Sheepherder Information

1. Is this application in support of a Schedule A or Sheepherder Occupation?	❏ Yes ❏ No

If Yes, do NOT send this application to the Department of Labor. All applications in support of Schedule A or Sheepherder Occupations must be sent directly to the appropriate Department of Homeland Security office.

C. Employer Information (Headquarters or Main Office)

1. Employer's name

2. Address 1

Address 2

3. City   State/Province   Country   Postal code

4. Phone number   Extension

5. Number of employees   6. Year commenced business

7. FEIN (Federal Employer Identification Number)   8. NAICS code

9. Is the employer a closely held corporation, partnership, or sole proprietorship in which the alien has an ownership interest, or is there a familial relationship between the owners, stockholders, partners, corporate officers, incorporators, and the alien?	❏ Yes ❏ No

D. Employer Contact Information (This section must be filled out. This information must be different from the agent or attorney information listed in Section E).

1. Contact's last name   First name   Middle initial

2. Address 1

Address 2

3. City   State/Province   Country   Postal code

4. Phone number   Extension

5. E-mail address

OMB Approval: 1205-0451
Expiration Date: 03/31/2008

Application for Permanent Employment Certification
ETA Form 9089
U.S. Department of Labor

E. Agent or Attorney In formation (If applicable)

1. Agent or attorney's last name	First name	Middle initial

2. Firm name

3. Firm EIN	4. Phone number	Extension

5. Address 1

Address 2

6. City	State/Province	Country	Postal code

7. E-mail address

F. Prevailing Wage Information (as provided by the State Workforce Agency)

1. Prevailing wage tracking number (if applicable)	2. SOC/O*NET(OES) code

3. Occupation Title	4. Skill Level

5. Prevailing wage
$
Per: (Choose only one)
❑ Hour ❑ Week ❑ Bi-Weekly ❑ Month ❑ Year

6. Prevailing wage source (Choose only one)
❑ OES ❑ CBA ❑ Employer Conducted Survey ❑ DBA ❑ SCA ❑ Other

6-A. If Other is indicated in question 6, specify:

7. Determination date	8. Expiration date

G. Wage Offer Information

1. Offered wage
From: $ To: (Optional) $
Per: (Choose only one)
❑ Hour ❑ Week ❑ Bi-Weekly ❑ Month ❑ Year

H. Job Opportunity Information (Where work will be performed)

1. Primary worksite (where work is to be performed) address 1

Address 2

2. City	State	Postal code

3. Job title

4. Education: minimum level required:
❑ None ❑ High School ❑ Associate's ❑ Bachelor's ❑ Master's ❑ Doctorate ❑ Other

4-A. If Other is indicated in question 4, specify the education required:

4-B. Major field of study

5. Is training required in the job opportunity?   5-A. If Yes, number of months of training required:
❑ Yes ❑ No

OMB Approval: 1205-0451
Expiration Date: 03/31/2008

Application for Permanent Employment Certification
ETA Form 9089
U.S. Department of Labor

H. Job Opportunity Information Continued

5-B. Indicate the field of training:
6. Is experience in the job offered required for the job?   6-A. If Yes, number of months experience required: ❑ Yes ❑ No
7. Is there an alternate field of study that is acceptable?   ❑ Yes   ❑ No
7-A. If Yes, specify the major field of study:
8. Is there an alternate combination of education and experience that is acceptable?   ❑ Yes   ❑ No
8-A. If Yes, specify the alternate level of education required: ❑ None   ❑ High School   ❑ Associate's ❑ Bachelor's   ❑ Master's ❑ Doctorate ❑ Other
8-B. If Other is indicated in question 8-A, indicate the alternate level of education required:
8-C. If applicable, indicate the number of years experience acceptable in question 8:
9. Is a foreign educational equivalent acceptable?   ❑ Yes   ❑ No
10. Is experience in an alternate occupation acceptable?   10-A. If Yes, number of months experience in alternate   occupation required: ❑ Yes   ❑ No
10-B. Identify the job title of the acceptable alternate occupation:
11. Job duties – If submitting by mail, add attachment if necessary. Job duties description must begin in this space.

12. Are the job opportunity's requirements normal for the occupation? If the answer to this question is No, the employer must be prepared to provide documentation demonstrating that the job requirements are supported by business necessity.	❑ Yes ❑ No
13. Is knowledge of a foreign language required to perform the job duties? If the answer to this question is Yes, the employer must be prepared to provide documentation demonstrating that the language requirements are supported by business necessity.	❑ Yes ❑ No

14. Specific skills or other requirements – If submitting by mail, add attachment if necessary. Skills description must begin in this space.

OMB Approval: 1205-0451
Expiration Date: 03/31/2008

Application for Permanent Employment Certification
ETA Form 9089
U.S. Department of Labor

H. Job Opportunity Information Continued

15. Does this application involve a job opportunity that includes a combination of occupations?	❑ Yes ❑ No
16. Is the position identified in this application being offered to the alien identified in Section J?	❑ Yes ❑ No
17. Does the job require the alien to live on the employer's premises?	❑ Yes ❑ No
18. Is the application for a live-in household domestic service worker?	❑ Yes ❑ No
18-A. If Yes, have the employer and the alien executed the required employment contract and has the employer provided a copy of the contract to the alien?	❑ Yes ❑ No ❑ NA

I. Recruitment Information

a. Occupation Type – All must complete this section.

1. Is this application for a professional occupation , other than a college or university teacher? Professional occupations are those for which a bachelor's degree (or equivalent) is normally required.	❑ Yes ❑ No
2. Is this application for a college or university teacher? If Yes, complete questions 2-A and 2-B below.	❑ Yes ❑ No
2-A. Did you select the candidate using a competitive recruitment and selection process?	❑ Yes ❑ No
2-B. Did you use the basic recruitment process for professional occupations?	❑ Yes ❑ No

b. Special Recruitment and Documentation Pro   cedures for College and University Teachers –
Complete only if the an   swer to question I.a.2-A is Yes.

3. Date alien selected:
4. Name and date of national professional journal in which advertisement was placed:
5. Specify additional recruitment information in this space. Add an attachment if necessary.

c. Professional/Non-Professional Information – Complete   this section unless your answer to question B.1 or
I.a.2-A is YES.

6. Start date for the SWA job order	7. End date for the SWA job order
8. Is there a Sunday edition of the newspaper in the area of intended employment?	❑ Yes ❑ No
9. Name of newspaper (of general circulation) in which the first advertisement was placed:	
10. Date of first advertisement identified in question 9:	
11. Name of newspaper or professional journal (if applicable) in which second advertisement was placed:	
	❑ Newspaper ❑ Journal

OMB Approval: 1205-0451
Expiration Date: 03/31/2008

Application for Permanent Employment Certification
ETA Form 9089
U.S. Department of Labor

I. Recruitment Information Continued

12. Date of second newspaper advertisement or date of publication of journal identified in question 11:

d. Professional Recruitment Information – Co   mplete if the answer to question I.a.1   is YES or if the answer to I.a.2-B is YES.   Complete at least 3 of the items.

13. Dates advertised at job fair From: To:	14. Dates of on-campus recruiting From: To:
15. Dates posted on employer web site From: To:	16. Dates advertised with trade or professional organization From: To:
17. Dates listed with job search web site From: To:	18. Dates listed with private employment firm From: To:
19. Dates advertised with employee referral program From: To:	20. Dates advertised with campus placement office From: To:
21. Dates advertised with local or ethnic newspaper From: To:	22. Dates advertised with radio or TV ads From: To:

e. General Information – All must complete this section.

23. Has the employer received payment of any kind for the submission of this application?	❑ Yes ❑ No
23-A. If Yes, describe details of the payment including the amount, date and purpose of the payment :	
24. Has the bargaining representative for workers in the occupation in which the alien will be employed been provided with notice of this filing at least 30 days but not more than 180 days before the date the application is filed?	❑ Yes ❑ No ❑ NA
25. If there is no bargaining representative, has a notice of this filing been posted for 10 business days in a conspicuous location at the place of employment, ending at least 30 days before but not more than 180 days before the date the application is filed?	❑ Yes ❑ No ❑ NA
26. Has the employer had a layoff in the area of intended employment in the occupation involved in this application or in a related occupation within the six months immediately preceding the filing of this application?	❑ Yes ❑ No
26-A. If Yes, were the laid off U.S. workers notified and considered for the job opportunity for which certification is sought?	❑ Yes ❑ No ❑ NA

J. Alien Information (This section must be filled out.   This information must be   different from the agent or attorn ey information listed in Section E).

1. Alien's last name	First name	Full middle name
2. Current address 1		
Address 2		
3. City State/Province	Country	Postal code
4. Phone number of current residence		
5. Country of citizenship	6. Country of birth	
7. Alien's date of birth	8. Class of admission	
9. Alien registration number (A#)	10. Alien admission number (I-94)	
11. Education: highest level achieved relevant to the requested occupation: ❑ None ❑ High School ❑ Associate's ❑ Bachelor's ❑ Master's ❑ Doctorate ❑ Other		

---

292 ◆

OMB Approval: 1205-0451
Expiration Date: 03/31/2008

Application for Permanent Employment Certification
ETA Form 9089
U.S. Department of Labor

J. Alien Information Continued

11-A. If Other indicated in question 11, specify
12. Specify major field(s) of study
13. Year relevant education completed
14. Institution where relevant education specified in question 11 was received
15. Address 1 of conferring institution
Address 2

16. City	State/Province	Country	Postal code

17. Did the alien complete the training required for the requested job opportunity, as indicated in question H.5?	❑ Yes ❑ No ❑ NA
18. Does the alien have the experience as required for the requested job opportunity indicated in question H.6?	❑ Yes ❑ No ❑ NA
19. Does the alien possess the alternate combination of education and experience as indicated in question H.8?	❑ Yes ❑ No ❑ NA
20. Does the alien have the experience in an alternate occupation specified in question H.10?	❑ Yes ❑ No ❑ NA
21. Did the alien gain any of the qualifying experience with the employer in a position substantially comparable to the job opportunity requested?	❑ Yes ❑ No ❑ NA
22. Did the employer pay for any of the alien's education or training necessary to satisfy any of the employer's job requirements for this position?	❑ Yes ❑ No
23. Is the alien currently employed by the petitioning employer?	❑ Yes ❑ No

---

K. Alien Work Experience

List all jobs the alien has held during the past 3 years.   Also list any other experience that qualifies the alien for the job opportunity for which the employer is seeking certification.

   a. Job 1

1. Employer name
2. Address 1
Address 2

3. City	State/Province	Country	Postal code
4. Type of business		5. Job title	

6. Start date	7. End date	8. Number of hours worked per week

OMB Approval: 1205-0451
Expiration Date: 03/31/2008

Application for Permanent Employment Certification
ETA Form 9089
U.S. Department of Labor

K. Alien Work Experience Continued

9. Job details (duties performed, use of tools, machines, equipment, skills, qualifications, certifications, licenses, etc. Include the phone number of the employer and the name of the alien's supervisor.)

b. Job 2

1. Employer name

2. Address 1

Address 2

3. City	State/Province	Country	Postal code

4. Type of business	5. Job title

6. Start date	7. End date	8. Number of hours worked per week

9. Job details (duties performed, use of tools, machines, equipment, skills, qualifications, certifications, licenses, etc. Include the phone number of the employer and the name of the alien's supervisor.)

c. Job 3

1. Employer name

2. Address 1

Address 2

3. City	State/Province	Country	Postal code

4. Type of business	5. Job title

6. Start date	7. End date	8. Number of hours worked per week

294 ◆

OMB Approval: 1205-0451
Expiration Date: 03/31/2008

Application for Permanent Employment Certification
ETA Form 9089
U.S. Department of Labor

K. Alien Work Experience Continued

9. Job details (duties performed, use of tools, machines, equipment, skills, qualifications, certifications, licenses, etc. Include the phone number of the employer and the name of the alien's supervisor.)

L. Alien Declaration

I declare under penalty of perjury that Sections J and K are true and correct.   I understand that to knowingly furnish false information in the preparation of this form and any supplement thereto or to aid, abet, or counsel another to do so is a federal offense punishable by a fine or imprisonment up to five years or both under 18 U.S.C. §§ 2 and 1001. Other penalties apply as well to fraud or misuse of ETA immigration documents and to perjury with respect to such documents under 18 U.S.C. §§ 1546 and 1621.

In addition, I further declare   under penalty of perjury that I intend to accept the position offered in Section H of this application if a labor certification is approved and I am granted a visa or an adjustment of status based on this application.

1. Alien's last name	First name	Full middle name
2. Signature	Date signed	

Note – The signature and date signed do not have to be filled out when electronically submitting to the Department of Labor for processing, but must be complete when submitting by mail. If the application is submitted electronically, any resulting certification MUST be signed immediately upon receipt from DOL before it can be submitted to USCIS for final processing.

M. Declaration of Preparer

1. Was the application completed by the employer? If No, you must complete this section.	❏ Yes ❏ No

I hereby certify that I have prepared this application at   the direct request of the employer listed in Section C and that to the best of my knowledge the information contained herein is true and correct.   I understand that to knowingly furnish false information in the preparation of this form and any supplement thereto or to aid, abet, or counsel another to do so is a federal offense punishable by a fine, imprisonment up to five years or both under 18 U.S.C. §§ 2 and 1001. Other penalties apply as well to fraud or misuse of ETA immigration documents and to perjury with respect to such documents under 18 U.S.C. §§ 1546 and 1621.

2. Preparer's last name	First name	Middle initial
3. Title		
4. E-mail address		
5. Signature	Date signed	

Note – The signature and date signed do not have to be filled out when electronically submitting to the Department of Labor for processing, but must be complete when submitting by mail. If the application is submitted electronically, any resulting certification MUST be signed immediately upon receipt from DOL before it can be submitted to USCIS for final processing.

ETA Form 9089   *Page 8 of 10*

OMB#ll25-0001

U.S. Department of Justice
Executive Office for Immigration Review

Application for Cancellation of Removal and Adjustment of Status for Certain Nonpermanent Residents

---

PLEASE READ ADVICE AND INSTRUCTIONS BEFORE FILLING IN FORM

PLEASE TYPE OR PRINT

Fee Stamp (Official Use Only)

PART 1 - INFORMATION ABOUT YOURSELF

1) My present true name is: *(Last, First, Middle)*

2) Alien Registration (or "A") Number(s):

3) My name given at birth was: *(Last, First, Middle)*

4) Birth Place: *(City and Country)*

5) Date of Birth: *(Month, Day, Year)*

6) Gender: ❏ Male ❏ Female

7) Height:

8) Hair Color:

9) Eye Color:

10) Current Nationality and Citizenship:

11) Social Security Number:

12) Home Phone Number: ( )

13) Work Phone Number: ( )

14) I currently reside at:

Apt. number and/or in care of

Number and Street

City or Town   *State*   *Zip Code*

15) I have been known by these additional name(s):

16) I have resided in the following locations in the United States: (List PRESENT ADDRESS FIRST, and work back in time for at least 10 years.)

Street and Number - Apt. or Room # - City or Town - State - Zip Code	Resided From: *(Month, Day, Year)*	Resided To: *(Month, Day, Year)*
		PRESENT

PART 2 - INFORMATION ABOUT THIS APPLICATION

17) I, the undersigned, hereby request that my removal be cancelled under the provisions of section 240A(b) of the Immigration and Nationality Act (INA). I believe that I am eligible for cancellation of removal because: (Check all that apply.)

❏ My removal would result in exceptional and extremely unusual hardship to my:

	UNITED STATES CITIZEN	LEGAL PERMANENT RESIDENT	TEMPORARY STATUS	NO STATUS
spouse, who is a	___	___	___	___
father, who is a	___	___	___	___
mother, who is a	___	___	___	___
child/children, who is/are a	___	___	___	___

With the exception of absences described in question #23, I have resided in the United States since:

(Month, Day, Year) _____.

❏ I, or my child, have been battered or subjected to extreme cruelty by a United States citizen or lawful permanent resident spouse or parent.

With the exception of absences described in question #23, I have resided in the United States since:

(Month, Day, Year) _____.

Please continue answers on a separate sheet as needed.

(1)

Form EOIR-42B
Revised January 2006

PART 3 - INFORMATION ABOUT YOUR PRESENCE IN THE UNITED STATES

18) I first arrived in the United States under the name of: *(Last, First, Middle)*

19) I first arrived in the United States on: *(Month, Day, Year)*

20) Place or port of first arrival: *(Place or Port, City, and State)*

21) I: ❑ was inspected and admitted.

❑ I entered using my Lawful Permanent Resident card which is valid until _____ . *(Month, Day, Year)*

❑ I entered using a _____ visa which is valid until _____ . *(Specify Type of Visa)* *(Month, Day, Year)*

❑ was not inspected and admitted.

❑ I entered without documents. Explain: _____ .

❑ I entered without inspection. Explain: _____ .

❑ Other. Explain: _____ .

22) I applied on _____ *(Month, Day, Year)* for additional time to stay and it was ❑ granted on _____ *(Month, Day, Year)*

and valid until _____ , or ❑ denied on _____ . *(Month, Day, Year)* *(Month, Day, Year)*

23) Since the date of my first entry, I departed from and returned to the United States at the following places and on the following dates:

(Please list all departures regardless of how briefly you were absent from the United States.)

If you have never departed from the United States since your original date of entry, please mark an X in this box: ❑

1	Port of Departure *(Place or Port, City and State)*	Departure Date *(Month, Day, Year)*	Purpose of Travel	Destination
	Port of Return *(Place or Port, City and State)*	Return Date *(Month, Day, Year)*	Manner of Return	Inspected and Admitted? ❑ Yes ❑ No
2	Port of Departure *(Place or Port, City and State)*	Departure Date *(Month, Day, Year)*	Purpose of Travel	Destination
	Port of Return *(Place or Port, City and State)*	Return Date *(Month, Day, Year)*	Manner of Return	Inspected and Admitted?

24) Have you ever departed the United States: a) under an order of deportation, exclusion, or removal?......... ❑ Yes ❑ No

b) pursuant to a grant of voluntary departure?......... ❑ Yes ❑ No

PART 4 - INFORMATION ABOUT YOUR MARITAL STATUS AND SPOUSE *(Continued on page 3)*

25) I am not married: ❑ I am married: ❑

26) If married, the name of my spouse is: *(Last, First, Middle)*

27) My spouse's name before marriage was:

28) The marriage took place in: *(City and Country)*

29) Date of marriage: *(Month, Day, Year)*

30) My spouse currently resides at:

Apt. number and/or in care of

Number and Street

City or Town   State/Country   Zip Code

31) Place and date of birth of my spouse: *(City & Country; Month, Day, Year)*

32) My spouse is a citizen of: *(Country)*

33) If your spouse is other than a native born United States citizen, answer the following:

He/she arrived in the United States at: *(Place or Port, City and State)* _____ .

He/she arrived in the United States on: *(Month, Day, Year)* _____ .

His/her alien registration number(s) is: A# _____ .

He/she was naturalized on: *(Month, Day, Year)* _____ at _____ . *(City and State)*

34) My spouse ❑ - is ❑ - is not employed. If employed, please give salary and the name and address of the place(s) of employment.

Full Name and Address of Employer	Earnings Per Week *(Approximate)*
	$
	$
	$

PART 4 - INFORMATION ABOUT YOUR MARITAL STATUS AND SPOUSE *(Continued)*

35) I ❑ - have ❑ - have not been previously married: *(If previously married, list the name of each prior spouse, the dates on which each marriage began and ended, the place where the marriage terminated, and describe how each marriage ended.)*

Name of prior spouse: *(Last, First, Middle)*	Date marriage began: Date marriage ended:	Place marriage ended: *(City and Country)*	Description or manner of how marriage was terminated or ended:

36) My present spouse ❑ - has ❑ - has not been previously married: *(If previously married, list the names of each prior spouse, the dates on which each marriage began and ended, the place where the marriage terminated, and describe how each marriage ended.)*

Name of prior spouse: *(Last, First, Middle)*	Date marriage began: Date marriage ended:	Place marriage ended: *(City and Country)*	Description or manner of how marriage was terminated or ended:

37) Have you been ordered by any court, or are otherwise under any legal obligation, to provide child support and/or spousal maintenance as a result of a separation and/or divorce? ❑ Yes ❑ No

PART 5 - INFORMATION ABOUT YOUR EMPLOYMENT AND FINANCIAL STATUS

38) Since my arrival into the United States, I have been employed by the following named persons or firms: *(Please begin with present employment and work back in time. Any periods of unemployment or school attendance should be specified. Attach a separate sheet for additional entries if necessary.)*

Full Name and Address of Employer	Earnings Per Week *(Approximate)*	Type of Work Performed	Employed From: *(Month, Day, Year)*	Employed To: *(Month, Day, Year)*
	$			PRESENT
	$			
	$			

39) If self-employed, describe the nature of the business, the name of the business, its address, and net income derived therefrom:
_____

40) My assets (and if married, my spouse's assets) in the United States and other countries, not including clothing and household necessities, are:

Self
Cash, Stocks, and Bonds............... $_____
Real Estate.................................... $_____
Auto (dollar value minus amount owed)....... $_____
Other (describe on line below)...................... $_____
_____ TOTAL $_____

Jointly Owned With Spouse
Cash, Stocks, and Bonds............... $_____
Real Estate.................................... $_____
Auto (dollar value minus amount owed)....... $_____
Other (describe on line below)...................... $_____
_____ TOTAL $_____

41) I ❑ - have ❑ - have not received public or private relief or assistance (e.g. Welfare, Unemployment Benefits, Medicaid, TANF, AFDC, etc.). If you have, please give full details including the type of relief or assistance received, date for which relief or assistance was received, place, and total amount received during this time: _____

42) Please list each of the years in which you have filed an income tax return with the Internal Revenue Service:_____

PART 6 - INFORMATION ABOUT YOUR FAMILY *(Continued on page 5)*

43) I have_____*(Number of)* children. Please list information for each child below, include assets and earnings information for children over the age of 16 who have separate incomes:

Name of Child: *(Last, First, Middle)* Child's Alien Registration Number:	Citizen of What Country: Birth Date: *(Month, Day, Year)*	Now Residing At: *(City and Country)* Birth Date: *(City and Country)*	Immigration Status of Child
A#: _____ Estimated Total of Assets: $_____	Estimated Average Weekly Earnings: $_____		
A#: _____ Estimated Total of Assets: $_____	Estimated Average Weekly Earnings: $_____		
A#: _____ Estimated Total of Assets: $_____	Estimated Average Weekly Earnings: $_____		

44) If your application is denied, would your spouse and all of your children accompany you to your:

If you answered "No" to any of the responses, please explain: _____

Country of Birth - ☐ Yes ☐ No

Country of Nationality - ☐ Yes ☐ No

Country of Last Residence - ☐ Yes ☐ No

_____

_____

_____

45) Members of my family, including my spouse and/or child(ren) ☐ - have ☐ - have not received public or private relief or assistance (e.g., Welfare, Unemployment Benefits, Medicaid, TANF, AFDC, etc.). If any member of your immediate family has received such relief or assistance, please give full details including identity of person(s) receiving relief or assistance, dates for which relief or assistance was received, place, and total amount received during this time: _____

_____

_____

_____

_____

_____

46) Please give the requested information about your parents, brothers, sisters, aunts, uncles, and grandparents, living or deceased. As to residence, show street address, city, and state, if in the United States; otherwise show only country:

Name: *(Last, First, Middle)* Alien Registration Number:	Citizen of What Country: Birth Date: *(Month, Day, Year)*	Relationship to Me: Birth Date: *(City and Country)*	Immigration Status of Listed Relative
A#: _____ Complete Address of Current Residence, if Living: _____			
A#: _____ Complete Address of Current Residence, if Living: _____			

PART 6 - INFORMATION ABOUT YOUR FAMILY *(Continued)*

IF THIS APPLICATION IS BASED ON HARDSHIP TO A PARENT OR PARENTS, QUESTIONS 47-50 MUST BE ANSWERED.

47) If your parent is not a citizen of the United States, give the date and place of arrival in the United States including full details as to the date, manner, and terms of admission into the United States:_____

_____

_____

48) My father ☐ - is ☐ - is not employed. If employed, please give salary and the name and address of the place(s) of employment.

Full Name and Address of Employer	Earnings Per Week *(Approximate)*
	$

49) My mother ☐ - is ☐ - is not employed. If employed, please give salary and the name and address of place(s) of employment.

Full Name and Address of Employer	Earnings Per Week *(Approximate)*
	$

50) My parent's assets in the United States and other countries not including clothing and household necessities are:

Assets of father consist of the following:

Cash, Stocks, and Bonds................................ $_____
Real Estate.. $_____
Auto (dollar value minus amount owed)....... $_____
Other (describe on line below)...................... $_____
_____TOTAL $_____

Assets of mother consist of the following:

Cash, Stocks, and Bonds................................ $_____
Real Estate.. $_____
Auto (dollar value minus amount owed)....... $_____
Other (describe on line below)...................... $_____
_____TOTAL $_____

PART 7 - MISCELLANEOUS INFORMATION *(Continued on page 6)*

51) I ☐ - have ☐ - have not entered the United States as a crewman after June 30, 1964.

52) I ☐ - have ☐ - have not been admitted as, or after arrival in the United States acquired the status of, an exchange alien.

53) I ☐ - have ☐ - have not submitted address reports as required by section 265 of the Immigration and Nationality Act.

54) I ☐ - have ☐ - have never (either in the United States or in any foreign country) been arrested, summoned into court as a defendant, convicted, fined, imprisoned, placed on probation, or forfeited collateral for an act involving a felony, misdemeanor, or breach of any public law or ordinance (including, but not limited to, traffic violations or driving incidents involving alcohol). *(If answer is in the affirmative, please give a brief description of each offense including the name and location of the offense, date of conviction, any penalty imposed, any sentence imposed, and the time actually served.)*

_____

_____

_____

_____

55) Have you ever served in the Armed Forces of the United States? ☐ Yes ☐ No. If "Yes" please state branch *(Army, Navy, etc.)* and service number: _____

Place of entry on duty: *(City and State)* _____

Date of entry on duty: *(Month, Day, Year)* _____ Date of discharge: *(Month, Day, Year)* _____

Type of discharge: *(Honorable, Dishonorable, etc.)* _____

I served in active duty status from: *(Month, Day, Year)* _____ to *(Month, Day, Year)* _____

56) Have you ever left the United States or the jurisdiction of the district where you registered for the draft to avoid being drafted into the military or naval forces of the United States?

☐ Yes ☐ No

Please continue answers on a separate sheet as needed.

Form EOIR-42B
Revised January 2006

PART 7 - MISCELLANEOUS INFORMATION *(Continued)*

57) Have you ever deserted from the military or naval forces of the United States while the United States was at war? ☐ Yes ☐ No

58) If male, did you register under the Military Selective Service Act or any applicable previous Selective Service (Draft) Laws? ☐ Yes ☐ No
If "Yes," please give date, Selective Service number, local draft board number, and your last draft classification: _____

_____

59) Were you ever exempted from service because of conscientious objection, alienage, or any other reason? ☐ Yes ☐ No

60) Please list your present or past membership in or affiliation with every political organization, association, fund, foundation, party, club, society, or similar group in the United States or any other place since your 16th birthday. Include any foreign military service in this part. If none, write "None." Include the name of the organization, location, nature of the organization, and the dates of membership.

Name of Organization	Location of Organization	Nature of Organization	Member From: *(Month, Day, Year)*	Member To: *(Month, Day, Year)*

61) Have you ever:

☐ Yes ☐ No   been ordered deported, excluded, or removed?

☐ Yes ☐ No   overstayed a grant of voluntary departure from an Immigration Judge or the Department of Homeland Security (DHS), formerly the Immigration and Naturalization Service (INS)?

☐ Yes ☐ No   failed to appear for removal or deportation?

62) Have you ever been:

☐ Yes ☐ No   a habitual drunkard?

☐ Yes ☐ No   one whose income is derived principally from illegal gambling?

☐ Yes ☐ No   one who has given false testimony for the purpose of obtaining immigration benefits?

☐ Yes ☐ No   one who has engaged in prostitution or unlawful commercialized vice?

☐ Yes ☐ No   involved in a serious criminal offense and asserted immunity from prosecution?

☐ Yes ☐ No   a polygamist?

☐ Yes ☐ No   one who aided and/or abetted another to enter the United States illegally

☐ Yes ☐ No   a trafficker of a controlled substance, or a knowing assister, abettor, conspirator, or colluder with others in any such controlled substance offense (not including a single offense of simple possession of 30 grams or less of marijuana)?

☐ Yes ☐ No   inadmissible or deportable on security-related grounds under section 212(a)(3) or 237(a)(4) of the INA?

☐ Yes ☐ No   one who has ordered, incited, assisted, or otherwise participated in the persecution of an individual on account of his or her race, religion, nationality, membership in a particular social group, or political opinion?

☐ Yes ☐ No   a person previously granted relief under sections 212(c) or 244(a) of the INA or whose removal has previously been cancelled under section 240A of the INA?

If you answered "Yes" to any of the above questions, explain: _____

_____

_____

PART 7 - MISCELLANEOUS INFORMATION *(Continued)*

63) Are you the beneficiary of an approved visa petition? ☐ Yes ☐ No

   If yes, can you arrange a trip outside the United States to obtain an immigrant visa? ☐ Yes ☐ No If no, please explain:

_____

_____

_____

_____

64) The following certificates or other supporting documents are attached hereto as a part of this application: *(Refer to the Instructions for documents which **should be attached**.)*

_____   _____

_____   _____

_____   _____

_____   _____

_____   _____

_____   _____

_____   _____

_____   _____

_____   _____

_____   _____

_____   _____

_____   _____

_____   _____

_____   _____

_____   _____

PART 8 - SIGNATURE OF PERSON PREPARING FORM, IF OTHER THAN APPLICANT

(Read the following information and sign below)

I declare that I have prepared this application at the request of the person named in Part 1, that the responses provided are based on all information of which I have knowledge, or which was provided to me by the applicant, and that the completed application was read to the applicant in a language the applicant speaks fluently for verification before he or she signed the application in my presence. I am aware that the knowing placement of false information on the Form EOIR-42B may subject me to civil penalties under 8 U.S.C. 1324c.

Signature of Preparer:	Print Name:	Date:
Daytime Telephone #: ( )	Address of Preparer: *(Number and Street, City, State, Zip Code)*	

PART 9 - SIGNATURE

APPLICATION NOT TO BE SIGNED BELOW UNTIL APPLICANT APPEARS BEFORE AN IMMIGRATION JUDGE

I swear or affirm that I know the contents of this application that I am signing, including the attached documents and supplements, and that they are all true to the best of my knowledge, taking into account the correction(s) numbered _____ to _____ , if any, that were made by me or at my request.

_____
(Signature of Applicant or Parent or Guardian)

Subscribed and sworn to before me by the above-named applicant at _____

_____
Immigration Judge

_____
Date (Month, Day, Year)

PART 10 - PROOF OF SERVICE

I hereby certify that a copy of the foregoing Form EOIR-42B was: ❑ - delivered in person ❑ - mailed first class, postage prepaid

on _____ to the Assistant Chief Counsel for the DHS (U.S. Immigration and Customs Enforcement - ICE)
    (Month, Day, Year)

at _____
         (Number and Street, City, State, Zip Code)

_____
Signature of Applicant (or Attorney or Representative)

Form EOIR-42B
Revised January 2006

Department of Homeland Security
U.S. Citizenship and Immigration Services

OMB No. 1615-0007; Expires 08/31/08

AR-11, Alien's Change
of Address Card

Name (Last in CAPS)	(First Name)	(Middle Name)	I am in the United States as a:

☐ Visitor ☐ Permanent Resident
☐ Student ☐ Other _____ (Specify)

Country of Citizenship	Date of Birth (mm/dd/yyyy)	Copy Number From Alien Card

A

Present Address (Street or Rural Route) (City or Post Office) (State) (Zip Code)

(If the above address is temporary) I expect to remain there _____ Years _____ Months

Last Address (Street or Rural Route) (City or Post Office) (State) (Zip Code)

I work for or attend school at: (Employer's Name or Name of School)

(Street Address or Rural Route) (City or Post Office) (State) (Zip Code)

Port of Entry Into U.S.   Date of Entry Into U.S. (mm/dd/yyyy)   If not a Permanent Resident, my stay in the U.S. expires on: (Date - mm/dd/yyyy)

Signature   Date (mm/dd/yyyy)

Form AR-11 (Rev. 01/20/06) Y

AR-11, Alien's Change of Address Card

This card is to be used by all aliens to report a change of address within ten days of such change.

The collection of this information is required by Section 265 of the Immigration and Nationality Act (8 U.S.C. 1305). The data is used by U.S. Citizenship and Immigration Services for statistical and record purposes and may be furnished to Federal, State, local and foreign law enforcement officials. Failure to report a change of address is punishable by fine or imprisonment and/or removal.

ADVISORY: This card is not evidence of identity, age or status claimed.

Public Reporting Burden. Under the Paperwork Reduction Act, an agency may not conduct or sponsor an information collection and a person is not required to respond to an information collection unless it displays a currently valid OMB control number. We try to create forms and instructions that are accurate, can be easily understood and that impose the least possible burden on you to provide us with information. Often this is difficult because some immigration laws are very complex. This collection of information is estimated to average five minutes per response, including the time for reviewing instructions, searching existing data sources, gathering and maintaining the data needed, and completing and reviewing the collection of information. Send comments regarding this burden estimate or any other aspect of this collection of information, including reducing this burden to: U.S. Citizenship and Immigration Services, Regulatory Management Division, 111 Massachusetts Ave. N.W., Washington, D.C. 20529. **Do not mail your completed form to this Washington, D.C. address.**

Mail Your Form to the Address Shown Below:

Department of Homeland Security
U.S. Citizenship and Immigration Services
Change of Address
P.O. Box 7134
London, KY 40742-7134

For commercial overnight or fast freight
Department of Homeland Security
U.S. Citizenship and Immigration Services
Change of Address
1084-I South Laurel Road
London, KY 40742-7134

This page intentionally left blank.

CERTIFICATION BY TRANSLATOR

I, _____, certify that I am fluent in the English and

_____ languages, that I am competent to perform this

translation and that the attached document is an accurate translation of the document entitled

_____.

_____   _____

Signature   Date

_____

Name

_____

Address

_____

INDEX

G

good moral character, 31, 72, 74, 75, 79, 105, 196
government employees, 37
grandparents, 77
green cards, 3, 6, 7, 11, 12, 20, 24, 26, 27, 53, 54, 55, 57, 58, 68, 70, 80, 89, 90, 91, 94, 100, 118, 127, 136, 137, 139, 141, 145, 152, 153, 157, 164, 165, 170, 171, 174, 176, 182, 185, 186, 187, 188, 189, 190, 191, 193, 195, 196, 197, 198
grounds of removability, 71, 180

H

health conditions, 21, 73, 131, 144, 148, 149, 153
hearsay, 178

I

immediate relatives, 17, 18, 19, 24, 25, 26, 27, 35, 43, 83, 84, 85, 91, 96, 97, 98, 99, 107, 151
Immigrant Petition for Alien Worker (form I-140), 48
Immigration and Nationality Act (INA), 12, 71, 72, 77, 152, 180, 188, 191
Immigration and Naturalization Service (INS), 7, 12, 13, 68
immigration benefit, 9, 63, 152, 190
immigration court, 7, 58, 60, 61, 62, 63, 71, 90, 115, 121, 126, 129, 130, 131, 137, 138, 139, 143, 152, 154, 156, 169, 171, 175, 176, 177, 178, 179, 181, 183, 184, 191, 193, 196, 200
immigration judges, 23, 57, 58, 60, 62, 63, 71, 72, 75, 90, 125, 126, 137, 138, 155, 161, 171, 175, 176, 181, 182, 188, 191, 199
in status, 6, 39, 43, 62, 117, 122, 174
income, 23, 111, 145, 146, 147, 148, 149, 196
individual hearing, 63, 125, 178, 181
insurance, 21, 74, 146, 149
Internal Revenue Service (IRS), 129, 147, 198
investor, 51, 52, 134, 135, 136, 158

J

joint sponsor, 146

K

K-1 visa, 40, 41, 84, 105, 151
K-3 visa, 41, 84, 107

L

labor certification, 12, 43, 44, 45, 46, 47, 48, 68, 84, 85, 97, 110, 111, 113, 114, 151, 178
late amnesty, 68
lawful permanent resident (LPR), 3, 9, 25, 27, 38, 72, 75, 90, 104, 146, 148, 153, 155, 186, 188, 191, 195
lawyers, *See attorneys*
LIFE Act, 12, 41, 68, 113
loans, 21, 134

M

malpractice, 204
managers, 38, 44
marriage, 8, 18, 19, 20, 22, 23, 24, 26, 27, 31, 34, 40, 41, 42, 64, 68, 85, 86, 87, 88, 89, 90, 92, 94, 99, 101, 102, 103, 104, 105, 107, 108, 109, 113, 115, 117, 119, 122, 128, 130, 136, 143, 164, 167, 168, 169, 176, 186, 195, 196
    bona fide, 20, 23, 24, 40, 49, 63, 88, 89, 90, 103, 104, 106, 107, 108, 117, 128, 133, 152, 167, 168
master calendar hearing, 137, 177, 178, 179
Matter of Lozada, 203
medical examination, 113, 114, 120, 131, 143, 144, 153
medical records, 60, 73, 74
military members, 80, 96, 146
mini-amnesty, 33, 68
motion to remand, 63

N

name change, 27, 85, 86, 87, 88, 94, 99, 101, 129, 130, 186, 198
National Benefits Center (NBC), 157
National Security Entry-Exit Registration System (NSEERS), 156
naturalization, 3, 12, 26, 85, 86, 88, 94, 99, 101, 105, 108, 141, 157, 164, 186, 187, 195, 196, 197, 198